The RockStar's : Survival Guide

The RockStar's : Survival Guide

"No one ever told me when I was alone; they just thought I'd know better."

- Axel Rose: Better - Guns N' Roses

"Say less and you will get more."

-Digger Jones

"It's better to power up than to drain out! This goes for any facet of life, from martial arts to sports, from research to music."

- Digger Jones

Chapters

The Beginning

God's Gift 2 Women

Industry Peeps

Small Achievements

Bad Parenting

Grandma Nokamus

Yellow Butterfly

Final Crackdown

Acting to Fund Music

Comedy School is No Joke

A DJ's World

The Church

The Mock Club

The Night of the Living Dead

Angel Investors

Burning Jerusalem

Great Session Musicians

Shadows and Machines

Burning Jobs

Hidden Acceptance Letter

FunHole

Album Art

False Profits

Yellow ButterFlop

Vocal Lessons & Choirs

New Legacy

Bass Player Fiasco

Emotional Retards

New Legacy II

Music Video Shenanigans

The Show

Plane Crash Records

Industry Discrimination

Digger's How To's...

Stay Healthy

Mixing Genres

Unique Gigs

Flake

Song Synapses

Thoughts On The Music Industry

Best Advice Ever!

Extra Thoughts

Show Me the Money

Disclaimer:

Let me first say,

This account is a how-to book, an autobiography and a self-help book. It was a cathartic experience writing it. I absolutely love the music industry, with all its components and radio features. I absolutely hate how old arrogant white trash gatekeepers have ruined the industry and the joyful process of getting on the radio. Many books have already been written on how to be a rock star or the life of a rock star. However, many of these books have been written by people who "have made it". By the time they write the book, they are fucking delusional. Instead, this is going to be written by someone who "didn't make it", but should have. It is a real life, down to earth survival guide. Welcome to *The Rock Star's Survival Guide*. This is my gospel.

Chapter 1: The Beginning

My nickname is ***Digger***. My grandma gave it to me when I was born. I supposedly was a blue baby and the doctor said I wasn't going to make it. Rumour has it, I was fighting for my breath all night. Then, early in the morning, I started breathing after my grandma had been praying for hours with a rosary. She was delirious by then, when suddenly my family burst into cheers and my grandmother started crying:"He's such a little Digger."

And it stuck! I still get Christmas cards to Digger thirty years later. In fact, there are some family members who don't even remember my real name. Growing up, it was so embarrassing. I would be on a breakaway in hockey and my mom would yell:"Go, Digger!"

I would score and skate over to the bench and my friends would be like, "Yo, did your mom just call you a what I think she called you?"

In university, however, I took the name and ran with it. I changed my stage name to Digger Jones and became ***DJ Digger Jones***. Check it up on social media if you don't believe me!

I have always been a good musician with a good ear, but I only really started taking music seriously after a heartbreak that left me stunned in grade twelve. I mean, I was always a good musician growing up, but sports, art and acting interested me more. Growing up, I was also eyed by girls a lot because I am good-looking. Do you know how much pressure comes with being good-looking? How much envy and responsibility burden a good-looking person that isn't rich? My mom would always say: "You think you're God's gift to women or something." Now I realize I am. I always liked talking to girls and this would become a great selling point for my music later on.

My Childhood

My parents were pretty sadistic. They knew that their lives would suck. Therefore, they used to brainwash me into thinking I was a bad kid, in order to have a reason to "punish" me for everything. "Punishment" was to actually get me to do all the hard work around the house. I was a bit of a slave to my parents growing up. In fact, one day, after sneaking out of the house to go play hockey goalie with the local kids, I got grounded for my entire childhood. I was so good at sports that all the kids in the neighbourhood pleaded with me at my window to play goalie. Even though I was grounded, I snuck out the window, while my parents were not home, but I made a crucial error coming home through the front door and forgetting to lock it again behind me. I got caught by my parents, so I lied. They found out I had lied and grounded me for a year. That's right, I slipped out a tiny window, maybe a symbol of a small window of success, to play goalie and I got abused for a year because of it. I remember excelling in sports so much because of wanting someone to notice me and take me away from my abusive parents. Every time I could, especially when my parents would go out, I would sing in my room, practicing either choir songs from school or hip hop songs on my cassette player. It was my outlet when I couldn't go out and play sports.

Choir Boys

I spent countless hours in choirs when I was growing up. I auditioned for a choir in primary school and the rest is history. I always sang around the house, especially when I was doing dishes. I preferred playing sports. But if I had to be stationary, I turned to arts, theatre and music. When I walked into the gymnasium for choir auditions in Grade Five, I was nervous. I thought everyone sounded so good when I heard us all sing *'O Canada'* every morning. For some reason, when each student went up individually to sing with just the piano, they all sucked. I remember only myself and another Spanish boy named Diego having great solo voices, everyone else just kind of blended in behind us. The girls on the other hand were something of angels. I would listen in amazement at how every young girl sounded great. I was the only boy who could sing the soprano notes with the girls. I loved when the choir conductor would assign me to sing a part with only the girls. I loved harmonizing with girls, I still do. I find their voices so pure and untouched by screaming, drugs, violence and other vocal digressers. I sang in every choir, every year from Grade Five to Grade Ten. I was the lead in every theatre production from *Fantasia's Mickey Mouse*, to *Billy Ray Cyrus* rendition of *Achy Breaky Heart*, when that was a thing.

I have a natural ability to be in front of people and the camera, either dancing, singing or acting. When I was sixteen, I was in the *Teen Challenge Gospel Choir* for a year, in which I travelled across Ontario performing in churches, festivals and even stadiums for Christ. When I first came into the choir, I was instantly liked for my ability to sustain high notes with power. Other good singers felt jealous of me at first. Nevertheless, when they sang with me and I allowed them to have the spotlight and I harmonized well with them, they eventually loved singing with me. I remember there was a gifted singer in the program who had some mental problems. He initially felt like I was stealing his thunder, and the other guys in the choir also made him feel like that when I would get the solo songs over him. When I saw that this crushed him, I walked over and shared a secret with him. I told him that I was going to talk with the choir director and have him compose a song that was perfect for two separate male solos and one duet at the end, and the choir would sing the choruses behind us. This made him very happy. It turns out he wasn't having problems with sharing the spotlight. He just didn't want to be cut so high and dry after the year he had put in. We arranged a beautiful piece to end every show, and not a dry eye was found in the crowd from that day on. The choir would sing a few songs, I would have a solo and then I would give my testimony about how Jesus had saved my life from an abusive father, an overwhelmed mother, and now I sang to praise God. The truth is I liked singing in the choir, and although some of the songs were corny, the melodies were sophisticated, and my choir director rocked. After I would give my testimony, the choir would sing a few more songs, then we would have our big duet, and people would just flock to the *merch* table. I think the year I was in the Teen Challenge Choir was one of their most lucrative seasons.

Chapter 2: God's Gift 2 Women

Summer Camp

As soon as I graduated from high school, I got an awesome job working at a summer camp. I met a Chinese liaison who was travelling from Taiwan. Her group of Taiwanese kids were the best. They all loved me. I would play personal concerts for the group almost every night. They loved knowing they were the first people to hear a new song I wrote. I enjoyed hanging out with that group. I actually cried when that group left, because it felt like I had found a new family. This seemed like an inevitable end to our summer.

The following year, at the same camp, I met an Italian girl. We clicked right away and she loved that I would sometimes play songs for her in the garden behind the campus. A decade later, I am still in touch with her. I actually wrote a song for her called *Good Knight* with my band A Close Encounter. Finally, she boarded the bus to the airport and I never saw her again. "We grew close without making love", is one of the lines of the lyrics to the song.

University Fling

In university, I met a tall elegant Chinese girl who absolutely adored my skills as a guitarist. She inspired me to keep writing songs even when all else seemed hopeless. Olivia was her name and we dated each other for about a year. I remember Olivia being a great student. She actually would wake me up in the middle of the night before an exam, motivate me to study a little more and memorize key concepts. We were so different, yet so well matched. She was a great Economics student and I loved Arts. Call that a perfect couple. I wrote songs for her. The song *Fed Up*, has a part where I sing, "just hold her". That was for Olivia.

Ultimately, Olivia and I broke up. I made a stupid decision one time to ask her if she wanted to take a detour to see my uncle with me before he died. I am not kidding, I actually took a girl to an apartment, in the poor end of town, where my family gathered around a half-dead body and we all saw him breathe for the last time. My uncle looked tragic. He could hear us but could not move or speak. The family had to see him like that for his last breaths. I played the song *Meet Again* for him on his death bed, which would become a re-occurring theme, for all my friends and loved ones, who die along my path, I would play *Meet Again* for them at their funeral. It was all too much for Olivia and after we left, she pretended to be fine. The next morning when we parted ways, I never saw her again. She stopped returning my calls. She eventually went back to China, since she was only in Canada for a semester for an exchange program. Before she left, she called me and we had a nice farewell talk and that was it. I never saw her again, but we both knew it was awesome while it lasted.

Romance & Music

After I broke up with Olivia, I was a mess. I wondered around in heartbreak looking for anyone to ease the pain. Once, I was coming back from visiting my family in Northern Ontario, and I was on the subway. I saw a cute Russian chick sitting alone. When I first met her, there was instant chemistry. I started talking to her and she smiled right away, which is always a good sign. We talked for a while and I got her number. I happened to have some beers in my bag and asked her if she wanted to share a drink with me. She was relatively new to Canada. To survive, she juggled with two jobs. She worked as a piano teacher and a staffer of a virgin olive oil factory. But trust me, she was no virgin. Therefore, beer was something she liked. Her name was Anastasia. I nicknamed her KGB. I told her I played in a band, and she said she taught piano. KGB and I biked to my house, where I brought her into my room and pretended to listen to her piano lesson. When she was showing me a certain scale pattern, I leaned in and kissed her cheek. She stopped, and I could tell she couldn't think. I tried to lean in again and she got up and said it is better to meet another day. I felt like I had crossed the line. I was sure she would never return my call again. To my surprise, a couple nights later, we met up and ended up going back to her place, a dingy apartment in the sketchy part of Toronto. I grabbed a pizza on the way and a bottle of Vodka, just in case. She even put my songs from my band on her home theatre system and I got excited. We ended up making love with my own music playing in the background, which was a first for me.

After that, I phoned her up and we met a few times at a local coffee shop. At the time, I was taking piano lessons, and knew of all the best piano spots on campus. I took her to the same music college where I had taken lessons. The rooms were secluded and nothing is better than some good piano music to set the mood. Musicians should be getting laid the most, but often our romantic, sentimental passion is mistaken for creepiness. Musicians are passionate, intelligent and great mood setters. When I took KGB to the nice piano room, it had these great big bay windows and the sun was setting, so it was perfect timing. It was beautiful! I made love to her right on the lid of the grand piano. What a Beethoven.

Near the end of my university program, I was part of a Public Speakers Club. The members loved me there because I was well spoken, good-looking, and capable of bursting into songs during my speeches. It was Canada Day and the group decided to go to Ribfest, which is a local festival in Toronto filled with pork ribs, live music and a lot of alcoholics. I will never forget the cover band asked if anyone in the audience knew *Ice Ice Baby* by Vanilla Ice. I put up my hand, walked on stage and the band broke out into a perfect rendition of it. I rapped the first verse verbatim then in the second verse I switched it up and freestyled my own verse and the crowd exploded into a roar of approval. I ended up jumping off the stage into the crowd, like a mad man and they actually caught me. That is one of the defining times in my musical life before I got famous.

Rock Star Rack

I met this awesome rocker chick while I was rehearsing with my band. My band used to jam at this rehearsal space every weekend. When this new chick got hired there, it was awesome. She was a gorgeous rocker chick. She used to wear a baggy work t-shirt and her breasts would still be bursting out of it. In fact, I remember it was hard to concentrate on music when she came around. Her name was Lisa and she had pink hair, tattoos and a tongue ring. When no one was around it was so easy to talk to her and I started building rapport. I knew we were both attracted to each other.

One time I was talking to her and my band showed up. I instantly felt nervous talking to her, not wanting to take things too fast because I liked the place I was rehearsing in, and I knew the manager didn't really like me. I didn't want to screw things up. I talked to her, but it was all mechanical, not natural. Although I did call her up a few times after that, nothing materialized from it.

I realized Lisa just liked the attention. Plus, it was even more pressure that all my band mates wanted to fuck her and were jealous when I talked to her. To make matters worse, I felt the pressure that if I didn't get her, I would not make it as a star in the music business. Does that even make sense? Pressure plays mind games. Luckily, I went on to make it in music and kept that truth in mind.

I even had a microcosm of what the music industry would be for me. It's ironic. When I was an insecure teenager terrified to try to take women, I would just play my guitar at camp fires and parties and all the women would circle around me in awe. Following a breakup, the only people to listen was a bunch of dudes from my high school. Sometime life shows you a riddle in the form of a glimpse of the future.

Pepper Spray Incident

One day, just after graduating from university, I was on my way to a band practice. I saw some prick and his brother walking down the street. I knew these two drug dealers from high school and we didn't really like each other. As I passed by them, they noticed me and tried to start a fight. I knew they trained in martial arts, and I had my guitar with me, so I tried to avoid them. As I turned away, Prick pushed me from behind. I turned around and said: "Thank you, you're going to jail. Then you can fight as much as you want."

Prick got scared when I said this and tried to provoke me to fight him so that he wouldn't be in the wrong. I walked to the local plaza to call the police, because I had left my phone at my girlfriend's house. I waited half an hour and cops didn't show up. The goon brothers had already run off, so I left and went to practice. I would have thought nothing of it, if I hadn't seen them in my area the very next day, near the same plaza.

It was fate, or some psychotic plan, but whatever it was, what happened next is Hollywood material. I got off the bus and they were at the bus stop. Prick's brother Priss was asking people for cigarettes. I thought: Maybe some MMA fighters smoke?

This time I had my phone with me and I pulled it out to start recording them. I tried to keep it casual and keep my distance, thinking they wouldn't see me, but one of them noticed,

"Hey you! What the fuck!"

I looked up and saw them running across the street at me. They tried to fight me, but I kept backing away far enough until they stopped. I called the police.

"Hi, yes, I called about an assault yesterday and now the same people are trying to fight me again."

"Where are you?" the dispatcher asked.

"The same damn plaza!" I yelled.

"Where are the assailants?" asked the dispatcher.

"Right in front of me with their fists up! What the fuck! Are the cops coming this time?"

"Sir, get as far away from them as you can until cops arrive. They will be there in about ten minutes. Are you in any serious danger?"

"Yes!" I hung up the phone.

Do you know how hard it is to deal with two rabies-infected dogs for ten minutes? To make a long story short, Prick ran across the street when I was waiting for the police and attacked me. He managed to grab my phone and literally snapped it in two right in front of me. I had important recordings from my band on that phone, so I literally went nuts. All the years of him stalking me, talking shit, taking my girls, and now robbing my music while assaulting me, I fucking went nuts. I attacked him and managed to knock him on the ground. I had been working out a lot those days, so I jumped on him, screaming and throwing punches. He tried to kick me in the face while lying down, but missed. I landed a really strong downward thrusting strike right on his chin. I knew he would try to grab me in a choke hold when I tried to punch him, so I waited for his hand, then kept landing punches on his face until I broke his nose. His brother Priss ran over and tried attack me from behind. I saw him from my periphery and kicked him in the balls. I didn't care about the phone. I only wanted my SIM card back. Not only was it in his pocket, but it also had my music on it.

As I tried to get the SIM card, Prick reached into his pocket and the next thing I knew I was getting pepper-sprayed in the face. They tried to beat me up while I started to go blind, but luckily some lady was recording everything on her camera phone and ran over. This lady would later testify in court. The goon brothers noticed that people had seen them try to rob me and they took off running. I could see, for a split second, out the corner of my eye, and I started chasing them. I knew if I didn't stay with them, the cops would come and they would be gone forever with my phone, and everything would have been for naught. So I chased them. The younger brother Priss tried to block me, so Prick could hop a fence. I had to football juke Priss, then stiff arm him in the face as he slid into a group of people. The people started pushing him, and I kept chasing Prick. I chased Prick, yelling for help behind him for several blocks.

When Prick finally stopped, out of breath, in a Spanish guy's back yard, he tried to convince the Spanish family that I was a crazy guy stalking him. When the cops showed up, they already had my guitar in their possession. The cops also already had the pepper spray can and immediately arrested Prick along with Priss. For a split second it was the best feeling I had ever experienced in my life. Then the sweat from the chase had dripped the rest of the pepper spray into my eyes and I went temporarily blind. It was the worst pain I had ever felt in one moment. It felt like I went through a war. I started screaming, and crying, as snot ran down my nose. The paramedics had to put saline water in my eyes. For the rest of the day I was exhausted, even when I gave my video testimony, which probably looked even better in court, I was a mess. It looked like someone hit me with a baseball bat in the eyes. The two goon brothers went to jail for six months and never bothered me again. The best feeling I had ever felt in my life. Who the fuck carries pepper spray around every day?

Be careful of those who demand the most money for their services but behind the scenes try to either drag out their work or rush to get it done. The biggest lesson I have learned in life is the following:

People like to confuse things all the time in order to give a meaning to their lives, because when it is all going natural and fluid, most people are nowhere to be seen. When things are working out for you, they are hiding in shame, whereas when it starts getting confusing, chaotic and glitchy, they all come out of the woodwork. It is the only time they feel comfortable. Bad people glitch things to slow them down so they can catch up to life and feel a part of something, instead of feeling ashamed of how shit they are at life usually.

The next chapter will address some of the people I met in the music industry. Some of them are like the people I just mentioned, while others were a real blessing to work with.

Chapter 3: Industry Peeps

Producers

I honestly do not really like producers. I blame these people for the garbage that has flooded the music airways today. Those assholes have shaped the music industry into a watered-down version of television dramas. To make things more annoying, producers have huge egos, usually do a lot of drugs and have more money than the musicians that are doing all the work. I remember in music school, studying about producers and watching teachers promote producers like they were the Jesus of the industry. Everyone wants to be a famous producer, but really it is like a director in the film industry. A director can be a visually artistic genius, who is hungry and trying to prove his worth to the industry and will create a masterpiece that goes down in history as such, whereas other directors will take a great storyline, with great actors and still somehow ruin it. Out of all the producers I learned about, I at least respected producers who used to be musicians. At least, those guys know how hard it is to be a musician. They can relate and communicate better with musicians. They understand the dynamics of a song as a songwriter rather than as a fan or a capitalist.

I always hated the emphasis and love given to what is referred to as *"Merlin the Magician"* type producers. These are the type of producers people aspire to be the most, even though I think I have figured out their formula. They walk into a room and tell a band how to change their song that they have been working on for months. In five minutes, they change it to a hit single, when really what they just did is cookie cut the song into something that radio stations and labels will gladly promote, since it is the same formula our ears have been programmed to enjoy. It is not a revolution. It is the standard, the status quo. I have heard of producers taking some serious time and effort with bands in rehearsal spaces and studios, moulding and crafting songs with the band almost like a co-writer. I do appreciate this too, because an outside perspective can simplify an overly complicated riff, harmony or instrumentation overlap, but many times it is just another guy's opinion. That opinion may have more clout in the industry. But there is a plethora of stories of bands and artists that rejected a producer's weird or watered down suggestions. Moreover, because those bands and artists refused a producer's input, they got all the glory when the world saw the masterpiece the way it was supposed to be shown. I have produced all of my albums and I love producing. That is truly making music. Composing is good, but if another musician can compose better than you, but you understand how to reach millions of ears, the collaboration between both of you will be legendary. Deal with musicians' egos, keep your own ego in check and you will be a good producer.

Audio Engineers

Those are the scientists of the music industry. Sometimes, however, scientists can be very anti-social weirdoes, who cannot relate to people. That is why they work with ultra-sociable producers. On many occasions, audio engineers' opinions about your song are so flawed that it's comical. Do not let them toy with the production of the song, because their little adjustments are often childish sounding, gimmicky or just too esoteric. They have literally listened to so many songs and types of music that what tickles their fancy as musically artistic is leap years ahead of the average fans and may literally be in left field or in the case of mixing my album disaster, left ear.

Recording Studios

Recording studios are a strange domain. They are either so professional as well as efficient, that it is hard and expensive to even get into the studio or they are money grubbing bastards that are cheap knock offs and just hire their space out. There is a fine line between those two types and I have been in places that seemed legit, and then when you give them the money, they turn into the cheap knock offs.

Mastering

What the fuck do mastering people actually do, turn the fucking volume up? I swear these are just places where they pour baby blood on the record and ask Satan if it is a hit album or not. No, seriously, I actually really respect mastering. I have seen how they do it, and it is far more of a craft than mixing. Although mastering has fewer components, it means there is less places to hide errors. I know they play with the volume of a mixed track, but it goes far beyond that. They use tubes, analog consoles, pressure grids, volume boosts and sonic manipulation. In addition to their tool kit, they have an ear for every frequency known to the human ear. They do not just make the album coherent and volume consistent; they also take out distracting frequencies and can make an album bright or dark with just volume boosts. Mixing is like prepping tracks to fit together. Mastering is gluing them together.

Sound Guys

A sound guy can make a show run smoothly from backstage or can be the single most important ruining factor. They are usually guys who have been in the music industry way too long. They almost always have long hair and a bone to pick. They hate most bands, because they have heard everything before as well. They are seriously jaded when it comes to music, because they have seen great bands that they loved get the short end of the stick, while pop princesses they hate get the spotlight. They know it is an industry run by evil devil worshiping assholes, since Lucifer was a musician, remember. Sound guys can make you sound like a record or wreck your show to sound like a cell phone recording.

Rehearsal Studios

I have been to so many of these dumps that it gets annoying after a while. I think so many musicians had similar complaints, that now you will get these upstart companies with pretty nice room sizes and equipment, but they will charge you a pretty penny, anywhere from 20-30$/hr. When you think of it, it is all a rip off. These places charge mega bucks for rooms that are usually vacant. I know because I have lived beside one of them. It is a form of monopoly of facilities. Nowadays, everyone is renting out space, even recording companies have rehearsal studios in their back lots. My advice, get a garage and jam in it. My dad's friend owned Cat Eye Studios in Toronto in the 1980s. It was one of the first rehearsal spots for emerging bands. This guy was making a killing until some mobsters told him that he had to sell it to their guy. When my dad's friend refused, his warehouse was burned to the ground, he was randomly put in jail and he eventually lost his mind. I never knew why, until I met the owner of The Rehearsal Factory in Toronto. That owner apparently was the son of the mobster guy who was trying to force the sale. Apparently, this owner stalked my dad's friend so bad, he forced him out of the industry and then took all of Cat Eye customers and became a millionaire. What a nice story about how welcoming the music industry is.

Session Musicians

Session musicians are the hired contractors of the music industry. They are the labor force. Some of them can be world famous and expensive and others can be moderately talented but with serious baggage. They are either over-priced, arrogant, hard to book, and with less chops than they think, or they will have great chops but are emotional retards. You can hire by the union prices and get some decent musicians that have impressive resumes, but this will cost you more than the studio fees, or you can find an amazing busker, pay him $200.00 bucks to play on a song and own everything, like I did.

The Suits:

Promoters

Those are the paid "hype junkies". Promoters hype people up about your show. Be careful, they also love to undermine authority, play for the enemy behind your back and will take a cut from the top before you even see how much money was made that evening. They will bring gangsters, mafia and lawyers around to scare and intimidate bands and managers and will even threaten violence when it comes to payouts. They are cheap and scamming money is like a challenge of manhood to them.

Bloggers

Bloggers are great people to network with if you can actually get a hold of them. Most of them never respond to social media or emails, because they are constantly being bombarded with requests and spam. However, when they respond, some bloggers can be pretty rude. Therefore, you must have a thick skin when dealing with them. In fact, most bloggers will only talk to you if they know you are a devoted follower to their page and have done non-band related work for them. Only then can you plug-in your artist page or band. The worst is when you take the time to get to know a blogger, you add comments on their articles even if you don't like them, and finally they agree to listen to your album and then they bash it. Wow...really, thanks! Now I know why people blog, because they could never be real journalists for a multinational newspaper and they could never write a song to save their lives. Musicians write music, bloggers write subtle insults. Pussies! Go hide behind your computers like they are your digital turrets.

Booking Agents

Bookers will phone the asshole bar owners for you, but want 5% of everything. Even if they didn't get the gig or if the radio likes your song and wants it to be a hit, the booking agent is always hanging around wanting his 5%. When a venue is great, it is his doing; when it is shit, it is your fault.

Record Labels

Music is getting worse! The harmonic diversity is down, the texture, color, and quality has decreased. Pop music has become repetitive and progressive rock has become too complicated. Where is the happy medium of Queen, 2Pac, Led Zeppelin and Nirvana? Every dance song feels formulaic. One hears the same "bwah bwah" or "bing bing" in every dance song. One can also be under the impression that songs must have the same sound to get played, to fit the cookie cutter of what is trending.

For instance, I once listened to ten different dance songs at a club and I thought it was the same album. The same comment applies to listening to the radio. I will listen to five different stations playing different songs, but it sounds like the same band, filled with big sounding simple drum beats and "whayo whayo" (millennial whoop) vocals. Quick! Someone tell the labels the following: "Familiarity does not have to be boring and promoting stupidity". Supposedly, many scientific studies around the globe have proven that lyrical intelligence and sonic diversity are constantly decreasing on a gradient scale. "Play a million chords for four people or play four chords for a million people", as the old saying goes.

So many songs, especially in pop and rap, repeat the same lines, as an overt plan to make people stupid, like a systemic agenda to only allow their programmed artists on the radio. Everyone who is anyone these days, Brittney Spears, Rihanna, Lady Gaga, Adam Lambert, the list goes on, all had their songs written by the same guy. Swedish songwriter, Max Martin wrote everyone's shit hits. Now you're telling me that a great band from Canada can't get into the industry because their music is not dumb enough or written by Swedish Max? Fuck the music industry! It's better to listen to music than to make it. The industry has a bad cultural message in everything. That's why many people just stick to listening to Beethoven. If you or your band mates are over the age of thirty, the industry will pit you against a band with members in their twenties. You win, they get cut. They win, you get cut. It is a zero sum, zero forgiveness industry.

Money = Music Manhood

If you have money, like Drake, you can literally buy fans, with a little talent. Unfortunately, if you are the most talented poor musician, you must be a mental case or else why wouldn't anyone from the industry not have found you already. I found out the hard way that gaining likes on social media, true fans and followers has nothing to do with being organic; it all has to do with paying for a publicity agency to create algorithms that make you look more famous than you are. Those algorithms will entice people to buy into your music and not discredit you. Most of a person's first 100,000 views, likes or followers are actually bots.

Don't even try to have a baby as a rock star. You either have to have a child that is low key or have your mate look after the baby or you have a baby when you are famous and the world looks after it. Many great musicians have been derailed because of an unexpected pregnancy. I know very few who, during a tour, hooked up with a chick and had a kid. The record label and team will just forbid it and do everything they can to stop it (*Adjustment Bureau*). Yeah maybe the groupies can raise your child! Maybe your wife will be nice enough to look after the baby when you are on tour like the singer from Rise Against! Probably not though, so plan to a have a child before or after you get famous, not during.

What about rocking out for a good cause? Do you think Live 8 and SARS Festival gave all their money to charity?

Give me a break!

Everyone involved got paid and the leftovers went to AIDS or SARS. I remember seeing First Nations people doing *The Water Walk* and begging and pleading with a few semi-famous folk singers to come play for free at the opening ceremony. Very few famous musicians will actually do anything for any cause for FREE. This actually makes profit seeking NGO's look bad and obligated, so to prevent a run on donations, the organizations just stop it before it starts. If a famous musician does do a show for FREE, it is with a serious PR incentive for their team, not out of their heart.

Grants

The granting system is a façade. You will write a grant all week or all month, and do everything perfect and they will still give the grant to their friends. One time, I literally saw a grant being taken from my band and given to an acoustic francophone couple, because they knew the grant department chair. Frankly, that couple was terrible!

I grew up in Toronto, listening to Kardinal Offishall, a mediocre Canadian rapper, and I would never have expected ten years later to be competing with him for a small amount of granting funds. I mean, this is a person I grew up watching on MTV and who had all the "bling" in the world. Now, he is taking money from new emerging artists, exploiting his established name to edge out other "no name" musicians. Where did all his money go? It's like he's on musician welfare now.

I am sick of somewhat established artists taking all the grants for their mediocre tours and albums, when there is a plethora of great bands with great sounds, great stage presence and already great recorded albums. These musicians are left in obscurity and still get a big "fuck you but have a nice day" rejection letter come decision time. In music school, I had a grant writing class and I was able to hear first-hand from a granting judge what is expected in getting the grant nod. To be honest, it has nothing to do with music; it is all about how many fans you have. The grants will not help you get fans; they want their sticker on an already established artist who has fans. I saw a list of grant recipients, and you would be surprised how many names repeat every year. These mediocre musicians take money from emerging geniuses and never get famous again themselves, then ask for the hand-out again the next year. WTF!

Chapter 4: Small Achievements

Although I am kind of salty about my experience in the music industry, I know it will all pay off in the end. I had a few minor achievements in my rookie career. When I was in high school, I went from an intellectual stoner who skipped classes and then aced exams to actually trying hard and finishing my last year with decent marks. In my final year of high school, I seemed to catch up for all the things I missed. I started a band specifically for the end of the year's battle of the bands. No one even knew I was a musician. All my old gangster friends and my new Christian friends were so surprised when they saw my band mates and I jamming during the dress rehearsal. For the show, there were about a thousand people in attendance. It was a big thing at our school. Even family and friends from other schools would come to our show. To synthesize a lengthy story, I absolutely crushed it. I had girls crying, guys starting a mosh pit and teachers literally raising my grades just from that show. We were the opening act that night, and we started things off with a bang. I had gathered the band together with phenomenal musicians from my church youth group. I really enjoyed playing with this band. In fact, the bass player is one of the guys who later joined the army. He is the only one I do not begrudge. He was so talented the Canadian Forces hired him to be their bass player for their touring Jazz band. Nonetheless, that night our band stole the show.

There was another band of goons that had been preparing all year for this night, with high energy songs. One of the judges was even the father of a member of that band. Still, the crowd told the judges what was good. Our set list was only five songs and each one was iconic, well played, and a perfect complement to the next song. I sang an original song named *Praise* and it was well received. We heard uproar when we finished our opening song. It was a good feeling and it made us feel welcomed and comfortable the rest of the set. We then went into a few contemporary alternative rock songs such as *Crash* (DMB), *In Repair* (OLP), *Apparitions* (MGB) and then closed the set with a spiced up version of *People are Strange* (The Doors). As soon as we finished our set, the crowd jumped to their feet. My band actually mooned the crowd, but we had dropped our pants and were wearing shorts underneath that said "GO RAMS GO". The crowd loved this and I had girls run up to the stage asking for autographs and whispering, "Do you wanna fuck after the show?" It was incredible, I got my first taste of stardom that night and I never looked back. I actually just left with a hot blonde right after the set and I only found out the next school day that we had won. It was so boss.

Now that you have heard one of my best stories where I stroke my ego, it is time to hear one of my worst stories of being down and out, but still pulling off a miracle. I am actually most proud of this story. After high school, I didn't ride off into the sunset and go to an Ivy League school, although I should have. I instead became homeless and got in trouble with the law. I wasn't a criminal, but when you're poor and feel angry at the world for dealing you a shitty hand, trouble is always lurking around the corner. I made bad decisions, with so-called friends pushing those bad decisions on me, but then when I wanted a better life, all those "friends" seemed to disappear, like *Dust in the Wind*. A year after finishing high school, I recall trying to upgrade my credits at an adult learning center. I was living in the bushes beside my high school, because I hated the screaming and fighting of the local youth shelter. At the time, I was working a dead end job in a warehouse, trying to pull my life back together. I heard about an annual competition called "The Etobicoke Idol". I remember asking the bass player, who went to the army, if I could practice a few songs at his house for the upcoming show. He agreed and we jammed for the weekend. He could tell I was in rough shape, but I managed to hide my homelessness very well, with decent clothing and frequent showers at the YMCA.

During the next week, we performed for a small crowd at a local bar for the opening round of the competition. I only played two songs, but I absolutely crushed it. I played completely from my heart, with no ego, no assumptions, just a man with his broken heart and dusty acoustic. The crowd fell silent, and I thought they hated us. Then they shot up and cheered so loud the judges had to pass me on to the next round. I was so ecstatic that night. It was like this small achievement had given me something to live for, at least temporarily. It also helps when your bass player is a Humber Jazz grad with basslines and walk downs for days. People loved how his bass, my acoustic and vocals meshed so well together. It was like seeing a reincarnation of Kurt Cobain at the MTV unplugged concert before his death. To be honest, looking back, I could have died many times around that time, and that would have been my last unplugged concert as well.

The following show was much more intense. I saw people warming up in the halls, going over sheet music with their ensembles and even my asshole music teacher when I was young was there with his son. I had picked my slowest ballad, *Meet Again*, to be the final song since I knew the finger picking and message was sure to get me to meet the judges again. We were told to play three songs the week before, but when I walked into the larger bar that night, the greeter told everyone there would only be time for two songs per act. People were groaning, but I preferred this. I had three ready, but two were perfect, so it was to my advantage. I played *Drive* by Incubus first, because in a bar setting that song goes a long way. Apparently, the judges could see this too, by the reaction of the random bar goers not performing. Other musicians saw it as a cheat and frowned but I was homeless and didn't give a fuck what some pretentious music teachers thought. Next, I closed with *Meet Again*. I will never forget looking up and seeing even my old music teacher impressed with how I was able to slow everything down when it seemed like the night would be chaotic. Everyone loved the song *Meet Again* and I knew I was heading to the final round.

At last, the final round was set for two weeks later at the famous Etobicoke Ribfest. I had emailed organizers and asked if I could bring a drummer. They asked the Etobicoke Idol judges who declined but allowed me to bring a bongo player. They wanted acoustic unplugged vibes for the night. I was allowed to play four songs, as there were only four finalists. Like my high school battle of the bands, we opened the show. I was the youngest contestant and I guess they wanted to keep the younger audience members interested so they wouldn't leave the bandstand area after seeing some old guy come on stage first. The other three contestants were professional musicians. One was an old guy, who played a mean ukulele. Another was a Japanese piano player, who was my only real competition. The second youngest was a pop singer songwriter, who was there because of her looks. I opened the show and stole it. I played an original song *Treemen*, then I played *4am* by Our Lady Peace and I closed with *Semi-Charmed Kind of Life/Jumper* by Third Eye Blind. The crowd loved the last combined song and that sealed the win for me. After seeing the Japanese guy, who was the best musician of us all, mess up twice in his set, I was feeling confident. The old guy didn't get much attention since his style was a little out of place at a place where people just want to get drunk and listen to Third Eye Blind. The pop singer actually had a really good set and the drunk guys in the crowd loved her and let people know. I was nervous of the verdict because I somehow thought this was my one chance to change my life, like Eminem in *8 Mile*, an autobiographical film about a factory labourer from Michigan shooting for the stars with rap. I thought that if I won, some record producer was going to approach me from the crowd after the show and sign me. I thought I would magically go from being homeless to be loaded in a night, like I hear in the rags to riches stories in Hollywood. Think of my dismay when they called my name as the winner, I got a standing ovation, I got my award of $500, a gift certificate to Long & McQuade and a contract to record a single at a local studio, but no one came to my rescue.

I was happy to win but that was my first lesson in real stardom. You will get small accolades, but when will the real contracts come, who knows. The crowd cheered for me for five minutes and I felt like a star around them, then when I sat down and the closing band went on stage and I started eating my rib dinner, people forgot about me quickly. I looked over to the pop singer and saw that she was crying. Maybe she was thinking the same thing as me, that someone would rescue her from her quiet life of desperation and take her to Nashville. I got up and wanted to leave. My bass player agreed. As I was walking by the pop singer's table, I placed the music store gift card on her table and just kept walking. My bass player turned and said she was smiling. That week, I went to the recording studio and recorded *Treemen*. It was fairly well recorded, but the studio owner was hurrying things up since the studio had agreed to discounted rates with the prize for the contest. No record producer was at the studio waiting, and when I left that night and thanked my bass player for the awesome roller coaster ride that month, I went back home to my bush in the woods and cried.

Surprisingly, the next morning I was awoken by a phone call from a reporter. She worked for the *Etobicoke Guardian* and she wanted to do a piece on the finalists. We decided to meet in a local coffee shop that day. She came in and looked beautiful. We sat for a couple of hours, talked about my biography and my musical style. I played her a song and she took a few pictures. I could tell she had enough information, but was willing to still hang out a bit because we were attracted to each other. I told her I found her gorgeous and when I walked her to her car we kissed. I ended up taking her to a friend's house that night and having one of the best one night stands I had ever had. I called her the next day, thinking we were dating and she told me she was moving to Montreal to write for a bigger agency. I felt heartbroken but also like a man. Maybe that was my real prize. I later read the article she had written in the local paper and it made me look great. I still have it in my scrapbook. The whole experience was very bittersweet, and I would not take it back, but I will warn it is not for the faint of heart. I never got a record contract from that night, there were no A&R reps or famous producers, and the five hundred dollar prize money helped get me first and last month's rent, so it helped but was no rags to riches story.

It was a couple of years before I did any competitions after that. I just wanted to record in the studio, not compete with the dogs in the rat race anymore. I was a full time university student and I was just about to graduate and finally go back into music as a music student for the first time in my life. In this book, there will be times when I speak of Seneca College and my experience there. Apart from studying, recording and learning about the business side of the industry, I will have to admit there was one time that I actually felt like a star around stars. I had just entered the program around the time when Seneca College was holding a *Seneca's Got*

Talent contest. The grand prize was not a recording contract but it was money, and I was broke. I was so broke that I was living off the food bank of the school while attending it. I had come a long way from those nights in the bush beside my high school, however. I had graduated from university, had a part-time job in the library and a really nice basement apartment/studio. I was now a music student, which had been my dream for a decade, and I had great studio facilities at my disposal every day. With that being said, I still owed OSAP $50,000 and rent along with tuition far exceeded my part-time wages.

I nonetheless loved music and stayed the course. In the first month, I auditioned for *Seneca's Got Talent* and blew the competition away. It was easy in the first round to outperform the competition, since everyone and their grandma had signed up. It became comical hearing such out of tune singing and weird magician acts. When someone with a hint of talent shined, they instantly went to the second round.

The second round was also fun. It had about 20 contestants and ran all day in the student lounge. The best acts were a couple acoustic guitar acts, a great dance routine, a hilarious comedian/magician and my epic rap video spoof. Looking back on this, I should have saved this rap song *Bright Lights* till the final round, but I didn't know that competition would be so weak and I didn't want to get cut. Although the judges where all black students, who were rooting for their friends, I was the undeniable favourite going into the final round.

Five of us made it to the last round. Before the last round in the following week, I was approached by the judges, who were throwing a party for the finalists. Everyone from the school was invited and they had heard through other music students that I was a DJ. To save money and help me promote myself they asked if I would DJ the show right after the final round. I agreed, but later kind of regretted doing this because it took time and energy away from preparing for my final song. It seems that when life starts to give you higher levels of competition, it also gives you other random issues in life to make preparing for that competition harder as well. Of course, for the final round week, I had an insane amount of homework, problems sleeping because of noisy neighbours, and a four-hour set list to DJ the final party on my mind. For the final round, I thought it would be appropriate to play *Talking About A Revolution*, by Tracy Chapman. I sing this very well and I thought it would be a heartfelt ending.

After I played a great version of *Talking About A Revolution*, one of the arrogant female student judges got up and said: "That's it!" I was a little shocked and angered, seeing how much work I had put in to just get up to this point, but then I saw the humour in it. This black student, who was always up in people's faces about rights and racial equality, didn't even know the song *Talking About A Revolution* from one of the most well-known black female social commentary songwriters of the 20th century. Typical. I just walked off the stage knowing I didn't win and I would just be happy to get a medal. I ended up tying for third place and getting a gift bag of Seneca clothing and swag. It was alright, a little disappointing since I knew if I had played *Tracy Chapman* in the second round and waited to do my epic rap video spoof to *Bright Lights*, which the crowd actually knew and sang the chorus with me, I would have won.

Although I did not win, I was asked to DJ the final party and that was just as important to me. It was also bittersweet, but knowing that none of the finalists could ever transfer from acoustic rock to DJing a whole night of hip hop and house made me feel better. I will never forget that night. I cheated a little and used some mixes I already had from my days DJing for Varsity games at U of T, but yeah, a crowd loves a professional. Ironically, none of the judges for *Seneca's Got Talent* was at the party.

Bad Auditions

While attending Seneca, I started getting bored with mixing my own music, since I had been doing it for almost a year, nonstop, everyday. Near the end of the school year, I started getting into drumming more and more. I had practiced my chops on the school kit for a while when I was recording the drums for the *Shadows and Machines* album. Now, however, I had just bought an electric drum kit that I could play directly into my headphones in my basement apartment. I also started taking lessons seriously from the YouTube channel *Drumeo*. I connected with a band named *WaveLine*, since one of their members was a Seneca Independent Music Production (IMP) alumni. I knew I was drumming late in life, but I had heard so many so-called "professional" drummers that were just so terribly boring that I knew people would appreciate my energy and grooves, even if I had to still learn speeding up my drum fills and paradiddles. I didn't care, however, because drumming is so fucking fun. It is the best instrument for an athletic jock that has transferred into music. I liked the exercise and the energy. I landed an audition with this band for the spot of the new drummer and I practiced their material for about a month. All my friends and random students said it sounded great, so I went into the audition feeling confident.

When I arrived at the door of their rehearsal room in the same sketchy building my father used to rehearse in the East Side of Toronto, I heard the drummer audition before me absolutely crushing it. I almost just turned around and walked away, but the door opened just as I was about to. You know those times you don't know how bad you are until someone great shows you, it was one of those times. When I looked in, expecting to see Mike Portnoy, I saw a blonde girl. I was so amazed. What surprised me even more was when I found out that was the bass player and the kit was hers. They had been waiting for me. I got on the kit a little nervous. Then I heard the blonde girl play bass and she wasn't that good. This confused me. I wanted to just stop right there and suggest that I play bass and she stay on the kit, but the auditioned started. I played fairly well, only messing once and in the second song. The guitar player and I really started jelling by the third song. The singer on the other hand was constantly stopping the song to correct me and getting annoyed. It was the last straw when I saw the singer glance over at the guitar player and roll his eyes at my drumming, because I was drumming my heart out and it sounded pretty good.

We started an argument during the audition when I realized I was a better bass player than the female bass player who was a better drummer than I was. Why was I playing on her kit? What a weird dynamic. The guitar player could really tell I knew the songs and was a great musician. He was open to the idea of having me possibly help with another instrument. He could see the potential and I could see his potential. I had actually got in contact with this band through him. I had heard one of his songs on a previous IMP album, years earlier, and I loved his melodic soft metal style. While writing one of my scripts at U of T, I actually used one of his songs for a fight scene in *Three Axe Circle*. I contacted him when I got into IMP myself and he was nice enough to reach out and try to start something. I then heard his band and loved their sound. I found out that they were looking for a drummer, just when I was getting good at drumming.

The singer, on the other hand, was an asshole bully. He often went flat and when I started singing harmonies with him while drumming, he got really annoyed. I knew I was never going to play for this band, so I started trying to troll the singer, hoping he would snap and then I could just leave early. Apparently the band didn't want a drummer playing what they had told me to learn, they instead wanted me to play better than the previous drummer.

I was fired before I was hired.

Some people just audition musicians based on the chops and speed of their play. They cannot see the long term big picture, that someone with a little less talent may work harder, learn the songs better and become a great musician right in front of them and be loyal to them, instead of some guy who does fast blasts beats and then never shows up to practice. I kind of liked the catchy Nickelback type songs they had going, but touring with those tools would have been an ego battle nightmare just to order fast food on the road. I'm kind of glad it didn't work out because I would not want to be the drummer of a band that did all the music themselves. I would feel somewhat out of the loop creatively and melodically.

Chapter 5: Bad Parenting

Imagine you were born into a family that resented you being born. How hard would that be? Like you being born somehow took away their time and chance to become stars themselves. That is how I felt, being born into a family that wasn't ready and had pipedreams of becoming famous musicians.

My parents thought it would be cute and creative to name me Lyndsay, after some male musician in the 1980s. A note to parents: please get the sex right when naming your child. I know this new age trend is reverting back to the hippie days. However, in his quotidian life, a boy doesn't want to be named Ashley. Inversely, a girl doesn't want to be named Tony. Being named Lyndsay had an effect on my self-confidence early in childhood. I now realize that women love the feminine name, and it is a good cuddle joke after sex, but please don't put added pressure on your child's development. I guess it made me stronger, like Johnny Cash's song titled *A Boy Named Sue*. I later changed my name to Lynden, because it was unique, sounded cool and was similar to Lyndsay. As a child, my mother was constantly around men with her *DEADHEAD rock band, where drugs, sex and music was a nightly experience.

I will never forget the first time I was introduced to the band The Grateful Dead. I knew that my parents and all their friends worshipped this fat hairy guy named Jerry Garcia more than they cared about their own children. I didn't really know what the music was all about though. I remember being about ten years old and I was into a metal phase. I was listening to Metallica, Pantera, and Megadeath. My mom came home with a new album for me. She walked into my room, and said there was a new band called The Grateful Dead. I was so excited. I looked at the album cover and it was a skull. I thought the name was so rock and roll and the skulls and colours were *gonna* be the next Metallica. You can imagine my utter horror and disappointment when I put on the first song and some country singer came on saying "Keep Trucking". WTF!

Now that I am famous, I am going to have a shirt on stage that says "I'm grateful he's dead" with a picture of Garcia and a stop sign cross over his face. You know like, *Ghostbusters*!

When I was thirteen years old, my family moved from Vancouver to Northern Ontario. We were constantly moving and I changed schools every year. My mother stopped being a deadhead and became obsessed with Native American spirituality, which to me was a lot cooler. My mother had some Aboriginal friends with daughters. What I liked about those Native girls was that they didn't give a fuck. They told off their parents, smoked, drank, fucked and still seemed to have a lot of love and respect for their parents, elders and culture. They were all good at sports and liked school. When you're an Aboriginal child living up North, you hunt, fish, trap, go out with family and friends everyday and are constantly moving, not sitting around playing video games.

I come from a family of bad musicians. I don't mean terrible musicians. In fact, my mom makes pretty catchy folk songs with great choruses and lyrics. My dad is one of the best bass players I have ever met who didn't make it. When I say I came from a family of bad musicians, I don't mean they sucked, I mean they were bad people, who seemed to play music for other bad people. My mom never tried to increase her knowledge of chords so it was always G, C, D, Em until you wanted to blow your brains out. My dad could make a wicked walking bassline, but he would always be in bands with some of the most demonic-looking scum I have ever seen.

The Not So Good Family

I once knew this family of hillbilly musicians. They used to foil their acquaintances' plans to gain any success in the music industry. They were called the Good family and nothing good ever came from them. I had to live with this family for a year, while I was going through a slight depression after the summer camp and before university. I enjoyed playing music with their son, but he was an amazingly gifted guitar player who seemed to be depressed every time he touched the instrument. He told me that when he was young, his dad made him learn scales until he hated music. When I met him, he was into rap and producing. We used to get high a lot and make hilarious rhymes, which actually were so good I kept a few and used them for the *New Legacy* album. The rest of the family on the other hand was a bunch of emotionally retarded animals that did more drugs than *Sigmund Freud*. They played the same rifts over and over using different variations when they jammed. They only impressed non-musicians. Real musicians wouldn't even hang around with them, because they were boring and arrogant drunks. Worse yet, they seemed to be the guard dogs for the industry, never letting anyone past them. If someone managed to get past them, they would be the first to rat them out or criticize their music.

I later found out that this family of poor hillbillies was actually the forgotten offspring of The Good Brothers, a semi-famous country band that had minor success in Canada from the 1970s onward. The Good Brothers are goofs however and I smashed their CD the moment I got it. This is why! I remember The Goof Brothers – ha! – playing a show with Pat Burns, the former coach of the Toronto Maple Leafs, when I was a child. The show was terrible. This not so good family also had brothers that became the band The Sadies. I am not a fan, but at least The Sadies have listenable music. Little did I know, I would later sleep with their granddaughter. Girls like that are always in the way, demanding more and more attention, but giving less and less respect.

When will the industry stop trying to put these spoiled brat blondes in the spotlight over real musicians? We all know this is just a way for them to launder money back into their pockets by inserting pin up dummies that will give the money back to their firms, companies, dealerships and even restaurants. My message to record execs is...

"Stop hiring and promoting your clones as a way to cycle money."

In my crazy life of dealing with abusive family members, angry peers and a chaotic world that only lies, I have come across many people that had good advice but only delivered it out of rage. Many of the worst men in my life actually had some of the best advice. People like this just cannot overcome their own inner demons to pass the knowledge on correctly. I did learn that a secret society does exist. I am not a paranoid man. In fact, I believe I am very realistic. I do not want to join a cult, but I do not judge anyone for anything they believe in. The Illuminati may be dangerous, or may be necessary, or a bit of both. I do know that if a group of people feel threatened by your presence, they will do anything to make themselves feel comfortable again, even if this means making your life a living hell. They did it to me, and I barely wronged them. Imagine people who truly wronged them! It got me thinking about all the weird deaths in Hollywood, the music industry and politics. Maybe some of these famous people's deaths were assassinations and not just conspiracy theories. I have heard so much online about how the Illuminati runs the entertainment industry. Well, I don't know what happens on the red carpet, because I have never been there, but this is what I do know. The red carpet represents the blood of the people that were crushed to make the carpet exist.

Have you ever noticed that the word Illuminati has the word "naughty" in it? The following statements will be about what I have noticed the occult trying to do to me and others that are trying to push through to make it in the industry. The crazy Illuminaughty will try to set you up to fight or confront losers, usually the biggest angriest baby they can find. They will come around when you are injured, crippled, tired or vulnerable, because on an average day they would lose verbally.

They love to test people with insurmountable obstacles and then make the person feel "not ready" and a "failure" to deny them a spot on the red carpet. They like to make it look like everything has to do with a dirty association tactic of making someone feel like they have to overcome a loser to get success in another field. It is like a sick game of dealing with loser, who only get attention when things suck. It is like if the most arrogant bully loser became your class president in junior high… Hang on! Isn't that what is happening in America these days?

Moreover, the occult will use any excuse, or dirt from someone's past to block someone who is rising, so that the money can stay in their tight-knit circle. For example, this happened to me when I was training to join the University of Toronto's Jazz Choir. I felt like everything was trying to block me. I "randomly" got a new landlord, who purposely allowed construction workers to dust up my apartment with renovations just before a big singing audition. I have heard horror stories about people, who just before big competitions have had every type of sabotage thrown at them from a "mysterious force". It could be how Michael Jordan was allowed to remain the best at something. If you were to take away all sabotages, give the best motivation, the best facilities, the feeling that you are the best, the best team, and no needless energy wasters, you would find it easier to stay the best while your energy levels are still high. I am not saying that MJ didn't work hard or deserve some of the accolades. But GOAT? I do not think so. There were other athletes, who would have achieved more under the same conditions, who were sabotaged around every corner (i.e. Drazin Petrovic), in my opinion. The same can be said for the music industry. If you want to know how I was trained to spot errors in the occult world, read my first script, *Three Axe Circle*.

Chapter 6: Grandma NOKAMUS

Let me first start by saying my Grandma is a lesbian and it is a miracle that I am here. My grandmother came close to not giving birth to my mom and my mom almost didn't give birth to me. Furthermore, this book almost didn't get written. Feel privileged to read the material within these pages, because it is a priceless account of some hilarious failures and successes in the world of music. It is a miracle that my family exists. In fact, I think my grandmother is like one of the first lesbians. Imagine a Native Indian lesbian in the 1950s. Talk about discrimination.

One day, when I was young, I found out what "lesbian" meant, and I rushed to my grandma Nokamus, who was in the kitchen.

"Grandma, where's grandpa?"

"Oh grandma doesn't like men!" she quipped without paying any attention.

"You don't like me?" I asked with my eyes gradually becoming teary.

"Oh no, Digger," she replied upon grasping the meaning of the moment. "I love you very much. I just never really stayed with a man."

"If you are a *lesbinin*, then how am I here?"

"Well dear," she explained while laughing. "I met a World War II sailor one night, and we got drunk in a bar together and before we knew it, we had a one night stand and I got pregnant."

"What?"

"But you know, there is one man I would allow to do anything to me."

"Huh!?!"

"Elvis Presley."

Now my grandma was mad about Elvis. She has more pictures of Elvis around her house than pictures of our family. She has been to Memphis a handful of times and even to Elvis' house. You know you're a rock legend when you can cut through gender and sexual orientations and reach any man or woman's heart. Elvis was the King.

My grandmother's story of music, heartbreak and victory is legendary, enjoy:

I, *Nokumus* (Grandma),lived in the middle of the woods in a small town named White River (also the home of Winnie the Pooh).My parents had to make a tough decision to send us kids away, because there was no food. There were five kids. My name is Violet, the Tomboy, the adventurous and the musical. The five of us also lived with my great grandma. She was a tiny lady. We called her "Shomi". Her side of the family had the First Nations surname Matchinni, which means "Evil Man". I was sexually abused in White River, not by my father or a family friend, but by a one of the fathers of a girl in my school. I was abused at age ten. I don't know about my classmates, but I think the same man abused many of the children in town, because everyone knew everyone. I have come to realize, a lot of musicians were sexually abused in some way or another. In 1955, we finally had to move, because neither my mom nor my dad could afford to raise us. I was so happy to leave.

All five of my siblings were sent to a lady's house in Sudbury because she had the same last name as us, Legault. It is a French name, and Dad thought she would take care of us, because of our French kinship. We were only there for about six months. The Franco-Ontarian lady only took us in for the money. Although we ate well, she was ruthlessly mean. The French lady didn't like Natives. She used to call us "Mokish Cavash", which meant "Goddamn little Indians".

One time, the French lady was in bed with her bad leg, reading. My two brothers, Edgar and Albert, were running by the room playing. The French lady yelled, but they keep doing it. The French lady got up and tied a strong string around the door to the hallway stairs. The French lady went back to her bed using a cane and pretended to read. As the kids ran by again, Edgar the youngest boy tripped on the string and fell down the stairs. A loud bang was heard and Edgar was crying at the bottom of the stairs. The French lady got up, walked over the string, untied it and hid it in her pocket. She then yelled down the stairs: "See what happens when you're bad? God punishes you! Now go to bed, Mokish Cavash."

As the children walked up the stairs past her, Edgar, whose nose was bleeding, threw some of his blood on the French lady's night gown and ran into his room and locked the door. The French lady looked in shock at the blood. She stormed into her room, got a key from the drawer and walked over in a rage to open the door. The kids banged on the door, yelling at Edgar to open the door. The Franco-Ontarian lady opened the door and grabbed Edgar by the hair, who was already crying, and told him to hold out his hands in a fist. Little Edgar's fists already had blood on them from the fall down the stairs. I remember him holding them out expecting to get hit. The lady lifted her cane to hit Edgar's knuckles with the handle side, just then, I pulled Edgar's hand away and said:"You want to hit someone, hit me. Don't hit him, he's only a baby."

I knew I hated that place and I was going to run away. The French lady hated looking bad, so she stormed out of the room, but I knew it wasn't over. One night soon after that incident, I approached my closest sister, Evelyn. "I am gonna run away," I whispered.

"You're gonna die," Evelyn replied.

"Yeah, I'm almost twelve, I know what to do. It's around Easter holiday and I know father is in Faulkner Ridge for the weekend on a business trip."

"How you gonna get there?" Evelyn asked.

"I don't know, walk. I want you to come with me."

"It's a bad idea and I will scream if you run away now."

"What are you doing!" I blurted while looking around."I was just kidding! What are you trying to do, get me in trouble? Never mind, forget I said anything."

That night, possibly because Evelyn told on me, The French lady came upstairs with a stick. The French lady walked into the room, and I was standing in the shadows, waiting for her.

"Go ahead you bitch!" I exclaimed."You want to beat me, then go ahead, 'cause I got no use for you, you're rotten and no good."

I knew I was running away that night, maybe so did she. The Franco-Ontarian lady left the room in a huff. I dozed off briefly and woke up at the first sign of morning. I woke Evelyn up, staring directly into her eyes.

"I'm leaving little sis. Are you gonna scream? Eh?"

"I love you sis," said Evelyn prior to hugging me.

I picked up my bag and opened the room door slowly. I had to steal a little money from the French lady's purse to make sure I could make the whole trip. I then went into the bathroom and opened the window. I dropped out of the second story bathroom window and knocked myself out from the fall. I didn't even remember hitting the ground, because I passed out from the impact. I woke up five minutes later, checked if I had my little bag of lunch and left. I knew Evelyn was watching me from the window. Evelyn just watched me in adoration. I walked through town to the train station and bought a train ticket to White River. The ticket agent looked at me strangely. A train pulled in, I hopped on it and occupied a vacant seat, clutching my bag. A conductor came around checking tickets. I handed him my ticket. He noticed something and looked down at me.

"You're on the wrong train," the train conductor pointed out.

"What?" I quizzically asked.

"This train is going to Sault Saint Marie," he added.

"Ummm..."

"I'll tell you what, the next stop is Coppertone. You can get off and take the bus back to Sudbury."

"Ok."

When I got off the train in Coppertone, it was still early morning. I checked the bus times and noticed that I had to wait all day for the bus back. For a little girl, I was not stupid. I knew they were probably looking for me, and maybe had already called the cops. I didn't want to be noticed so I left the train station quickly, and went to find a place to hide. I walked down a back street, and came to a big patch of bushes, near a river and a farm field. I remember hiding in a small bush. I made a little lean-to. Looking back I see the irony. There I was, a small Native girl making a lean-to in the bushes to avoid the white man.

I gathered sticks, some branches and made a lean-to with one of my shirts covering the lean-to. I remember resting and rubbing my stomach, obviously hungry. I took out a bill from some of the money I had stolen from the French lady. I poked my head out and checked if the coast was clear. I remember heading to the corner store. I walked by a house with a lady gardening. After leaving the corner store, I quickly ran back to the hiding bush carrying a bag of chips. Then, I remember falling asleep. A rustling noise woke me. It was a dog, with no leash, sniffing around with a little old man walking the dog. I was terrified of getting caught. The dog came into the bush, where the old man could not see. It came right up to me, sniffing my face. I had to quietly cover my face without the sound of hard breathing. Suddenly, I couldn't help it. I sneezed loudly.

"Hey, who's in there?" asked the old man. "Rex, come here boy!"

I looked around in a panic and grabbed my bag and ran out the other side of the bush. As I walked down the same back street, I saw the same old lady gardening outside the same farmhouse I had walked by earlier. It was just before dinner, and the sun was setting.

"Are you OK? Are you lost?" the old lady asked from her garden.

"No, I'm just wondering around waiting for a bus. I took the wrong train, visiting my uncle in Sudbury."

"Oh, is that right? You must be bored to death walking around. Are you hungry? Here let me fix you up a drink or something."

The old lady took me into her house. The inside was a very beautiful country farmhouse. The old lady brought a cup of orange juice along with plate of bannock, a Native flat quick bread, out from the kitchen and watched as I ate.

"You know there's a missing girl," the old lady said.

"Well that's not me," I retorted with composure.

I remembered thanking the old lady and walking out the front door. Of course, the old lady watched me as I was leaving and then picked up the phone. I decided to walk along the railroad tracks back to Sudbury for the five miles instead, because I knew that the random old lady probably phoned the police. In the shadows, I walked along the train tracks, avoiding being seen by trains. I arrived back in Sudbury. It was late evening, already dark, about ten o'clock at night. I remember going to the train station information wall again and checking the train schedule. I left the train station and walked the crowded streets of downtown. There were movies, shows and lights everywhere. I saw a big neon sign for a country singer at the Sudbury Arena. I knew I couldn't just stand around, so I mixed in with the crowd, improvised as I went.

I checked my bag of money. A little money left. I bought a ticket and followed the crowd into the Sudbury arena. As I walked up to sit, the music got louder. When I sat in my assigned seat, I saw a female country singer on stage already playing a show. When I walked across the singer's line of sight to find a seat, I could tell the singer noticed me, a little girl by herself. Halfway through the last song, I left the crowd behind. I had a train to catch. When the train pulled in, I was ready and I got on. I did it right this time and got off in White River the next morning.

I didn't want to see my dad right away, because I was scared that he would give me hell. I didn't know what to do, and I was scared to go to any of my parents' houses right away. So I decided to go to a family I knew, a family I went to school with. My family knew them and I felt safe there. They were the Banaish family. I told them what happened. They phoned my dad right away.

REUNITED WITH DAD

When I saw my dad's truck pull up and my dad get out, I started to cry.

"What are you doing here?" asked my father in a caring and soft voice.

"You have to get those kids," I urged him. "You can't leave those kids there."

"What!" my father shot back with a puzzled look.

"She beats us and blames us for everything. She hates us, dad."

Dad needed to finish the weekend, then he came and saved us. Father got a hold of mom to help get the kids. Little did I know how much I was an inspiration to my family. I reunited the family, if only temporarily. When I saw my mom, I started to cry, as well. I got out of the truck in front of my mother's house and ran up to mom, crying and jumping in her arms. After that, we all moved to a nice little town named Franz, Ontario. It was a tiny little town, which I call the "magical music town". One week later, all my siblings came home and he met them as they got off the train.

"We're free, we're free, we're free!" shouted Evelyn.

THE MAGICAL LITTLE TOWN

In 1956, I went to school in Franz. Mom lived in Franz with her boyfriend Rosier. He was a kind man, a good substitute father, who treated the kids well. Mom was a housewife. Rosier worked for the railroad. Rosier and mom always puttered around the kitchen, looking happy and organized. My father continued to live in that dreadful town White River, and he would visit often. All five kids lived in Franz with mom, while father sent money. Dad was happy for mom, because she was happy with this new Francophone Ontarian. My father and

Rosier actually became friends. When my dad would visit, the two men would sit around the table, always talking fast in French and laughing over a cup of coffee.

Growing up, I hated school. I quit school when I was thirteen years old, around the end of grade school. I struggled doing math homework, and the teacher had no patience for any Aboriginal kids. I constantly got smacked by the teacher's ruler, and I had a hard time concentrating. My brothers Albert and Edgar were even worse, but at least they could flip the teacher the finger and go home. I felt like I was in jail. In Franz, the school only went up to Grade Eight. Back in the 1950s, Franz, like much of Northern Ontario, did not have a complete educational infrastructure that took anyone from Pre-School to Grade 12. Besides, trade schools, known as colleges in Ontario, did not exist. There was only one school house, one classroom. There was no-high school there, either.

Other than that, life in the town of Franz was a ball. It was real fun, a whole new experience. There were only three hundred people in town. I loved Franz. Some of the best memories of my life were there. A bunch of townspeople would always gather around a neighbour's backyard with a bonfire, playing the guitar, fiddle and hand drum. All the adults would be smoking, drinking, laughing and having a BBQ. The town was all one big family. Everyone smoked and played instruments. That's how my sister Evelyn and I first learned how to play the guitar. Evelyn was on rhythm, and I played lead. We both sang as well. We were a little duet. Evelyn and Little Vi were playing songs for the townspeople, while they sat around a bonfire. Everyone always clapped and cheered. I knew this made my mom proud.

I started taking guitar seriously that year when I was thirteen years old.

I remember walking into her room and seeing a new acoustic guitar with a big red bow on my bed. My mom bought me my first guitar in Franz. I played guitar for more than two or three hours a day. All the kids loved Franz. We only lived there a short time; only about two years, but I remember every day. As the kids grew up, we had to leave to find jobs. There were no jobs in Franz. Back then, there were only two stores, a hotel, the railroad, and a bunch of tourist going through our little town. Nowadays, it's just bush and trees. The only thing that still remains there is the big lake. The train still passes through the town but doesn't stop anymore.

I moved out when I was sixteen. I lived in a small room above a book store and had to steal food from work. I worked in the kitchen cafeteria, and got one solid meal a day with my meal plan. I remember walking by the book store and seeing a book about lead guitarists. I bought it, took it up to my dingy bedroom and read it as fast as I could. I was determined this time to improve my skills with the guitar and become famous. I worked night shifts and practiced in the day. I practiced guitar everyday and memorized that guitar book. I started to catch momentum. Then life got in the way.

I remember one day I was walking down the street with another girl. We decided to go into a coffee shop. A young naval officer walked in and introduced himself. His name was Bob. He was tall, well built with glasses and in uniform. He sat down, and we had a really easy conversation. He made me laugh.

Now, I knew I was a lesbian back then. I liked chicks and I was a tomboy, but this gentleman was fun. We always had a lot of fun and liked hanging out. He knew I liked girls and would actually try to help me get them. We chummed around a lot over a period of a month. He was like my friend. We slept in the same bed a lot and never had sex, which was normal back in the 1950s.

Once, I remember, this guy trying to hook me up with this gorgeous, wild, little Native girl. He tried to set everything up. I finally, however, gave into his charm. How did I have sex you may ask? Well, let me say, to this day, that was the only time I ever had sex with a man. Because of it, I had a daughter and she had my grandchildren. I guess we're all miracle children and it was meant to be.

During my adolescence, I remember Soldier Bob and I lying in bed as the lights were low, somewhat cuddling.

"You know Vi," Soldier Bob opened."I'm doing everything for you to get that girl."

"Yeah and..."

"Well, it's just, um, well, maybe now, you know, you could do something for me."

"What's that?" I asked.

"Let me make love to you," Bob declared.

"Are you off your rocker?"

"Probably," Soldier Bob confessed while leaning in for a kiss.

He convinced me late that night, only once, but that's all it takes. The next morning, I waited on a park bench as I called him over. He approached slowly. I guess he could see that I looked scared. It started to rain like a movie.

"Hey Sailor..." I greeted Soldier Bob.

"Hey. So why'd you call me out here. Is it something serious?"

"You know what," I announced."I'm pregnant."

"Pregnant..." Soldier Bob replied upon being taken aback. "What? It was once!"

"You must have some good sperm."

There I was, a twenty year old Native lesbian, with no real education, a shitty job, living in a room, pregnant with a soldier's kid. I knew this baby was a miracle child, though. That year,

I got pregnant with my daughter. I always say it was an accident, but I now know my daughter was no accident.

A ROUGH START

I ended up moving to Toronto after that, thinking I had a better chance in the city to raise money for my baby. I let my mother keep my daughter for a few months, until I could get back on my feet. Maybe that was a mistake, but that's what I did. A Native lesbian who is a single mother in the big city during the 1950s, that's what I did. I remember getting off a bus in Downtown Toronto feeling happy, with my head held high. I was dressed up, wearing high heels, sort of out of place. I was carrying a guitar and luggage bag and had a piece of paper with an address on it.

I remember going to the public washroom in the bus station. I looked at the bathroom stall and noticed I couldn't take both my luggage and the guitar inside the stall. Therefore, I placed the luggage right beside the stall and brought my guitar in. Of course, after I came out of the stall, my bag was gone. I remember looking everywhere in a panic, until I stopped and realized I could do nothing. I was about to start crying, all my clothes and belonging were gone. Then I got the idea, looking at my guitar. Everything happens for a reason.

I immediately walked out of the bathroom and started busking in the bus station. I started belting *Folsom Prison Blues*, a song by Johnny Cash. Some people walked by, obviously tourists, and dropped money. Then more people stopped to listen. I realized I looked good and professional. I was dressed up and had a sweet growl of anger in my voice. As I ended the song, people started to cheer and howl. I kneeled down to count the money, and was surprised at how much was there. Some people even came up to me to ask for an autograph.

"Hey can I have your autograph?" asked many kids in unison.

"Oh, I'm a nobody," I said with modesty.

"Well, you're going to be a somebody!" cheered some parents.

I came to Toronto in 1965, and have been here ever since; over forty years. I did everything myself. I never followed anyone. I went to Toronto as a fluke. I was twenty-one years old at the time, and my mom was still up in White River. I worked a bit, but because I had limited education, I couldn't find work up in the North. In Toronto, however, I worked in a restaurant to make sure I ate. I would practice guitar scales at night. I played the guitar almost every day, whenever I got off work. When I met a few people in Toronto that played in bar bands, my life changed forever.

I remember I was on shift at work once, wiping a table at the local diner. A little woman, about twenty-five years old, sat at the table alone. I took out a pad of paper to take the order.

"What can I get you?" I inquired.

"Your number!" declared the customer.

"What?"

"Hi, I'm Ella," finally announced the female customer. "I work across the street at the flower shop. You're kind of new, aren't you?"

"That noticeable, eh."

"Say, I happen to know some great gals we can go for a drink with sometime if you want to come."

"Sure, okay."

That night I met "Auntie Ella" in 1967, shortly after I moved to Toronto.

FIRST RISE TO FAME - THE ROCKETTES

You might ask, why I didn't start music lessons? Well, when you're new to a city, you don't know anybody, and back then it was hard to afford professional lessons. There was no YouTube. I met some girls, however. We did practices and formed a band. That's how I got started. We were called The Rockettes.

After that, I seemed to always be in a bar drinking with Ella, obviously trying to sort of befriend her, if you know what I mean. By then I met Ella's friends, a group of girls that would become my band. We would practice on the stage after closing time. The bartender and Ella would stop what they were doing and smile, enjoying the music. I played quite a bit for the first couple of years. I got my first taste of success in an all-female band called The Rockettes. We did paid gigs and toured Northern Ontario.

I remember once getting off the tour bus, wearing black glasses, in some random parking lot of some shitty biker bar. I was slightly bored with the lack of promotion, and I wanted bigger venues. A band sign read The Rockettes, and people were standing in line for tickets. The band would always play a cover of Anne Murray's *Snowbird*, with our own country twist. The crowd loved this. Ella was like our manager and always talked to the club owners. I remember that night eavesdropping our hired promoter talking to the bar's owner inside.

"They're pretty good," the promoter said."*Ya* know, they pass."

"I know a better band, that just lost a lead guitarist," the bar's owner replied.

"Oh!"

The promoter told me later that night. They arranged a meeting for me the next day. I remember walking in to an office, where a studio session was in progress. A band was playing behind a glass wall. I remember admiring how talented and tight the all-girl band sounded.

"They're beautiful!" I exclaimed.

"They're called Country Slang," specified the promoter.

"They don't have a lead?" I asked.

"That's why I brought you in," said the promoter while looking at me. "How would you like to join the band? I know all about you, Vi, I know you like chicks. Don't worry. I need you to keep them in check. Here, let me introduce you."

The promoter brought me into the live recording space as and I shook hands with my new band. All the bands I joined early were all-girl bands. We played country, blues and rock n' roll. Country Slang was starting to get local attention. Little did I know we would blow up. I was just happy to play with serious talent. I got really good, too. I even surprised myself on stage sometimes. I played lead guitar; there was a cute blonde who played bass and the other was on drums. We had a great rhythm girl, who sang and was a real comic with the audience, too. When the bar was empty, however, I would drink at a table with Ella. That's when I really started to drink, because I was in bars every night. After you're done playing a show, what do you do? You drink. I drank alcohol too much instead of learning new stuff. We played a show every night, Monday to Saturday. The only rest was on Sunday, to go to church and confess our sins for the week. I learned a lot of guitar licks. I didn't know how to read music or scales. I didn't know what I was playing. I relied on my hearing to recreate a melody on my guitar. I knew the chords' names but didn't know any theory. All I needed was the chords to the song.

"You know," our Rhythm Girl harrumphed on stage in front of the audience. "Our manager keeps trying to get us to take guitar lessons. We've all tried twice. None of us likes starting from the bottom and working our way up. Hey guys (turning towards the band's members), remember the teacher getting us to play, *Mary had a Little Lamb* and we would play it by ear and never read the notes, better than he could play? Well, this is for you, music teacher." The band Country Slang starts a country version of *Mary had a Little Lamb*. The crowd starts cheering.

It was good while it lasted. I wish it had continued longer. If it wasn't for my drinking, I might have been a famous musician the first time around. I wasn't concerned with making a hit song with the band. I wanted to play lead guitar for a superstar in their own band. But the first time around, I never did get there. I would go up on stage half drunk and not even know what I was playing half of the time. I played hung over. Sometimes I played my best when I was hammered. It's hard to explain, but I felt the flow. I remember standing on stage during a lead solo part, with my eyes closed, head in the air, sweat dripping from my head band, playing a great lead guitar solo. I know musicians who can't play at all drinking, who take their music like a sport, who train, perfectly sober, really fast, like a calculated machine. They play it exactly the way they practiced it. Not like the ones who flow into it, looking like their minds are floating in space.

FIRST TRIP TO NASHVILLE

I remember Ella and me walking the busy streets of Nashville. I waited in line to get on the stage at a random open mic night. Ella watched from a table. When I was twenty-four years old, I'll never forget the first time I went to Nashville, Tennessee. It was in my drinking days. It was always my dream to make it big in Nashville. There would be a whole bunch of them, come with their guitars and wait in line for their chance to play a tune. I remember I got up and sang a tune: *Johnny Be Good*, by Chuck Berry. The crowd got off their feet and started dancing. I swear I had everybody screaming. When I got off stage, I even had people ask for my autograph again. Can you believe that? They thought I was a star.

"It's not gonna be long before somebody finds you!" yelled an old country lady.

"Oh, don't worry about that," I replied. "Nobody's gonna find me. I'm a nobody."

"You're gonna be a somebody," the old lady shot back while looking at me deep into my eyes.

That night, I remember I was drinking and not shy. When I drank, I was so loose. When I was sober, I was so shy. When it came to getting onstage, it was no problem. I liked the crowds, the center of attention, but when it came to networking in a room, finding a record producer, I wouldn't do that. No way. Ella would get me drunk and encourage me, even force me at times, to get up and play.

One night in Nashville, I remembered a man all in black with a cowboy hat standing at the bar, smoking a cigarette, watching me play. He whispered something into the server's ear and pointed towards Ella. When I got off the stage and the crowd was cheering, the waiter came over to my table.

"Hello ma'am," the waiter greeted Ella and me. "A man left this for you," he added while handing us a business card.

"Oh my God!" I cheered. "That was Travis Tatum! You know, the guy from that famous Nashville duet."

I spun around to see him, but he was already gone. I flipped the business card over and saw a hand written message, with an address and a time.

"I got an audition!" I shouted.

"Congratulations," said Ella. "We should celebrate. Two more rounds, waiter!"

The next morning, I got off the public bus. Again, I was well dressed, but it was obvious I was a little poor. I looked at the card and the building's address again to double check.

♦

Then, I went inside. On the elevator, I clutched my guitar. I was nervous, sober and excited. Of course, Travis Tatum walked into the elevator with a group of people.

"Hi," I said shyly.

"I said book the band at half price," Travis Tatum talked to the person beside me without deigning to notice me. "They open my next show and if they don't like it, find another band."

I stood behind him unsure of what to do, so I coughed. Tatum looked behind, looked at me and said: "Wow! You look even better in real life."

He took my hand and added: "I'm *gonna* make you a star."

"Really?" I asked him.

We leaned into each other and kissed.

♦

The elevator rang. I woke up from my daydream. We had arrived at Tatum's floor. Tatum looked back again and then turned away, not recognizing me at all. I remember catching the door before it closed awkwardly.

"Mr. Tatum," I said shyly.

"Yep," he replied while turning around towards me.

"You wanted to see me."

"Oh, you're the girl from the bar last night."

The elevator door went to close again, and I awkwardly stepped out of the elevator.

"Walk with me," he told me.

The two of us walked down the hallway towards his office.

"I checked up on you. You play in that band named Country Slang, right? You're a pretty good guitar player for someone who doesn't know what she's doing."

"I beg your pardon!?!" I shot back.

"What I mean is, you have no formal training," Mr. Tatum clarified.

"But I like your raw sound. How would you like to be a session player for some of my shows? We're looking for a good looker, who can keep a lick in time."

We reached his office. Mr. Tatum closed the door and looked at me with seductive eyes. I feared what would happen next. "How long you been in Nashville?" he asked.

"Just a day," I replied with an obvious embarrassment.

"Got anyone taking care of you?" he asked while leaning towards my face.

"I'm a lesbian!" I blurted out.

Both of us started laughing.

"Oh, okay, um, well, ah, let's get down to business. Sign here," he ordered.

Tatum handed me a contract.

TOUR TORTURE

I started touring with Travis Tatum, and I remember getting off his tour bus to swarming fans, mostly teenage girls. I would always wear black glasses and a Native beaded leather jacket. His music was really catchy but corny. I worked for him for about a year and then there would be times, when he wouldn't call for months. I played as a session musician and lead guitarist in other bands. I got tired of playing other people's songs that followed the same chord progressions. I wasn't a songwriter at all though; I would just fill someone else's songs and make them better. I learned from a lot of great musicians. Sometimes on stage, Tatum would let some girl sing a song, and she couldn't carry a tune. I was so embarrassed to be there. This girl couldn't carry a tune, but she could remember everything. Sometimes, another guitar player came on stage. He was an older country-looking fellow. He played a bluegrass music style. He was extraordinary. I would just watch him in awe, smiling, trying to keep up. One night, as I was coming off the stage, Tatum approached me. "What a great show sis'. I want you to meet someone," he declared.

Tatum walked me over to a group of people standing around talking. One had a guitar on his back. It was the older bluegrass player. He was talking to a female country singer.

"Vi, this is Crystal Gayle."

"Oh my God!" I said. "I have listened to you my whole life."

"Well, that's good," Crystal Gayle stated. "I can't get these guys to listen to me for five minutes."

Everyone laughed.

"This is Mickey," Travis Tatum said.

In my life, I met some phenomenal lead guitarists. One fellow, named Mickey McGovern was one of the best bluegrass players I had ever seen. He never got the credit he deserved, and that night he told me: "Hey kid, walk with me."

We left the group and walked around the backstage talking.

"You know, Vi," Mickey started, "you don't have to play the song exactly the same way you did every time. Just make sure you hit the chords at the right time and you can change it up when you want. You don't have to play it note for note. Add a note or two sometimes or play it like the recording sometimes. Play your own thing."

I preferred it like that, but I got lazy and didn't learn and practice new riffs enough and once I tried to wing it on stage when I was drunk and I got fired from a gig. I am not too proud to admit this part.

Travis Tatum introduced me to a music producer. This producer had a shallow behaviour and faked around me, with a fake smile, but always judging and patronizing me. I was in the recording studio with the Country Slang girls. As the blonde bass player and I repeatedly played our parts, I caught the producer nodding to Travis Tatum behind our backs. I remember playing a really nice lead part that day. During one of the takes, when the band was improvising and playing a perfect take, the music producer interjected: "Hey, sorry, ladies, can we do that again, I seem to have lost that whole take? I know, I know, I'm sorry, can we roll it again?"

This was not the case. I actually saw what happened. The music producer had not lost a take. He was trying to confuse us with multiple takes, getting us to improvise and switch it up, so he could cancel the session later and steal the lead and basslines. I knew he would then delete the evidence on us and leave us with some other shitty take. Back then it was hard to copyright music. I caught him and started yelling at him. Country Slang left the recording studio immediately. Travis Tatum was trying to steal my band's riffs and undermine us. I remember after that, the band just sat around a motel room depressed. I was frantically listening to a rough recording of what I had just played for the song, trying to salvage my best take. I listened over and over, relearning everything by ear. I went back to Toronto with Country Slang. I was not in a good state of mind and was more drunk than usual, constantly messing up on stage. The crowd began to boo me off the stage one night.

"BOO... Get off the stage, drunk!" shouted many spectators in the crowd.

After that show the same promoter who introduced me to Country Slang approached me while I was taking down equipment. "All you do before and after a show is drink. You're finished, Vi," the producer announced.

THE FALL

My sister Evelyn and I sat around the kitchen table in Evelyn's home.

"Thanks, sis'," I expressed my gratitude, "for letting me stay here till I get back on my feet."

"Welcome to the world of us normal people. Time to get a job."

There was a knock on the door.

"Oh," I remembered, "that's probably Ella. I told her to come by, she said she might have a job for me lined up."

"Oh, that was fast," noticed Evelyn.

Ella walks into the kitchen, with a smile on her face.

I couldn't play music all the time. I had to get a job. I worked with Ella. I became a courier, to have freedom on the road, to think about my failure and minor successes. I played music on the weekends. When I started work, I never played for money again. Next to playing music, I loved being a courier. I settled down, got an apartment, instead of a room, and stopped trying to play six nights a week to pay the bills. I had to be famous drunk, because me sober was a different person. Now, when I'm sober I can sing my heart out. I was sober when I was a courier and drunk when I was a rock star, but I couldn't do both. I couldn't be a rock-star sober, and I couldn't drive drunk. Sometime, I dreamed of what could have been.

ONE MORE SHOT

I remember one day at the courier warehouse, I drove into the warehouse, and Ella was waiting by my parking spot.

"I want to introduce you to the new chick," said Ella."I met her at the bar last night after her first courier shift."

"Oh," I responded.

"You got to meet this gal, Joanie. She can really sing and play the guitar. I said we would go out for drinks tonight."

We decided to meet at a local dive bar, to have a good time. I started the conversation.

"So," I began, "Ella told me here that you playa mean guitar and sing."

"Well, I don't suck," Joanie stated.

Everyone laughed.

"Well, I'm trying to get back into the game," I replied to Joanie.

"Yeah, Vi here was a real hit for awhile with a band," Ella informed Joanie. "You ever heard of Country Slang?"

"Yeah," confirmed Joanie, "I think I might have heard a song. That was an all-girl band, right?"

"Yeah, I played guitar for them for a couple years," I added.

"Wow...then what are you doing here?" asked Joanie.

Everyone guffawed again.

"Long story," I commented. "Maybe I'll write a book about it. Anyways, I want to start another band."

"Well, I'm in," Joanie voiced her interest. "I think I can talk to a few others, too."

"Let's do it!" I affirmed.

After all this, I started another band late in the 1980s with Joanie. She played rhythm and sang. I was a little rusty but again, we did pretty well. We played paid shows. It was hard to get paid shows, but we did. We played in Hamilton, Toronto, you know, anywhere that paid and was close enough. We didn't perform big shows; we performed at small joints. We used to stuff the band into a courier van to travel to a show. I played in the '80s in bars, but I was still drinking. How did we find paid gigs, you may ask? Well, there is a whole world of people getting paid well to play and then there is a whole world of nobody knows you, you got to play for free. For example, anytime you play in Nashville, Tennessee, if you aren't already famous, you have to play for free. For instance, Terry Clarke played bars for years and never got paid. The only money received was through tips. Barbra Streisand, to name an artist most people now know, played in bathhouses, and Emmylou Harris played in beatniks, which are little, hippie clubs, festivals and coffee houses. She also started out only getting paid by tips.

Don't think I forgot about my daughter, Darlene. When I got a little more stable, after my stint with Country Slang, I sent for her and got my daughter back from my mother up in White River. Ella and I would talk about it back at her place, while my little daughter, Darlene, ran around having fun.

"Good to have her back, eh?" asked Ella.

"I feel like I missed the most important years," I bemoaned out loud.

"Are you kidding me?" Ella questioned me, "Now is the most important years."

Darlene ran into the house.

"Hey!"I cheered while grabbing her with a hug as she ran by."How would you like to learn the piano, sweetie?"

"Okay," agreed my little Darlene while running away.

I remember my daughter Darlene taking piano lessons. Little Darlene would sit at the piano, constantly hitting one note, on a really small child size keyboard, in extreme boredom. The teacher would peek over her shoulder.

"Timing," delivered the teacher."It's all about timing."

"I'm hungry," my little Darlene complained.

I tried to get my daughter to take piano lessons. But she hated it. The teacher was average, but she hated practicing on that little piano. So I said "what's the point" and cancelled the lessons. Soon after, I remember getting a great idea. One morning, as I sat at the kitchen table drinking coffee, I heard on this advertisement on the radio: "Crystal Gayle will be playing tonight, so get your tickets if you haven't already. Show starts at six o'clock."

"Hum..."

I immediately got up and left out the front door. My daughter Darlene must have come down for breakfast right after. By this time, she was in her early adolescence. She was obviously into rock music, wearing a Pink Floyd t-shirt. As she sat at the table to pour some cereal,I came back through the front door.

"Good morning, dear," I welcomed her.

"Hi," Darlene responded drowsily.

I remember this like it was yesterday. I kissed her forehead and slid the ticket to the Crystal Gayle concert near her bowl.

"How would you like to see Crystal Gayle tonight?" I asked my daughter.

"Yeaaaah!" Darlene shouted and hugged me intensely as if I woke her up with an invisible cattle prod.

"I got to work late, so...guess who will take you...Grandma...she's coming to visit today."

I got tickets for my daughter and my mom that morning, and they went that evening. They both loved it and before you knew it, my daughter was playing the guitar. I will never regret doing that! I used to play guitar at the kitchen table, and Darlene would watch me intently. I didn't teach her guitar, only let her watch. Kind of like a reverse psychology. Like basketball dads or hockey dads that don't let their kids play the sport, and then when they do, the kid is hooked for life. I could have sent her to watch a famous piano player, to inspire her, but it never even crossed my mind. Now that I think of it, if she had stayed with the piano, she would have become a natural at the age of twelve years old, but she liked the guitar, and she became pretty good herself.

"Mommy's got to play a show tonight," I told my daughter.

"Have fun!"

BAND LUCK!

We had an excellent drummer in this new band, in fact I think people came to just watch him play sometimes. Whenever there was a drum solo, he would play it flawlessly every time. Then one night he didn't show up. All members of the band were waiting in the rehearsal room for the drummer, looking at our watches.

"Maybe something came up," I opined.

"No," replied Joanie. "He just called me an hour ago and said he was on his way."

I remember our band walking down the hallway with our equipment about to leave. As we opened the front door and looked down the street, we saw ambulances and police cars at a scene of a car accident. We all looked at each other in disbelief. I remember us running over and, sure enough, we saw the drummer's motorcycle under a transport truck.

"Oh my God!" shouted Joanie.

"Where is he?" I asked a police officer. "Is he..."

"I'm sorry," the police officer declared. "You're *gonna* have to come this way..."

The band's members all started crying. We lost our star drummer that night. They said he slammed on the brakes to avoid a jaywalker and slid right into a transport truck in the next lane, which was speeding through an intersection to get on the highway. After that, we just stood around the rehearsal space, trying to regroup and play a tune. Everything was so sad, and it didn't look like we would continue. The drum seat was vacant. It was very hard to continue after that. We auditioned a few drummers, but it was pointless. I almost put the guitar down for life. Then one night, Joanie walked into the room with a new guy. He was a tall man, wearing a country hat and spinning two drum sticks in his hand. He looked a bit like Darlene's dad, Soldier Bob.

"This is my nephew Gary," Joanie spoke. "He knows all about what happened and would like to see if he can help."

"Now, listen guys," Gary announced. "I'm not saying I can be whoever it is you lost and I'm sorry for that. But, I do not suck at the drums. They are my life. So, if you don't mind, I'd like to get back to playing shows again, too."

Gary sat at the kit. The band started playing on time immediately. Everyone was smiling again. After that, we always kept a picture of our previous drummer in the corner of the room with a candle lit beside it.

Life seemed to go on after that. I was in a better state of mind and I signed my daughter into the local high school in Toronto called Runnymede Collegiate. Darlene was a good student. She loved Biology and Science. She had a good group of Russian friends, all of whom were really smart. My daughter graduated with flying colours and the whole family went out for her graduation dinner. I remember being so proud of her. The whole family sat around a table in a local restaurant, enjoying their dinner.

"So what's next, Darl?" I asked.

"I'm *gonna* get pregnant and have a kid," Darlene proclaimed.

Everyone at the table stopped immediately and looked up. Ella choked on her steak. Then, everyone realized it was a joke and started laughing.

"I have decided to go to music school for music performance," Darlene rectified.

"Wow!" Ella said.

I wish I could tell you my daughter became a professional musician and rode off into the sunset. Unfortunately, that's not how life works. Darlene struggled with music theory the same way I struggled with Mathematics. She started hanging out with the wrong crowd, the rock-star crowd. She met a guy and often would party and play music all night and struggle in class. To make matters worse, she ended up getting pregnant. Darlene dropped out of music school and had a rehearsal studio with her own rock band. She smoked in school to be cool and that went on to become a bad addiction her whole life. I remember her studio was in a local basement under a video game arcade. A group of people would funnel down the stairs to hang out every night. One time I went to take a look in the studio. I saw Darlene standing and holding a beer beside her boyfriend Steve, a long blonde hair bass player. The band started to play hard rock.

"One, two, three, four," Darlene counted.

As the loud music started, I remember seeing a bald-headed drummer playing very loud and my daughter's boyfriend Steve playing a wicked good bass line. Then, Darlene started to sing. I guess you can figure out that Darlene and Steve had a son, my grandson Digger. This couple was actually seriously together for five years. Everyone thought they were going to get married. They played in the same band together, and when they had Digger, they were inseparable. Till this day, I think my daughter was too young to have a child. It was the final push to get her to drop out of school. She wanted to party, but having a kid wasn't the excuse she needed. Maybe having Digger ruined her music career, who knows? All I remember was that I was in the same hospital at the time getting a back operation, when my daughter was to give birth.

So my sweet daughter wanted to drop out of school, to have her baby. Digger's parents were high school sweethearts. They had known each other since Darlene was sixteen. Darlene and Steve used to hang around on the couch at my apartment. One morning, I was in a bad mood and I woke up to go to work.

"So what are you two *gonna* do today?" Darlene asked Steve.

"I'm gonna check out this new bass at a friend's house," Steve replied."He said he'll lend it to me for our next gig."

"And you?" I asked Darlene while ignoring Steve.

"I'm tired, can I have 20 bucks?" Darlene asked.

"I want you to get a job or go back to school, one of the two," I declared.

"Yeah, yeah, I know."

"No, seriously, I've watched you two putter around here for months. Get a job, or school, or get out. Both of you!"

In order to drive my point home, I slammed the door, as I was leaving to go to work. I remember coming home from work and seeing Darlene having a beer at the table watching TV. Steve opened the door a few seconds after I had just closed it. I was in an obviously sour mood, and Steve looked hyped up on drugs and was way too excited about something.

"Good News, hun," Steve blabbered. "You know that guy that makes guitars? He just told me he wants to join the band, and boy, is he a wicked guitar player. He got us booked for the next month. It doesn't pay great, yet, but he said if we do well they'll book us as the regular band every weekend."

"Really?" asked Darlene without keeping a lid on her excitement. "That's great!"

"So you're gonna be rock stars, are you?" I asked."What about helping me with rent first, or better yet, buying your own food. I said a job or school."

"I just want to play music for my life," Darlene stated."Who are you to judge? You played music for years and have nothing to show for it."

"Get out!" I roared.

"What?" Darlene asked.

"You drop out, you get a job. I don't want to see you hanging around the house all the time."

"Steve and I are playing in a band, and that's final."

"Well, I hope it pays well, 'cause you won't be living here anymore. Pack your shit up. Both of you take the baby and go get a life. You leave tomorrow."

I yelled that at her and slammed the door to my room. I didn't think they would actually go through with it. Maybe I was a bad mom; maybe I was too harsh. Was I wrong? I knew Steve and her would struggle. I gave her an ultimatum: stay in school or get a job. Unfortunately, all she wanted to do was to play music, not even study it. Therefore, I kicked my own daughter out when she was twenty years old. It wasn't easy for me to do. People think it was easy for me to do. In hindsight, she was exactly like me, and that's what was hard for me to watch. I remember the next day, having the same argument and kicking them out. I remember shutting the door to my apartment, putting my back to the door and balling my eyes out. I thought about running out and getting her, and saying it would all be fine, but I thought if I did that she would forever be there, puttering around. I now see, I should have given her more time, I should have seen it was just a phase she was going through. Maybe I shouldn't have kicked her out at such a young age with a stupid boyfriend and a child. Nevertheless, that's what I chose and what she chose. We both had our reasons and regretted it for life.

After that, I went through a period of depression. I started drinking during the day. I was drunk at the wheel as a courier one day. All of a sudden, I got slammed into and spun off into the guardrail. Another car slammed into my back and one into that one. There was a pile up, and I was knocked unconscious. Inside the passing car sat Joanie, Evelyn and Gary. There were also OPP cruisers and fire trucks everywhere. Cars drove by slowly. A fireman held a crying baby in his hands. Firemen and cops were fighting a car on fire. I barely survived.

"Oh My God!" Joanie drove by me.

"Sis!" yelled Evelyn.

"Stop the car!" added Gary.

I survived...and that baby was Digger. On the way to my last delivery, before going to a gig for that night, I hit my band mates' car and almost killed everyone, including my own grandchild. I don't have to tell you how serious that car accident was. It was the moment that changed everything. That was my last chance.

Digger's parents were serious with their own band, and once they had a kid, they all hung out with the same people they knew since high school. They stayed together for as long as they could, but after about a year, things started falling apart. Digger's father told me one time he walked in on Darlene with another man. Darlene claimed Steve was acting like an arrogant, rude bastard, and she broke up with him. She said she had put up with him for too long and his pipe dream of being a rock star, without ever practicing. Darlene also said they had already broken up for months, when Steve randomly came back to get some stuff and she was already dating someone else. Ironically, I think Darlene never slept around, until after Steve broke her heart.

The story supposedly goes like this. Steve opened the front door of Darlene's apartment. The lights were off. Steve stumbled by the baby Digger that was sound asleep. Steve was obviously drunk. While walking towards Darlene's room, he heard moaning and laughing. Just then, he busted into the room and turned on the light.

"What the fuck is going on in here?" asked Steve.

A tall and curly black-haired man rolled off Darlene in shock, and immediately stood up to fight.

"What!"Steve bolted with his fists up."You got something to say?"

"Do you got something to say, asshole!" Darlene screamed at Steve, while separating him and the tall man she was sleeping with."What the fuck are you doing here, we're finished?"

The baby Digger started to cry from the other room.

"You know what, Dar?" began Steve. "Your male friends always got in the way, even when I loved you. A bunch of cock blocks and cowards. You know, I wanted so hard to be a good father, but now I don't even know if the baby is mine. You're a slut, keep sleeping with all our friends."

The two men started pushing each other.

"Get out!" Darlene ordered Steve.

Steve left to the other room, picked up the baby Digger, gave him one last kiss and left out the front door, leaving it wide open. Talk about a responsible father and a healthy home to raise a baby! Somehow, Digger ended up becoming the best person in our family, while having the worst hand dealt to him. I guess life is not about how you start; it is about how you finish.

After Darlene had Digger, Evelyn, my sister joined my band. Joanie and I started living together and getting serious in our own relationship. Joanie and I would take Digger for the weekend every week, in order to get him away from the shit storm that was going on at home. We would take him for some fun time. We sort of raised Digger ourselves. We took him away from the chaos at home, all that instability. At home, he had no one to cook for him, only loud rock music all the time and we tried our hardest to give Digger a real home.

THE COMEBACK

I remember after that car accident, I was not the same. I knew I had to finish strong in life. I often would stare out the window thinking. I looked at my grandson Digger in the carriage, and had a nervous breakdown right there, weeping in my hands, alone in my apartment. That car accident changed everything. I felt I had lost someone, and made it my obsession to change my life back to music. I had to become disciplined in order to become highly successful again. I had to plan a new life. I started going to AA meetings, listening intently. Suddenly, I heard a voice from behind me. "Vi?"

I looked back and saw the blonde bass player from Country Slang.

"Oh my God, what are you doing here?" I asked.

We laughed, realizing I said that kind of loud.

"The same thing as you, I suppose," replied the blonde bass player.

"Yeah, I'm trying to kick the habit, *ya* know. I guess it's never too late."

"It's never too late."

We talked for awhile, exchanging numbers and then went on our way. Later that night, I sat in a dark living room, watching Anne Murray play a show on stage. Just then the phone rang.

"Hello," I picked up the phone.

"Hi, you pretty little Indian girl," said the voice on the phone."Wanna come get a few drinks with the girls tonight?"

"Hi, Ella. No, I'm good. I'm not feeling too well, I'm *gonna* stay home tonight."

"I miss you," Ella added."Well, suit yourself. I was hoping for a designated driver."

We both laughed and I hung up. I went to sit back down on the couch. Then someone knocked at my door. I hid in the dark kitchen pretending to not be home.

"I know you're in there, Vi. I heard the phone ring."

"What? Who's that? When it rains, it pours," I said to myself.

"Coming," I said to the voice on the other side of my door."Hang on."

I walked to the door, looked through the peep hole and opened the door.

"Surprise!" Joanie hollered while walking in the apartment."How you doing, kiddo? I haven't seen you at work for awhile. I wanted to see how you're doing."

"Ah, you know," I replied with a shy voice in an attempt to stick to small talk. "Just taking care of some things."

"Vi, you can't hold that accident against yourself forever. Come on, let's go out tonight."

"And do what? Drink?"

"Well, sorry our favourite past time is so unholy for you now. Nobody told you to drink and drive," Joanie commented with a slight trace of anger in her voice.

"And no one told you to come here," I snapped back.

Joanie started to leave out the front door.

"Okay," she declared with composure despite her anger. "Well, when you pull yourself out of this guilt trip, your friends and family will be here waiting."

"Yeah, with a bottle...get out!"

I slammed the door and went back to sitting at the table, tuning my guitar. It was early morning before I knew it. The guitar book I had bought as a kid was open on the table. I started to warm up with scales. A knock came at the door.

"Come in!" I said.

Evelyn walked in with her guitar.

"Hi, sis," Evelyn greeted me. "Early start."

"Let's just say I got a lot of catching up to do."

"We have a lot of catching up to do."

"I kicked the bottle," I proudly announced.

"Good, I didn't kick coffee yet, got any?"

"Fresh pot on the stove."

Evelyn got up to get coffee, I went back to practicing.

"I got us lessons," Evelyn howled from the kitchen.

"So what, are we starting a band, me and you?"

"Guess so," Evelyn retorted as she walked back towards me and sat down.

We smiled at each other.

Evelyn and I sat in a room with our guitars on our laps, looking at a music stand with a simple music sheet on it. Both of us were confused at first, but remained focused, trying to listen to the teacher. I tried again to learn music theory fifteen years later. When I was younger, I liked just playing on my own, by ear. When I think of it now, I should have learned the notes, so I could do both. I could have had both the flowing style and the methodical musicianship. I could have both improvised and read notes exactly the way they were written. That is what makes the best musicians. It's so important to learn your notes. First slow like a child, letter for letter, word for word, then like professional reading notes as sentences, paragraphs and entire stories.

SISTERS START A BAND LATE

Evelyn and I practiced scales, chords and harmonized our voices together perfectly in a rehearsal room every day. Evelyn started to learn the piano a bit to complement my guitar. We both started to excel.

"So anything 7 is dominant like a C7," explained Evelyn prior to playing it on the piano.

"And you get a diminished C, when you flatten the 7th on a scale, from a minor interval", I added prior to caressing the strings of my guitar. "You know, we should busk on the street."

"What, for money?"

"For practice," I clarified.

"OK!" Evelyn said upon cogitating.

Here we were, two older middle age sisters busking on the street together outside the Skydome in Downtown Toronto. Our sound was very tight, and we looked professional. Both of us were singing, and I played wicked leads over Evelyn's piano. A crowd gathered, just like when I busked in the bus station during my first day in Toronto. As the song finished, the crowd clapped and people began to drop money in my guitar case. A man in a suit approached us. "Hi ladies, who are you two?"

"Better question is who are you?" I shot back.

We all laughed.

"I'm a record producer from LA," the business man added."I'm visiting for a couple of weeks and have been going from bar to bar, show to show, looking for a new crop of local talent. You're both kind a older than most. Have you done this before? (Looking at Me)You look familiar!"

"You ever heard of Country Slang or Travis Tatum?" I asked the record producer with a little giggle.

"Yeah, they were an all-girl band that had a couple of hits about a decade ago."

I point to myself and smiled.

"No way! What happened?" asked the record producer with disbelief.

"Alcohol," I summarized.

"Ahhhhh...and now?"

"I'm looking for a second chance."

"Well, I can't promise anything. However, if you are both serious and can play like that night in and night out, I will get back to you. Here is my card. There is an agent I would like you to talk to. In a strange *kinda* way, I believe in you. There's no doubt you need a little dusting up."

We all laughed.

"Well, let's clean you up and get you two going," the record producer asserted."Talk to the agent and I'll get back to you. Maybe you'll be able to open for the new hit in LA or Nashville or something."

The business man smiled and looked directly into my eyes and winked before walking away.

"What was that?" asked Evelyn.

"A second chance," I responded.

I felt this time was more stable. It was my second shot, and I wasn't going to waste it. I was picked! So I called the agent, and he booked us in his home studio, where the producer and his team would be there to size us up. Evelyn and I arrived at the producer's house early.

"Here, come in," the record producer invited us with a gesture from one arm."Thanks for coming."

Evelyn and I looked around in amazement.

"Wow, nice place," Evelyn visually assessed.

"Who have you produced?" I asked."The Beatles?"

Everyone laughed.

"Ever heard of Anne Murray or Buffy St. Marie?"

My sister and I looked at each other with a blank stare.

"Here," the producer indicated. "We'll be downstairs."

The three of us walked downstairs into a nice home studio. Another man in a suit got up from behind the work station.

"This is Hans," the record producer said. "The agent you spoke to on the phone."

"Nice to meet you, ladies," Hans welcomed us."Well, it seems like you've been here before, eh Vi?"

Everybody laughed.

"Well, nobody's here to steal any of your music or force you to commit to something you don't want," added Hans.

"Let's hear both of you play," ordered the record producer. "If there's a spot for you perhaps opening for one of our headliners, we'll fit you 'old bitties' in."

Evelyn and I played the same song we played together in front of the neighbours in the small town of Franz. The producer and the agent looked at each other and smiled. While we were playing the song, the producer was already behind the glass booth making phone calls.

Let's just say from there, everything happened very fast. Not like before, where we had to work through everything. Now things were just flying. Before we knew it, my sister and I were travelling around the world with a stage band, doing our little country duet, opening for names like Anne Murray and Buffy St. Marie.

LAST TOUR HOORAYS

I remember near the end, I was getting on a plane, while Evelyn signed a kid's book of autographs.

"You now I could really get used to this," vocalized Evelyn.

"Don't let it get to your head," I retorted.

We laughed.

I picked up my suitcase that had stickers from around the world across it. We traveled around the world that first year. Europe, Japan, even Australia like some good old country music. We even got Darlene to come on as a guest singer sometimes. The three of us would sing for packed crowds and behind the stage, Anne Murray and Buffy St. Marie would watch and discuss the opening act.

"They're good," admitted Buffy St. Marie.

"I know," declared Anne Murray."I like their style...kind of a Fleetwood Mac feel but with country twang."

"I'm *gonna* get them to open for all my shows."

"Let's just wait to see what Hans says," warned Anne Murray, as she obviously wanted us to open for her show.

"I think Hans got them a record deal."

Finally, music was what it was supposed to be. Not an ego trip, but a way to pay for trips. Evelyn and I would lay back, relaxing in a gondola.

"Where do we go next?" I asked.

"Say sis," responded Evelyn while looking at her pocket book, "we got that show in Nashville tonight."

I knew the Nashville show was the most important of the tour. I also knew all this was taking a toll on our older bodies. During one of the shows, Evelyn got dizzy and stumbled a little on stage. The crew quickly took her off stage, as I had to finish the show alone. I immediately came off the stage looking for Evelyn and Hans. Hans noticed me and rushed over.

"Where's my sis?" I inquired.

"They took her to the hospital," confirmed Hans. "I don't know what it is, but as soon as they find out, I'm *gonna* go get her, so just hang tight in the dressing room until I know more."

I sat in the dressing room so worried, waiting, staring at the mirror and the door in the mirror's reflection. Just then Evelyn walked into the room slowly, using a cane. I got up immediately and stated crying. "Oh my God, sis, are you okay?"

I went to help her, but Evelyn waved for me to stay seated.

"What did the doctor say?" I asked Evelyn.

Evelyn sat down and looked up at me for what could seem like ages.

"I love you, sis," Evelyn finally broke her silence.

"Oh, come on, sis," I begged her for a clearer answer. "Don't do that. What did the doctor say?"

"I got cancer, sis."

"No."

"Yep, it's been there for a while. He says I *gotta* stop all this,(pointing around) or else I won't have long."

"But we were just getting started!"

Evelyn fought pancreatic cancer for three months after that, but it was a losing battle. I tried to pay for all the bills, but Evelyn eventually just told me to save the money and take care of Darlene and Digger, because she was happy with what we had achieved and was waiting to meet her heavenly Father. My best friend in this whole world died shortly after. I decided to finally write my first song, as an old lady. I wrote the song for my sis.

EVELYN DIES

During the funeral, everyone from the family, siblings, old friends, famous people, band mates and crew, all stood around as the casket was lowered six feet under. You know, I always wanted to check the lineage of my ancestors. I am a half-bred, maybe what they call a Métis, a specific type of Native French Canadian. It's all determined by a certain lineage and geographic location. All I know is I'm Native and my family is Native. I have seen this world change from racism to one big rush. I am old now and I wish I could go back and tell that little girl up north to stick to one thing and go for it, stay away from the booze and be proud to be Native. I was a Native, in a time when that was dangerous. I was a lesbian in a time when that was evil, and I was a rock star in a time when country music was fading. Now I am a mother and a grandmother, in a time that is getting shorter and shorter. Alcohol ruined our family. I pray for the Native families struggling with alcoholics. I pray for all the musicians trying to make it, stumbling through bars. I love you guys, I love you. I make tobacco offerings for all these prayers and I hope you do one day, too.

THE LAST SHOW

When I was very old, they asked me to play one more show in Nashville, since they knew what had happened. I told them I'd play only one song, the only song I ever wrote. I had my back to the audience, as I shed a little tear for my sister on stage. I then turned around and spoke into the microphone: "This one's for you, sis'."

I sang an acoustic solo song I wrote with my grandson Digger: *Meet Again– Shadows and Machines*.

As I sang my final song, I looked down at the audience and saw a little Native girl wandering in the crowd all alone. The little Native girl looked up at me. I stood there wondering if this little Native girl was alone, maybe a runaway, like me, or maybe a member of the next generation of musicians, the circle of life. The crowd cheered. Fin.

Chapter 7: Yellow Butterfly

I honestly had one of the worst mothers a child could get stuck with. She would constantly put so much pressure on me and would randomly flip out over the smallest things. She was ruthlessly unpredictable. Of course, everyone in my family thought they were just fine and no one sought counselling help. I never really had a strong relationship with either of my parents. When a conversation would start to deal with issues, especially about our past, they had every excuse in the book, which just became so tiresome to talk about after awhile. I just couldn't stay around them. It was emotionally and mentally exhausting. Everything would become a challenge of my timing and temperance, even though they will deny this until death.

For example, I will mention an oddity. My mom dated a rich and annoying nutcase, who had a PhD in Philosophy. This guy was in his fifties and still lived off his parents' fortune left to him. Luckily, my mom was cashing in on some of that. The strange thing was, however, this guy hated me. Whenever my mother and I started rebuilding our relationship, he would threaten to leave her. He was dangling his wealth in front of her as though it was a carrot. Whenever my mother and I had an argument or a falling out, he would be the first back supporting her. I am thinking of the great film series *Highlander*: "There can be only one!"

When I was homeless in my late teens, I met a lot of chicks, who always seemed to be hanging around my street punk friends. Surprisingly, a lot of these chicks were hot. The truth about this underworld, however, is when all the fun and games are finished, the only chicks still around are the ones you don't want. Those are the chicks who are still trying to be popular, when the night is over. When most of the guys are either horny or lonely, they start to finally notice those chicks. I later found out from my dad that my mom was one of those types of "always around girls". In fact, my dad told me once, that my mom slept around when they were dating, and that he wanted to get a DNA test to prove if I was his child. What a *Jerry Springer* episode! I'm a bastard from a slut, great...and I have a name, Digger...WTF!

In my final year of high school, I was nineteen and one of the oldest kids in the school. I remember playing in a band, and we were the best band around. My band was a group of friends that knew each other from the church. We were all great musicians at our respective instruments. I play rhythm guitar and vocals. I remember during our high school's battle of the bands, I had a few chicks in the front row hold up a sign that read "I want your baby" as a joke. Well, to one of them it wasn't a joke. My band won the battle of the bands, and afterwards, when everyone was going home, this one chick named Courtney Love approached me.

"You guys were great," Courtney said. "What are you doing tonight? Want to get a drink?"

It was like how a guy picks up a chick. I FELT LIKE A ROCK STAR. That was the moment I found my true calling: to be a rock star. Courtney Love and I left together. We went back to my house.

Take care of the ones who love you, even if you don't love them that much from the outset. Be careful of love and infatuation. Watch what you say to people who love you! Do not burn bridges and always try to end things gracefully. Help people build confidence by showing confidence around them. Confront tissues, but let others speak, even if it's hard. Most importantly, just hold your girl sometimes, let her cry and show her how much you care. Do not seek women to take care of you. Even though security is nice, independence is nicer.

Now, let's get back to my mother. I have always respected my mother's hard work and determination, but her choices at the end of something always failed. It got so hard watching constant failure after a while. My mother was a gifted vocalist, who could reach incredible heights (Loreena McKennitt, Stevie Nicks) and had a great ability to write thought-provoking lyrics along with cool melodies. I loved a few of my mom's songs growing up. To this day, I believe my mother should have been a vocalist in music school and trained as a pianist secondarily, not the guitar. I believe she would have been better than Jann Arden, from her piano, instead of always being around asshole rock musicians with her acoustic guitar. My mom loved that acoustic guitar, and her folk influence will always influence my slower acoustic ballads. However, my mom was way too naive, idealistic and vulnerable to be around asshole arrogant rock musicians, because they fed her ego, not her bank account.

To make matters worse, my mother started to improve her life, and then plummeted even further. You see, my mom moved to Vancouver, met a full blooded Native medicine man, had my younger brother and really started pulling herself up by her bootstrap. At the time, even her music skills and song writing started improving. Two of my mother's best songs, to this day, are *Ticket To The Sky* and *Stay Wild*. Those inspired me to take music seriously at a young age. I never wanted it to become an obsession; I wanted it to just stay fun. For some reason, my mom decided to come back to Ontario, maybe to see family or maybe to hang out with her old "wasteman" friends. All I know is when we moved back to Toronto, my mom had another child, my youngest brother and her music never sounded the same again. My mom met some drug dealer black guys when she was poor, and they hurt our family. She would perform at festivals, but it was from a place of pain, not a place of adventure. I am proud of my mom for overcoming so many obstacles and allowing me a chance to enjoy music. I am also proud of my mom's hit singles. Although I could never tour with her in a band, I would allow some of her songs to open a show for me and would gladly collaborate.

Chapter 8: Final CRACKDOWN

I have always felt sorry for my father. He is widely known in many music circles in Toronto as the best bass player to never "make it". Before this plethora of new age kids with the talent to burn it up on any instrument came the older veterans, who had to work hard at it for decades and pave the way for this new generation. My dad is one of those veterans. Never classically trained, my dad learned by ear and then by a system that he created himself to follow guitar players. My dad knows scales, modes, transposition, modulations, you name it. Unfortunately, he can't tell you how he knows or how to explain it. He told me that when he was a teenager, he literally locked himself in a room for weeks on LSD and hunted the mysteries of music theory, until he developed his own take on theory, much like Allan Holdsworth. My dad said he understood complex ideas with just a simple look at the fret board, like seeing a pattern. My dad was notorious for listening to a song once and playing it back perfectly, even adding embellishments. My dad has played in jazz ensembles, metal bands and wedding polka bands, you name it. He was a nerd growing up. Because his father didn't have the time or money to get him into organized sports, he just started playing the bass guitar. Then, when my dad was in high school, groups of poor Italian kids in his neighbourhood picked on him. After my dad had been beaten up and bullied one too many times, with no help from his poor English father, my dad said he became reclusive and started looking more towards music.

My dad is not an anti-social person, so being reclusive started to become lonely. He said he turned to marijuana and LSD, because all the nerdy rock musicians were doing it in the early 1970s. Later, my dad said that he met some musicians, who had ties with the Hells Angels, and he started playing shows with them. By then, he started to make money in music. That is also when he met my mom, who was brought to one of these big jam session parties by some friends from high school. My mom and dad played in a band together and also had their own side projects. My dad was starting to get famous in his side project called *Sussex Drive* and when they got a chance to open for a little Canadian band that was starting out called *Rush*, my dad said his band mates all got cold feet and they got dropped by the production company funding the tour. My dad said he fell into a depression after that and started spending more time with my mom and drugs. Well, folks, that is when I was born, into that heartbreak.

My mom and dad split up shortly after my birth. My mom started her band called *Coma Toast* and my dad started a band with a friend called *Temple of Sound*. Both had moderate success, with one of my mom's songs becoming a folk classic at the time and my dad doing a song for the *Expect No Mercy*, a film starring Billy Blanks. *Temple Of Sound* performed the titular theme song for the film *Expect No Mercy* and had a little bit of airplay on Q107. Nevertheless, my dad said it wasn't worth all the stress. The movie company paid for them to have a producer who consistently wanted to muffle the bass. Then, they hired a Jewish audio engineer, who basically ruined the bass heavy song and made it into an over compressed guitar-driven pop song. My dad said he was also not ready for any sort of success. He was hanging around drug dealers and people who only knew the fast lane. He also had already lost the love he had for music in his teenage years. My dad was involved in a car accident in his twenties, where he had some brain damage and he received $50,000in compensation. Of course, my dad didn't know what to do with his money, so he wasted it away getting addicted to crack cocaine, women and instruments that he would later pawn just to pay rent.

To this day, my dad still has his precious Rickenbacker bass. Fun fact: there are only 500 units of that model of bass made in the entire world. One Rickenbacker bass costs about 10,000$ and my dad still has it in and out of pawn shops to this very day. I wish I could tell you my dad got it together, married my mother and became a professional musician, music movie supervisor or music teacher. But no, life is mean, and my dad is a painter on welfare with mental issues. To make it more sad, he still plays his bass to every song from *Rush* in his garage drunk late at night. My dad's name is Steven Jones, aka Psychotic Steve. He looks like a member of the band *Foreigner*. Like every rocker from the 1980s, from Twisted Sister to Europe, he has long hair down to his ass, tight ripped blue jeans and not a penny in his pocket. My dad later told me one time when he was drunk that he made a deal with the rulers of this world to block me musically. I didn't know what he meant, but it scared me. Who knew making music for the public would be so hard? My dad is now like the best bass player who would play for the devil in hell.

I used to hold all these things against my dad, but now I use it as motivation. To make an analogy, think about how Micky Ward, the British boxer, used his brother's rise and fall in boxing to motivate him to a world title. In fact, the best way I can describe my dad is in the stand-up routine by Chris Rock. I heard that American comedian say two of the funniest things I have ever heard that apply directly to my father. Number 1: "If you're a priest, you better marry a nun. If you're an alcoholic, better marry someone who likes to drink. If you're a Catholic, better marry someone Catholic. If you like death metal, better marry a head banger. And if you're a crack head, well, you get the picture." Number 2: just like my dad, at least Chris Rock's dad never hit children, because he was never around.

THAT'S NOT EDWIN, THAT'S SOME SCRUB

I once had a so-called friend in junior high school, who used to come around my dad's studio in Downtown Toronto. I loved going to the studio with my dad, but I made the mistake of inviting this "frienemy" to come with us one time, when my dad's band was preparing for a big show at the *El Mocambo*. Yes, you history buffs, this is the same club where the famous Irish band *U2* first performed. As we were walking into the old rehearsal factory on Wellesley Avenue, a tall gentlemen was coming out. This guy had funky spiked hair at the time and looked a bit like a punk rocker. My dad stopped immediately, walked over and started talking to him. My asshole friend and I waited about fifteen feet away but still within earshot. Of course my idiot friend threw this: "Who is this guy? He looks like a wannabe rock star. What a loser!"

My dad and the guy looked up, frowned and kept talking. About five minutes later my dad walks over and says:"Which one of you idiots said that?"

"Who do you think?" I defiantly quizzed him.

"Do you know who that was?" replied my dad.

"Bono?" asked my friend.

"Edwin!" my dad corrected my friend.

"No!" I breathed with disbelief."You mean Edwin from *I Mother Earth?*"

"No, it wasn't," my idiotic friend bitched."That was some scrub. I know what Edwin..."

"You're an idiot," my dad interrupted my friend. "And you are not coming around here again."

"I've been listening to *I Mother Earth* all summer. Was that really him?" I asked my dad one last time.

"Yeah," my dad confirmed. "You're lucky he was in a good mood. He was wishing us good luck for the show tomorrow... He is preparing for a solo career he said."

"Wow."

"I'm sorry," my idiotic friend stepped in."The guy looked like a..."

"Shut up, man!" I told my friend.

The more I think about my childhood and all my musical experiences, the more I realize I am a product of the music industry. I'm the next *Kurt Cobain/Jimi Hendrix* reincarnation. I just had to go through pain to get there. Speaking about being a product of the music industry, the following artists and bands are the greatest influences on my music career in no particular order except chronological. I give these artists and bands all the credit for making life bearable and running with the musical torch so well that I will do my best as they pass it on to me: * You may laugh at this list, but these are the bands that saved my life.

Rock:

- Our Lady Peace
- The D.M.B.
- Jamiroquai
- Rage

- Coldplay
- Billy Talent
- P.O.D
- Linkin Park
- Creed

- Pink Floyd
- Oasis
- Dream Theatre
- Alexisonfire
- Fleetwood Mac

*Throw in a touch of *Chuck Loeb, Michael Buble* and *Chris Botti* and you have my role models

Chapter 9: ACTING TO FUND MUSIC

"America Ambush"

My first experience in acting came when I was fifteen years old. It was the summer of my Grade Ten year and I was hanging around some suspicious older guys. They knew my cousin, who had friends slightly older than me. Those guys ended up being my friends, because I was really good at stealing and shop lifting. I am not proud of it, but when I was a teenager, I had an uncanny ability to sense when eyes were on me and when the confusion lent itself to me getting away with anything and blending into a crowd. I had two goon friends who had nothing really going for them in life and only did extra work once in awhile to pay rent. I was idealistic and excited to be on the silver screen. I met them at the pickup point and we all jumped on a bus for a four-hour trip to some countryside set. My goon friend smoked a big joint with me and two girls he had just met. This got me way too high before the shoot. He then told me that the only way to get noticed for a credit or lines is to blurt out something appropriate at the perfect timing. He said I should look up and cry "America" when the American women approached. This so-called friend said he was playing a German guard and when I would yell "America", he would come over and fake hit me with his rifle and we would be in the movie.

Here is a word of advice, always learn about your movie before you get involved. The movie I was in was a TV movie for CBC, Canada's state broadcaster, called *Haven*. It follows a British woman buying and freeing prisoners. It had nothing to do with America! This is why it took me a decade to get back into the industry. I thought I was blacklisted, but then I learned that no one knew and no one cared. The scene was about a British woman coming to a poor town full of Jewish refugees to use her government papers to free some of them. Suddenly, I was dared by my goofy friend to scream out "America". I did it during the most important scene where the woman walked by and the close-up came on the poor destitute Jewish children. I reached out my hand, pulled her dress, had the camera swing towards me as a house caught on fire in the background and I screamed "America". "CUTTT!" The director instantly screamed. "Who just yelled 'America'? This is a British scene! Who the fuck just screamed 'America'?"

I looked at my friend, who just shrugged his shoulders, pointed at me laughing and then looked down laughing to himself. I realized he tricked me into sabotage. Some other extras started shoving me to put my hand up, but I was terrified of the consequences. Therefore, I immediately snuck behind them and blended in with the crowd out of enemy eyes.

"I will spend all day finding out who that was and I will make sure you never act in another movie for the rest of your life," declared the director to the cast and the extras."Who the fuck was that?"

The director had to literally spend hours looking over footage and bringing all the extras up to look at each face. Over an hour later, and possibly thousands of shooting dollars later, the members of the crew found me and immediately ordered security agents to remove me and sent me home early. I even got a letter in the mail with my pay stub stating that I was not welcome on any other set organized by that production company again. Little did I know that would be my first taste of fucking with asshole producers. I have been doing it ever since.

First Day on the Job!

When I was in my late twenties, I started acting as an extra in movies to fund my music ambitions. Here are some hilarious stories about what it takes to be in the movie industry and what kind of bathroom experiences I had on sets from all the chilli they kept feeding the extras. At the time, I was desperate for money and I had gone to a few productions. It seemed like the easiest job in the world. The first role I had was great. I arrived on set and was immediately greeted by the set director and wardrobe director. They got me to dress up in a fiber optics worker outfit and got me to wait outside at 6:00 a.m. in the morning. It was for a movie called *The Hummingbird Project*. I was actually pretty impressed with the whole film crew setup and organization. In the scene, I am circling an imaginary hole in the ground as some B actress runs through the park. It was my first taste of fame and I liked it. I could not understand why the actor I shared the truck with kept complaining. The next scene wasn't for another four hours and we were sent back to "holding" (where extras wait). I thought to myself: "This is amazing. I get paid to sit around and mix my own music. I also do music on the side and feel like I am hitting two birds with one stone. Hey, if I had an online business, I could literally be getting paid to do two things at once." The next scene was a stroll down a busy street of Toronto, which passed for Wall Street. Everything had changed. The street signs were American-looking; the payphones looked like they were from New York; and even the food venders looked different. I got to walk beside a beautiful actress resembling Halle Berry. We dropped fake money into a black Santa's Salvation Army glass ball, as he rang a fake bell that made no sound, as we crossed a fake street, to get a fake frozen hotdog from a fake hotdog vender. I was so amazed how expensive feature films could transform a whole city block into being fake.

As this scene was progressing, Salma Hayek would run out of an office building screaming that she quits. I was never really allowed to look towards Selma, even though I wanted to, because that would have ruined the continuity of the scene. I had found out then that Jesse Eisenberg was also in the movie and somewhere on set. Later in the day, after doing the frozen hotdog scene about thirty times. We were on a small break. I happened to be walking to the bathroom and literally saw Salma Hayek walking in-between scenes by herself. She looked at me and I actually looked away at first because it didn't look like her. She instead looked like a chubby prop set worker at first. I think Selma got offended that I looked away and she then looked at me hard. I then saw it was her and I froze a little, unsure if I was allowed to approach the "star" actress. I had never been on a set like this before, and it was my first day, so I actually had more balls than I should have. I stopped and blurted out: "Wow, I am a big fan of all your movies!"

"Oh, thanks," she replied without realizing I lied.

"I'm sorry I didn't notice you at first."

"I know, this scene has me dye my hair blue, wear a chubby suit and scream like a mad woman."

"I'd still give you an Oscar for it," I lied again.

"Wow, thank you (score)."

"This is my first time doing this."

"Oh it is your first time on this set?"

"No, it is my first time in a movie ever!"

"Wow, congratulations, welcome to the industry."

Then the unexpected happened. Selma then reached out her hand and shook my hand. (Never wash that hand again.) Just then Jesse Eisenberg walked up and asked: "Hi, who are you?"

"My name is Digger, and I just got into acting to pay the bills for music."

They both laughed.

"It is his first set ever," Salma Hayek told Jesse Eisenberg.

"First couple hours," I clarified.

"Wow, congratulations," Jesse Eisenberg told me.

Jesse Eisenberg then shook the same hand. I felt like I belonged.

"I'm just glad it was with you two," I told Salma Hayek and Jesse Eisenberg.

Everyone laughed (Double score).

Just then the set director walked over. "Hi, can I help you?" the set director asked.

"Om, yeah I was just looking for the bathroom."

"Down the stairs to the right...and please do not bother any cast or crew."

"Nice to meet you, I promise to behave."

Everyone laughed except the set director, who stared at me so hard that I thought I was going to be arrested or fired on the spot. I felt like I didn't belong.

I was so angry, the girl I had seen in so many of the hottest Hollywood scenes was now covered up like a fat hermit. Of course, on the only day I am on set with her, so far, I see Salma in her worst looking role of her career. WTF. To be honest, however, she is not the best actress and I think she got a boob job to only stay relevant in the industry. Sorry, Salma!

The rest of the day was easy, just waiting for the final scene, in which I had to walk out of a back alley behind Jesse and walk the other direction. Only the back of my head would be on camera. I got paid a hundred dollars for seven hours of work and free food with lots of downtime. I thought every acting experience was going to be like this, and boy was I wrong. I now know why my co-actor in the fiber optics truck complained so much.

Dancing with the Scrubs

My next movie shoot was for a series from Netflix called *The Umbrella Academy* that had no famous actors in it. I got a chance to be a club goer in a very terrible club scene, with terrible club music. In this scene, the production company had rented two entire nightclubs in Downtown Toronto. The one saving grace was that all the women in the scene were dressed sexy, and I got to dance with them. Of course, leave it up to the film crew to ruin everything in the name of art. I soon got harassed by a crew member, who kept trying to take me out of a good shot and in order to replace me by some black guy, who could not dance. The black guy looked so awkward standing there trying to dance.

"Hey you," an ugly crew member looked at me."I told you to go sit in the back tables."

"Get someone else to sit back there in obscurity," I shot back at the ugly crew member. "And quit trying to get the black guy to take my spot, because you think he looks cool. The brother can't dance and he is ruining the shot. No offense."

"No, I can't dance," admitted the black guy."That's cool."

"You *wanna* quit or be fired?" the ugly crew member asked. "Your choice."

"Hey man," I replied."I'm a good looking guy who knows how to dance. If you knew anything about movies, you would keep me here instead of trying to push me into the background."

He got upset and stormed off to try to get me in trouble for disobeying his orders. When the director came over and saw me dancing he whispered something to the asshole *oompa loompa,* and he fucked off. Some film crew guys on set are the biggest losers in the world. They are usually ugly, angry and slightly stupid, since no creative bone runs in their body. Be careful of them trying to sabotage your style. They look like a bunch of Hells Angels offspring too. Because I didn't listen to him, I got to dance with the group I wanted to the rest of the day. The only problem was that this got so boring after literally standing and fake dancing for four hours. I felt like my life and talents were being wasted away.

Blind FBI agent

Another time, I ruined another scene, but it wasn't my fault. I had been casted as an FBI agent on the show *Titans* (Batman & Robin Netflix). I had a really nice beige suit that set me apart from all the other spooks who were wearing black. I also had beige sunglasses that when I asked the wardrobe director if I should remove them, he assured me that they looked very realistic and added to my character. I was put behind some desk, and as we continued to do an office scene with multiple agents walking around trying to look busy, I was approached by a continuity director who whispered: "Hey, can you not look at your watch from now on."

"OK, why?"

"The director didn't notice that you had glasses on, and we have already shot this scene like twenty times, so now they are telling me to tell you to act like you are blind."

Everyone around me overheard that and started laughing.

"I'm blind?"

"Yeah, they fucked up, so just go with it and kind of hand things to people using your hearing."

"And my third eye!"

Everyone started laughing.

"OK people, back in your places," the continuity director ordered.

People started walking by the desk whispering hilarious insults. The following is a transcription of how we filmed the scene.

FBI Agent #1: Hey, can you pass that file over there, oh sorry, you can't, you're blind.

FBI Agent# 2: Hey, maybe you can solve this case with your psychic powers, since you somehow know where to hand the files.

FBI Agent # 3: Hey Chief, I'm over here. They didn't give you a gun, did they?

Freezing For Shazam

A few times I got to be a SWAT team member because of my size. For example, you see me for exactly 1.3 seconds in the show *See No Evil* as a SWAT member. Eventually, I was always casted as some big miner or factory worker in the background. The worst is not the acting, for I love the camera. It is the disregard for extras. Some crew members of production teams treat extras like cattle for a hundred dollars a day. I mean, come on! The production company and film crew are always so disorganized, stopping and starting, calling out teams then cancelling, and forgetting to utilize people at their highest energy levels. I had many nights, where I would literally be standing in the freezing cold for seventeen hours. To make matters worse, the film crews and directors seem to always be fat, white trash, angry, emotional people, that are always eating. Let's see if that last statement gets me into Hollywood.

For example, I was a carnival goer for the movie *Shazam*. This production was so top secret that they lied about the production name when casting even extras. They emailed us all and told us we would be in a movie called *Franklin*. I thought I was going to be in a movie about a talking nerd turtle. About a hundred extras were cramped into a trailer with limited seating, to the point that some of them had to sit on their suitcases. It wouldn't have been so bad if it weren't freezing and if the film crew hadn't kept getting us to come to the shooting area, then cancelling and having us go back to "holding". I didn't even have enough space to mix my music on my laptop. Instead, I actually would go to the portable washrooms and try to warm up as much as I could. It was a terrible experience. When the food finally came four hours late, it was chilli. Of course, I got sick and had severe diarrhoea. I had diarrhoea all night and knew this would be the last time I would ever do low-life and low-paying work as an extra again. I am a better actor than most the people I saw on camera anyway. I just needed a shot. It became a running joke that extras would try to compete with each other by seeing who could endure more suffering at the hands of the exploitive production company. We all received such a low pay it was a strange phenomenon. I ended up hating the *Shazam* movie after getting a slight case of pneumonia, having the runs all night, standing in the cold for hours and then being expected to return at 6:00 a.m. the next morning. No fucking way! That is the day I quit being an exploited and underpaid extra. No more "Freezing For Shazam, the pedophile version of Superman", no way!

Acting School Was a Joke

After music production school, I was accepted into the acting department of the same college I attended. I only stayed in the program briefly, because it was a big waste of my money. When I told a teacher I had a finished penning a feature length script and I wanted to shop it around, she responded that she knew no connections in the industry to get it out there. I knew those teachers could teach me only how to fail like they did, not how to get to Hollywood. Even in acting school, I had terrible acting peers, who tried to block me and constantly complained to teachers about being offended at something I did or said in my performances. Even in comedy school, it seemed like everyone was angry. A school full of angry comedians is the worst. I am lucky I figured it out young and had a chance to go to Hollywood, where at least the money made up for the bullshit I had to endure. I always respected people who excelled in one thing and then did music successfully after. People like athletes that actually had hit songs, like Shaq, Damian Lillard and Roy Jones Jr. I also respect Russell Crowe, Gary Sinise, Kevin Bacon and Kiefer Sutherland, actors known for having wicked bands during and after acting.

Chapter 10: Comedy School is No Joke

I did stand-up comedy for a while, and I didn't like it at all. Maybe because I had some terrible venues filled with mostly other hostile comedians and drunk people that are there to heckle or wait to be offended. I realized that I am a funny guy and I have great stage presence, regardless of what the haters thought. I never needed to go to school to learn how to be funny. In fact, playing a concert with the banter between songs is exactly like snippets in a stand-up comedy skit. When I realized that being a front man in a band is also like being an actor, politician, artist, stand-up comedian and rock star all at the same time, I dropped out of clown school.

In Humber Comedy, a comedy event organized at Humber College, I met some of the angriest self-righteous teachers I have ever met. Ironically, none of them was successful in the industry, but they kept trying to convince the students that they were. The only people to go to their events were people affiliated with the school. I remember being constantly centered out by one teacher in particular. He knew I was a graduate of the University of Toronto and it was like having a target on my forehead. "Oh, what's Uni boy doing here, with us College scum," I heard in my head.

I remember playing a concert for one of my stand-up routines. I played *Dive* and *Dog Walkers*, because those are my somewhat comedic songs. Instead of people being impressed, they were downright offended, and criticized everything they could. I knew it was the wrong place for me and I just was buying my time before I left.

One teacher in general wanted to try to provoke me into a fight, to ruin my credibility before I left. He looked like a combination of a goony hockey player and Harry the Sasquatch from *Harry and the Hendersons*. At the time, I must have had some of the funniest outburst I had ever had, knowing I was just trolling him before I left. After being centered out for the hundredth time, I confronted the teacher in front of the class. I knew I was one of the best students, and I was in a real good mood that day. No one, especially some asshole pylon teacher was going to ruin that. "Are you OK?" I asked the teacher.

The teacher went silent and stormed over to me.

"Excuse me!" Harry the teacher finally trumpeted.

"Yeah, I got it. Don't do blow. Why do you feel like you always have to have the last word? I mean, I'm not undermining your supreme authority, but it looks like you're trying to pick a fight right here in improv class."

The teacher clenched his fist and I was so hoping for him to swing, so I could go ninja on him. However, he just got the class to stop everything and listen to him vent. I just rolled my eyes, and I swear I heard the horns from the *Charlie Brown* parents coming out of his mouth.

Of course the next day, I was pulled into the principal's office, where I formally complained against his false accusations and left the program. I then made a formal complaint to Humber College's HR department and I left. The entire program was full of weirdoes and hot heads. The aggressive comedy teacher, who had laughed so loud in people's ears, was investigated and was eventually let go. I did not feel comfortable being trolled by emotional crack head babies, who thought they were funny. Some people are just purposely in the way. I think that bully teacher was just insecure and arrogant about recently being selected to be in the worst *McCain* French fry commercial on the planet. In the commercial, a blonde comes to the door, and he is dumbfounded. Later she ignores him and a black guy hits on him. Bhaaa, a career plummeting before it starts.

About six months later, I went back to the college to promote my upcoming album release party, and I put a few posters up. A teacher who was retiring also wanted a copy of the album. As I walked up to an old teacher of mine in physical comedy class, I was rudely ignored. Of course, self-righteous female teachers always think that students should bow to them and that nothing a student does is more important than the failures they have amounted to. As I approached the table with a friendly smile, she was already defensive. I tried to just put a press kit on the table and say: "My upcoming album release. Have a look!"

"Excuse me," the mean teacher snorted off. "We're in the middle of a..."

"Still cutting people off I see. It's okay, you're always trolling hallways trying to get good people in trouble and even arrested to make your pathetic life seem less sad. Anyways I *gotta* go."

Of course, the teacher followed me up to the main office and was going to complain. However, when she walked in, the secretary was already looking at my press kit and was impressed, asking questions, and the angry teacher saw me give the CD to the secretary right in front of her. "It is for the teacher who just retired," I instructed the secretary. "When you see him again, please pass it to him. He requested it, and he'll know exactly what it is."

"Will do," the secretary replied. "Thanks and good luck!"

The mean teacher was stunned. I winked at her and walked out quickly before I was arrested for trespassing. Teachers teach; winners do!

Chapter 11: A DJ's World

In my years as a DJ, I met some very nice European DJs, and a whole bunch of asshole DJs, who were either pretentious rich kids with bad taste in music or gangster DJs with bad taste in friends. Many of these beat makers had a small glimpse of fame that went to their head and now were impossible to work with. They often think they are more talented than they are, and can't see an opportunity when it smacks them in the face. I did get to go to France for a DJ workshop, and while I was there, I noticed everything was old-fashioned there, even the modern hotel I was staying at. The walls and bricks were all old-fashioned. It was beautiful, but a little odd to me. There was something a bit strange that I couldn't figure out, but that night, I saw something that I will never forget.

I was DJing a party on a U.S. Navy ship docked in France that night. It was a big deal and I was sharing the responsibilities with a friend, who was well established in Europe. We were invited to a grand dinner with sailors, crew workers, navy officials and entertainment guests. I will never forget that after dinner, I saw waiters and porters taking huge leftover roasts and throwing them in the dumpsters beside the dock. I then saw, to my amazement, French citizens literally climbing into dumpsters to get the remains of these roasts. People are starving across the seas. No wonder they look at Westerners as spoiled. I asked one of the waiters why they didn't just give the leftovers away, and he responded that people would say they got sick off them and they could sue the navy.

That night, I DJed the party, but I could not get that image out of my head. When I came back to Canada and saw people in the club scene, I actually was a little disgusted by our disregard for human life over consumption and oblivious greed. Drunken people were dancing, when there was nothing to really celebrate about. I met some more DJs that year, but I couldn't really relate to their overly hyped up energy or even the music (top 40s) that was becoming popular. I felt like I was continually playing a soundtrack for dumb people to get dumber. Every night, I would try to add my own flare, my own beats or cool music that I had found and enjoyed for its true energy and positive vibes, but those days seemed to be getting shorter. Furthermore, the idiot playlist seemed to be getting longer. I had to take a break from DJing to re-evaluate my life and the music industry in general. That is why I wrote this book.

Other than my little moral dilemma, if I didn't care about what I played, I could honestly say that being a DJ is the easiest job in the industry. It always made me laugh and/or cringe when I would meet DJs, who thought they were musicians, especially after meeting the great musicians in my life. I have a message to all those DJs. You don't make music; you spin what is already famous. You crate dig, which is fun. However, those are not musical works. Therefore, quit trying to get recognition for creating music. And to those who make their own beats, you make beats usually by piecing together pre-made loops and samples to make a Lego song. True DJs compose; they do not loop.

I Am One Hell of a DJ!

I remember DJing while in university. I started getting really into it. I always liked the ability to play someone else's music all night long. It felt like I was getting paid to party. Sure, the week leading up to the venue may have been full of some editing with software, some sampling preparation, some venue research to know what to play and some crate digging to get new material. Nonetheless, compared to other terrible dead end jobs I had prior, this was a walk in the park.

I knew I was getting good at DJing, when I threw a couple parties in university and everyone would just call me DJ. In fact, that's how I got the name Digger Jones through a random person at a party over-hearing me say my nickname was Digger, the person blurted out: "DJ Digger Jones in the house."

DJ Digger was born.

Of course, back in high school, I found myself at every party, hanging around the DJ. When he got too drunk, I always became the DJ. I was able to see if the crowd was feeling a certain direction, or when a new group showed up, things should change. I was also keen on hearing requests from drunken girls, and knowing if they were appropriate for the party or just drunken rants.

In university, I took it pretty seriously. I acquired a Pioneer DDJ turntable, a Korg authentic analog turntable, a licensed Serato program, about ten thousand songs ranging from country to deep house, and even my own pair of heavy duty Yorkville speakers. I would often have parties of more than a hundred people. After getting my feet wet, I was hired by the University of Toronto to DJ Varsity Games. This was fun, as I could often hype the crowd and even the team into pulling off upset wins. I found that the crowd loved my song choices more than my manager, who kept trying to get me to play Justin Bieber and Jason Derulo. My manager wouldn't know a hit song, if it kicked him in the balls. I eventually left a song playing, that I knew he didn't like, right through a basketball time out. The game had to be delayed, as I walked up to the Spanish manager and threw the expensive headphones at him saying I quit. Some people in the crowd actually started cheering when I did this. To make my disc-jockeying skills good enough for my album and for eventual professional hire, I even took a semester at the famous Scratch Lab in Toronto taught by DJ Starting from Scratch. I am a good music creator, producer and finder, but I am an average scratcher. I leave scratching up to the BBoys. I love to make my own music and add it to my playlists when have to DJ a night of others' music.

Chapter 12: The Church

Church Music

I have a right to voice my opinion on the issue of music in church. I have invested a lot of time and energy in being a part of a church. Therefore, my opinion is based on long-term observations, not theological studies. To me, the church has the worst emotional music I have ever heard in my life. I have played in many church bands, and to be honest, other than a few catchy songs, there is not much room for musical creativity. Either church music is old hymns, which are played for an aging congregation, usually by a really good piano/organ player, or it is trying to be contemporary with Christian pop-rock songs, which usually have decent chord progressions, but the worst melodies, lyrics and dynamics I have ever heard. After a while, all the songs start to sound the same and the overly emotional, "drag on" way the bands play them just becomes a theme song for mentally unstable people, who feel guilty, to come to the front of the stage and cry to God.

Booking My First Venue

When I first had the idea of doing an album release party, I started checking venues in the city. Most were either too big and expensive or too small and dusty. I did find a few average ones, but location becomes an issue when you are just starting your career. I should have chosen the Drake Underground or *The Supermarket*. This is because those two venues have a strong magnetism on residents of the nearby residential neighbourhoods, notwithstanding who plays any given night. Many random people come out every night. Instead, I picked a venue in the middle of a dying College Street around an Italian neighbourhood that had no pull.

The Church

I always had a good feeling about a Toronto club I will refer to as "The Church". I had done research on this place, when I was trying to book the final show for college. I liked the layout and the acoustics. I knew my concert wouldn't be extraordinarily big, so this venue seemed like the perfect location. I had been to the venue a few times for other events and I liked the spacing as well as stage.

I remember phoning the owner to book the club for a weeknight anytime in the next three months. He agreed to have me come to his office to discuss it. His office kind of surprised me. I thought a well-groomed club would have a nice office like some of my professors' in university. Instead, I walked into some back closet, with a small desk and papers scattered everywhere. Said office even had no windows. Moreover, the calendar pinned to the wall had more eraser marks than a kindergarten spelling test. He offered me a Friday night in two months, assured that it was an empty day and that it was all mine. I paid the deposit of a thousand dollars. This was my first experience with bar owners and how shady they could be. What happened next made me furious and ruined my show. By the time my concert date was approaching, out of the blue, I got a phone call stating that he had already pre-booked the entire day with Universal Music and one of their "tool" musicians.

The truth is, I had asked for any vacant date, I had watched him with my own eyes, phone the artist for that day, cancel their show, erase his name off the calendar, write my name in pen, shake my hand, take my money and send me a confirmation email. In actuality, Universal Music treated this club and owner like their own personal slave. They had financial backing, so they phoned him, argued that they wanted the Friday night show, threatened to pull future business away and got him to put them in my spot.

This fat liar then phoned me a month later, after the promotional material and flyers had already been printed, telling me he had switched the date and location on me. He tried to force me to do my concert in his tiny basement lounge, while another concert would be playing above me. Really?

I immediately screamed at him on the phone:

"There's no going back for me, you fat fuck. It's not like I can just postpone another month. Everything is in the works! The promotional material has been printed, posters are already up with the agreed time and place. You greedy fuck, you just took their larger deposit and now are trying to punk me. Fuck Universal Music! They already have enough money to do a show anywhere and terrible artists to do it. I am better than their sheep artists, and when someone comes to you for a private show for a new up-and-coming artist, you try to punk him, give me my fucking deposit back and hope I don't sue you."

I hung up. I thought about suing him for printing costs, negligence and emotional stress damages. In fact, it may have worked, but I was already in the midst of planning and implementing my show, so I decided to just get my deposit back, cut my losses and never enter that shithole church again.

Ironically, I actually felt that I had to go to the church club the next day to perhaps persuade the owner to allow me to remain with the arranged date. I thought by showing him the flyers and press kit that were already printed, he could easily re-arrange with Universal Music another date or venue. It was a Friday evening, exactly a month from my show. I phoned the club and no one answered. I thought about just going down there and knocking on the doors, which is what I did. I took a cab, with my brother inside, to the venue, in kind of a sour mood, to see what the fuck was going on. In general, if you've been dealing with a club all this time and have a contract with them, it is not your problem that they overbooked/have bad time management skills. In this case, there was no huge discount, however, and if I did nothing, I would be the loser. When I knocked on the door, a young doggish looking skinny guy swung the door open.

"Yeah!"yelled the doggy guy.

"Hi," I greeted him."I'm wondering if..."

"Come on man, hurry up."

"Awww...Is Tony in?"

"Who's Tony?"

"The owner!"

"I don't know. I'm just the sound guy for the act tonight."

"Well, I need to see the owner. He screwed me by changing a date on us when we already printed flyers."

"Well, take it up with him. I don't give a fuck."

"Apparently! Anyways, if you see him, can you tell him Digger was..."

"Listen man, you're taking time away from me setting up the sound for someone else."

"Are you looking to provoke a fight or something?" I responded.

"What? Fuck you!"the sound technician swore before slamming the door.

"No, fuck you and Tony, and whatever show you are doing, asshole, "I replied while walking away towards the cab."And tell Tony when you see his fat ass, I'm suing him."

I didn't sue him. In fact, I researched if a person can sue a concert venue if they change dates and locations on short notice. This is what I came up with, after a free consultation with a law office:

Most examples came from nightmare weddings, where the banquet hall either failed to deliver a service or tried to change a date or location to accommodate another event. The only thing a person can do is to ask for the deposit back; and if the owner disagrees, you can sue, via small claims court, if you have a written contract and a witness. To get damages or promotional costs back is very hard, however, unless the venue is rented by a large management company that has spent thousands on promotional material. Big companies sue, so venues won't fuck them. Indie artists have a burden to prove when suing, so venues constantly fuck them.

Even if the venue is affecting ticket sales and other vendors' profits, such as a table of merchandises, attendants, security, film crews, reporters and catering, everything must accommodate the venue, not the other way around. I learned that when scouting for a place (like when renting from slumlords), the owner will get you excited about all the great things the venue has to offer, free of charge, but on the day of the event, this is what I experienced. The difference between a wedding and a concert is that the wedding can just go on and the other events will have to accommodate around it, whereas two concerts cannot happen on the same stage at the same time. These venues are protected by hearsay, in court, like gangs are protected by political connections. They always do the damage then leave and make good people have to pick up the pieces.

If a vendor cancels at the last minute or does not show up, you can sue for the return of your deposit and any other payments. This is tantamount to witnessing the vendor performing below standard or not delivering the product it promised.

For example, if the banquet hall you book for your wedding reception gives you a smaller space than you paid for or becomes unavailable, you can sue for your deposit. A Louisiana court awarded a judgment to a couple whose justice of the peace failed to show at their wedding. All of these issues can be decided in small claims courts.

Small claims courts are meant to help individuals resolve disputes without the time and expense associated with a traditional trial situation. No attorneys are involved. Normally, there is a plaintiff, defendant and judge. Depending on where you live, the amount in dispute can be as high as $5,000. Any disputes involving larger amounts of money than what small claims allow typically must go through the traditional civil court.

Once you get to court, you need to bring in any evidence you can gather to prove your point. If you had a contract with the vendor, this is the best option. It is difficult to argue against the written terms of an agreement. If you did not have a written contract, bring witnesses to an oral agreement you made. If you have photos or receipts, those will help. Essentially, you need any writing or physical proof you can find to help prove your case. The bottom line is that you need to show the judge exactly how the vendor ruined your big day.

I eventually got my deposit back from The Church club via e-transfer and never got any printing costs back. I was so angry that, not only was I being fucked by the owner, but I was also being punked by his random sound guy. Right there in my anger, I had a genius and somewhat ballsy idea.

"Go across the street and book the bigger, better venue."

I ended up doing it, with my personal cab driver waiting and my brother in the back seat. I walked across the street to a somewhat popular club that I will refer to as "The Mock Club".

Now, I don't care if you have experienced a great indie show at the Mock Club. That is not what I am writing about. I am writing about the small details that I always notice, while most people do not. When I walked into the Mock Club, a famous band was rehearsing on stage (Metric). I was instantly impressed by the size, but not the seating. The club had a nice balcony, but everything was so dark and drab that it looked like a bad nightclub trying to be a concert venue. The stage was a little small, but the owner showed me all the assets that would make the concert a hit. He showed me things like a smoke machine, special lighting effects, a sound board directly off stage, and even multiple back drop projection screens. The bar was fairly large. There was a lobby, with an ATM, a small kitchen, and even a side bar across from the main bar. The venue's owner was of Italian heritage as well, but the exact opposite of the fat Italian across the street. Speaking about stereotypes, I expected an Italian neighbourhood dwindling in luxury and population with clubs run by shady Italian Mafioso.

The Mock Club's owner was skinny and somewhat fashionable. I was deceived into thinking he was a stand-up guy. His office was pretty organized and he had more staff than the club across the street. I walked into his office and placed one of my press kits on his desk. He looked up. "Hi," he welcomed me.

"Hi, I'm Digger Jones, and I plan to have a big show for my upcoming album release in about a month. Tony the asshole from across the street just switched the date on me, so I'd like to switch my venue to here."

"Wow... I see," the owner replied after a brief suspension of disbelief.

"Does this shit happen a lot with him?"

"Actually yes," he confirmed with a chuckle. "We have had many people complain about his disorganization, and then they come over here and we take care of them."

"Great, I'd like to book any weekend you got, and for whatever price it will cost me."

"How much you deposit for him?" he asked with wide eyes.

"I deposited one thousand dollars!"

"Yeah, I can do that. Here let me check my schedule."

The owner flipped through his calendar and stopped on April 26th, 2018.

"Well, on a short notice like this...what is it? About six weeks...I can't give you a weekend night. That is for sure."

I must have looked disappointed and was about to leave.

"But..." the owner came out of his thoughts. "I can put you in on the Thursday before Kid Cudi, a somewhat famous DJ. What do you think?"

"Well, it's only a day's difference, and I can do a music video in the afternoon and then the concert all night? The day is only me, right?"

"Only you! The club is all yours for the entire day."

"Deal! I'll send you a few promotional posters to put up around the venue, when we reprint with the new date and location. Thanks," I said prior to shaking his hands.

Now that sounded pretty reasonable, no? Well, nothing worked out the way I had planned after that. In my case, none of the venues wanted to throw in freebies for their inadequacies. There was also no free merchandise table. In fact, the owner was a complete asshole and would not even give us a table at the beginning. In retrospect, I see that I made his establishment look like shit by "tricking him" into thinking I was already famous and had great pull. He got suckered like me, looks good on him.

VENUES

This is my personal opinion on Toronto venues, in which I have played. If you are looking to book your big night and have never played these events, take notice:

- The Danforth Music Hall was too big, like Massey Hall, and the Opera House.
- The Dakota Tavern was too small. I hate playing in basements.
- Horseshoe is a dive bar, and Cameron House is even worse.
- Lee Palace is similar to a cave.
- Most of these venues are rented by a production company or label/management, and they pay the artist to play, that's it, not the artist doing it himself. Just squeezing in talent into dives.
- The Phoenix Music Hall is a pretty good venue, but I hate the east end.
- The Drake Underground is nice.
- In general, I have played in churches and convention centers with better ambience than Toronto's bar scene.

Chapter 13: The Mock Club

Here are the events that conspired to ruin my special day:

After I transferred the deposit to The Mock Club, I started planning and implementing the music sets to make this day work. I found out that the owner was a complete pompous, douche bag, who acted like he was a king sitting around his own place. I had an agreement with the owner to only pay a thousand dollars for a deposit that I would get back if the place was packed. He later changed it to fifteen hundred. Part of the failure was my fault, because I thought:"If I built it, 'they' (audience) would come."I thought that if I got a big venue, more people would come. We had no Ticketfly, no Ticketmaster and no online ticket sales on my website. What did I expect?

I learned that these venue owners acted like they knew the industry, when in fact, they couldn't entertain a toddler. None of them played in bands, could dance or even knew what it took to do an entertaining show. Even top entertainers (The Weeknd) are actually not that good on stage. They lack basic fundamental stage presence, and even if they have somewhat of a false arrogance up there, "it is always easier to perform when you are already adored, than to fight to gain fans, like me". I, however, am used to doing more than what's expected.

I hate when venues make everything confusing, with little help. The owners of those venues often make an artist do everything, while they laze around. Then, when it comes to transitional periods like dinner breaks, opening and closing, they rush everything and throw out things that don't belong to them. I lost my headphones at the venue, my specialized newly printed business letterheads and a bunch more.

To make matters worse, the sound guy was so bad. He was actually enticing me to fight him, in order to ruin my show or challenge me to stop him from ruining my show. I realized this was all a setup to get me to do something rash and end up in jail. The sound guy was taking precious time away from my sound mix on stage by spending five hours to mic a boomy drum kit. A lot of venues in the city actually suck. People don't want to admit it, because it makes them look like they just wasted their money. This, however, creates a bunch of salty musicians and venue owners, for the next musician booking.

I realized that timing is everything to the sonic waves and audio capabilities of an audience. In other words, no matter how good your band sounds, the audience will think you suck or are less than good, if you allow the opening acts to stall you, play long-winded sets and exhaust your audience's ears before you even get on stage. People actually got frustrated that too much audio noise was happening before my set. After that, no one could really appreciate the beautiful saxophone parts or soaring lead guitar lines. Please avoid audio fatigue in your audience.

As an added dagger in my heart, I later found out that there were thirty screaming teenage fans outside the Mock Club, who couldn't get inside because the club wasn't all ages. In fact, the security wasn't aware that the show was all ages, either. What a fucking waste of promoting and handing flyers out at Leaf Nation!

Now that I was on a roll, I started to figure out that Toronto's music scene was a conspiracy against me. I knew people would love my music, but I also knew that there were some heavy hitters not too keen on letting people hear my work. I should have listened to the warning signs. A friend, who came to the show told me the Mock Club felt like a cave to her. Here, I thought it was one of the best venues in the city, but I soon realized it is where the acts go to die.

Here is the nightmare leading up to the night I decided to leave T-dot:

This is the story, from start to finish, from when I first entered any studio to when I finally left Toronto, in search of a new acting career. My parents had been musicians for decades and only experienced heartbreak, so I thought I would make a final push for them.

The Beginning:

I asked for financial support from my mother and her rich boyfriend in 2009. They sent me a two hundred dollar cheque and a note attached saying: "Here, this is for recording your first album". I ripped the cheque up and mailed it back. Everyone in the industry knows two hundred dollars won't give you an hour in most studios, and you won't even get the drum kit set up in an hour. I knew I had to finance the project all by myself.

Instead, I recorded a few songs in some guy's attic that I met at the local church youth group. This guy was in a band that formed out of our church. They were called J Walk, which is a pretty catchy and clever Christian band name. Those teenage Jesus lovers were phenomenal musicians. They had a great sounding band and hit songs, but they had a terrible singer. Back then, I wasn't ready to intervene and experience fame with the band J Walk. In high school, I couldn't see the forest for the trees. In retrospect, I should have approached the band and said that I was willing to be the lead singer and band manager. I have an incredible vocal range and love to write lyrics. I, instead, opted to do everything myself. I wrote, recorded and hired my own band. Years later, while in university, I had my first song, *Find It for Yourself*, play when I was in jail for texting a girl that she was a bitch, that is another story. How is that for heartbreak? Everyone at the old church I attended saw my battle with failure and they all expected me to die. I knew this. Besides, like Hugh Glass in *The Revenant*, this motivated me to stay alive and thrive as my revenge only could come with fame and fortune. Those who were opposed to me, all tried to create a plan to kill me, to prove that they were right, because they were salty that I punked them. To quote Fetty Wap's song *RGF Island*: "Fuck all the haters, I left them behind me."

Chapter 14: The Night of the Living Dead

That same night, when everything was going wrong, I was met with hostility by a famous Toronto rappers entourage. I cannot say his name since I don't want to get sued, but he is BIG. Of course, this rapper wasn't in Toronto at the time; he was busy in Los Angeles. However, his goony entourage sure was in town. When everything was going wrong at my show, his people obviously started a problem with my promoter. My promoter was a recent acquaintance, who helped us get our stuff out into the market. I, on the other hand, did most of the online presence and physical distribution of promo material myself. I handed out flyers and created radio, as well as newspaper ads (more on this later). Because my band was somewhat grassroots and beyond our comfort zone, the asshole poster boy from T-dot, didn't come over and say: "Wow, Digger, you are great, you did all this yourself? Here, maybe I can put a good word in for you, get one of my people to help for your next show and maybe one day, you can even open for me."

No, instead it was like: "Oh, some dirt bag thinks he's better than me at rapping, and oh shit, he plays guitar, sings, raps, DJ's and produces... Kill him."

All I know is those thugs started an argument at the back of the club, stating my promoter owed them money. When we discussed what this was all about and realized they were just trying to intimidate us, I threatened to call the police and they left. Luckily, I was almost done with my set when they came back. I had already performed my hit singles and was about to end the show with a bang. Then, I saw the goons trolling in the back of the club again. Suddenly, a fight broke out and the lights came on. The owner of the club ran onto the stage and said the concert was finished and that police officers were on their way. When the concert ended, there were five black SUV's outside, with some of the biggest dreaded bodyguards I've ever seen. They kept trying to fight the venue owner and promoter, demanding money. I had my investor run over to me as soon as I finished my last song, and I was walking down the backstage stairs. "I think they might have guns," she warned me.

I was instantly ushered out of the Mock Club's backdoor by security guards into a cab, and we took off like a bat out of hell. A SUV tried to follow us, but we dipped onto the highway and were gone. My band mates seemed to be part of the problem as well, texting me constantly, asking for more money, which they didn't deserve. I learned a valuable lesson that night. People of that ilk will sulk and complain when it comes to working hard to get a set perfect. However, as soon as the show is over, they save all their energy to intimidate and demand money to the death, wanting all the credit.

After the show, my emotional retarded drummer did not want me to take the drum kit back to the studio myself, as he wanted to keep it as leverage to get more money. When I asked for my keys back from him to the studio, he started stalling. A few of his wildly aggressive friends came up to me questioning why I wanted my keys back. I responded: "Because they're my keys, and it is my studio, and I want my kit back. Do I have to explain myself?"

Now, I have dealt with assholes in prison and in my family, so whenever guys try to pull a tough guy act, I call their bluff. I always just remind them I can get the police in two minutes. Everybody's tough until the police arrive. Does that make me a rat, or a genius? In this particular situation, they all could see that I was serious and would get cops there in two minutes. Then they could fight real tough guys in jail all they wanted.

I turned and left that argument on the side of the road. I paid the cab driver a hundred dollars to fly to my studio, even skip a few stop signs, because I knew the SUVs would be flying behind us. I knew the cab driver, as he was my friend and personal Uber driver. He knew something bad had happened and was very helpful. This was one of the scariest moments of my life. We pulled up to the studio, I ran in, dropped off the drum kit with my driver and my investor. We hustled to get everything in the studio before the SUVs showed up. We were all scared and exhausted, but we kept going. Thank God for God's protection and for our hard work. We slammed the door, locked the studio, ran back to the car, and hid in the local parking lot with the lights out. Sure enough, two SUVs pulled up, started banging on the doors and calling people on their phones. We just stayed in the car, unseen and recorded everything on our phones. Then, when the people were distracted by another band pulling up to the neighbouring studio, we snuck away in the cab back on the highway.

I spent a very long night at my investor's apartment, worried that they would somehow find out where she lived. Thank God for an obscure Asian society that has no connections to the mainstream Canadian society! It was tantamount to going off the grid. We made reservations for my equipment and merchandize to go into storage and I literally paid for a train ticket to Vancouver the next day and was gone.

Instead of re-enacting in my own way the scene from *8 Mile*, in which Eminem has to overcome his fear and rise to the occasion in front of a packed house, my experience was the exact opposite. I had spent a year preparing for this show. I handed out flyers in Jurassic Park, Leafs Nation, secondary schools, universities, clubs and various subway stations. I had posted flyers all over Downtown Toronto. Speaking about traditional media outlets, I bought a radio ad and even a large ad in *Now Magazine*. All this should have been enough for a huge show. Fifty-five people showed up, and another thirty people outside who were not allowed in, because they were underage. What a draw.

This felt like my one shot that never came.

All in all, I look back and remember that I did an amazing job. I outperformed the opening rock band with the prose of my songs' lyrics, a better performance, and even better banter with the audience. My sets also included a dance routine, a stand-up comedy portion, and a music video while all this was going on. I even closed the show with five hip hop songs that I produced, DJed, and performed by myself, while playing lead guitar and rapping incredible lines, flawlessly. I was like a one-man band, all with inadequate equipment.

Just give me a real chance, with a real production budget, and I will fly, I thought.

Chapter 15: Angel Investors

I have a friend named Angel Wang, who invested her hard-earned money in every part of this journey. I knew Angel from high school, fifteen years ago. She ended up becoming my greatest ally in this music mess. She believed in my music, my determination and my many talents as an artist, scriptwriter, actor and musician. Angel was a true angel investor, but she did it with her own hard-earned money. She was not some rich philanthropist just trying to look like a generous donor for PR. No, Angel went through the mess with me, even when she knew she would not make her money back for a while. I was loaned about fifty thousand dollars and I invested twenty thousand of my own money. She nonetheless knew she was investing in a loss, to experience the joy of large returns later. Angel was pissed when all these people literally robbed my time and money, which was in fact her time and money. She told me that she would find a way later in life to make them "pay" for everything they "hustled", one way or another.

There was one problem, however. Angel was not good at promoting or anything to do with the music industry. She had no sound advice or experience. As a result of that inexperience, we threw money at places we shouldn't have and didn't hire an expensive publicist team like we should have. I struggled with insecurities, because of her doubt and fear of controversy that made me chicken to perform my song *Burning Jerusalem* on its own. It was not my money and I felt like the money may disappear at any time, so I rushed things. Here is some priceless advice:

Never rush a concert, because no one will show up. Take the time to promote a concert properly, with guaranteed ticket sales, and if a lot of people are coming, and you are behind schedule, then rush.

Even though things didn't go as planned at the beginning, I never used her for a single dollar. I appreciated every penny and I found the best deals for everything. In fact, I overworked myself and then paid her back everything with interest later in life.

It took me a few years to get the album making serious passive income, but when I did, Angel Wang was the first to get paid. I will always remember that she gave up her hard-earned money to help me when I was nothing and no one else cared. She is awesome and deserves the credit, as the lead investor for the first three albums. Now that my music career has started to launch and I have helped endorse USBs as the new CD, I have sold my USB packages with albums, wave files, posters and a music video, all hanging from a branded lanyard. DJ Digger Jones was the first to do it! No more being on a tight leash and chasing a dwindling carrot hanging in front of my wide eyes. Now, since sales have sky-rocketed, I will always remember the girl who was the first. Thank you, Angel! None of this could have happened without you. It was hard, but it was worth it.

Chapter 16: Burning Jerusalem

I wrote most of the material for the *Burning Jerusalem* album in 2016, while attending Seneca College. I would write in a library cubicle to stay focused. I often had a written story about a documentary I had watched or a clever insight I wanted to make a song about. In the library, I was able to craft the lyrics perfectly. When I wasn't in search of the perfect rhyme, I sometimes would go into the local forest or park. Once there, I could sit and write in the serenity of nature. It's funny how some of the lyrics in the *Burning Jerusalem* album are handcrafted out of shear intense hard work, like a machine in the library, while others are free flowing like the wind caressing the trees of a forest. I knew this album would be my harder rock material, so any songs I created that year that were either somewhat metal, I categorized them for my *Burning Jerusalem* album.

With Seneca College's audio rooms and equipment, I recorded three of that album's songs: *Burning Jobs, Burning Dido* and *Noah's Song*. Some of the drum takes had to be re-recorded in the new studio. However, *Noah's Song* was perfect as it was, and I pleaded with the Seneca teachers to allow it to go on our end of year collaboration album. Of course, they denied that request. Upon graduation, I had thirteen songs created, but I had never played any lead guitar or bass lines to any of them. I had just finished memorizing the lyrics, writing all the chord progressions and had basic ideas finished. I rushed into the studio anyway. This is because I felt it was a perfect way for me to flee post-secondary education, my retarded family and my shitty life. I didn't care if it wasn't perfect, because I knew I had an uncanny way of winging genius material in the studio.

So off I went into a studio that I had just learned about, without any real studio worthy instruments. I heard about the studio through a random guy I met on the subway. The chap was reading Uta Hagen's book *Audition*. We started talking on the train about acting classes, since I had just graduated from both Seneca's Music and Acting programs. I also knew I would eventually be going from audition to audition. He told me that he was returning from a voiceover clinic for cartoons. I asked about the studio, and he gave me a brochure. It looked like a small studio that only did voiceover and radio interviews, not full-length album recordings. There was a name attached to the brochure. When I went home to look it up, I saw that the studio's owner was somewhat of a child star and had done work for some *Nickelodeon* cartoons I had watched growing up. Impressed, I called to get more info. A voice picked up and it sounded like the female receptionist. The voice was very high pitched and childlike. I asked to speak to the owner and the person on the other end said he was the owner.

"He," I thought.

Anyway, I asked about the facilities and he assured me, in a high pitched voice that the studio was fully equipped with top of the line Pro Tools rig, Apollo interface and a Neve console. Well, I later found out this was all untrue. We would have problems later with trying to downgrade the sample rates of 96k to 44.1k, which actually cost me a whole day in the studio, because the three songs I had already recorded at Seneca College were in 96k.

When I arrived at the studio a week later, to take a tour and talk about prices, I was amazed at how sketchy everything seemed. Firstly, I couldn't find the house number on the home studio, because it was an Aside. I thought the studio would be in the house. The lights were all off, and nobody was there. I walked outback and saw a garage that looked soundproof, but the lights were off. I checked my watch and I was punctual. I waited on the patio for ten minutes, thinking the child star was just running late. It was starting to get dark outside as the sun was setting. Then about fifteen minutes later, a bunch of real B-level actors came out of the garage, laughing and schmoozing. They all looked at me and went quite. I stood up, walked down the patio stairs and asked for the owner. The shortest, child-like figure came over and gave me the limpest handshake I had ever felt. I felt sick. I then asked: "Is there a better time to come back?"

The child star assured me that it was a great time, and continued to show me the studio. The studio was tiny. The garage had a mixing room, a small floor and a tiny vocal booth. I should have just walked away when I saw this. But when the child star saw that I was shocked by the size, he assured me (manipulated me) into thinking that all the equipment was top of the line, as he promised. "Whatever we don't have in size," the child star began his misleading pitch, "we will make up for you by getting you our best audio engineer, our best plug ins, our best instruments. And we will go above and beyond with studio time and extras, by offering you our studio for four hundred dollars per day, which is less than half of what other studios charge." (This would later become $600/day)

I looked and saw that this studio did have everything I needed. It just was a miniature of other studios. I knew I could do a lot more in a personalized studio with more time, instead of rushing in a major studio. We agreed to record the whole album for a flat fee of four thousand dollars. The child star then said mixing time would be negotiated at a rate of $500/song for another $6,000. This was the first time I had learned that mixing is more expensive than recording. So there was my first invested $10,000 of someone else's money. Now, I am neither a greedy nor lazy guy, so I really wanted to do the best I could in the shortest amount of time I could for Angel Wang, without short changing my album. In general, the album is a masterpiece of songs, decent recording, with some terrible mixing, over-compressions and weird audio effects that the Jewish mixer threw in, probably because he didn't like the album name and wanted to throw a wrench into the project.

I went into the studio on the first day with my Fender Telecaster, Fender Acoustic and Fender Champion amp. I like Fender. In most studios, if you are not doing bed tracks with the band (drums, bass, rhythm guitar at the same time), you usually do everything to a click track and start with the rhythm guitar or bass line. I spent the first day in the studio, trying to do as many rhythm guitar bed tracks as I could, because I knew session musicians were coming in on Day Three. We were having tuning nightmares from Day One, because the main studio guitar was a Gretsch with washer tuning keys that only can change pitch slightly. I swear the whole album in a tiny bit sharp because I couldn't find the right hex key to adjust the guitar properly. Fortunately, it was a very slight tuning difference.

I did, however, feel a bit rushed from the start, because I knew the studio owner and producer were just out to make as much money off me as they could. With that being said, I didn't want to rush anything, especially with the rhythm guitar, because it is the framework you add every other instrument onto. I did every song perfect for the first two days, with only a slight adjustment in the song *Emotional Retards'* chord progression, since there are like twenty chord changes. In fact, we didn't add too much lead guitar to *Emotional Retards,* since the chord changes acted as the melody itself.

After two days of rhythm guitar work for the entire album, I could tell the engineer was already trying to stall me. He didn't like the fact that I wanted to do the rhythm tracks to five songs each day as he argued it is better to "take your time and do three a day perfectly". I had to explain to him that I had played these songs for a decade already, a hundred times over and I could probably do the whole album in one take. He reluctantly acquiesced, which was perfect, because the session musicians arrived on the third day, as I was just finishing the basslines for the ten previously recorded rhythm tracks.

Chapter 17: Great Session Musicians

The best part of this whole experience with the *Burning Jerusalem* album was the session musicians. Everyone was so professional and knew my songs already, even to the point of correcting one of my chords as not a minor 7th, but minor 9th, and another as Sus 2 not Sus 4. It actually felt great to work with Humber Jazz students, who knew theory better than me, and could transpose on the spot. They all liked my music and were fired up to get going. Since I had played most of the instruments for the entire album, I had two songs designated for all four of them. I had a Cuban drummer play on the album singles, and I even had him redo the drums for *Into My World*, since the timing actually slows and fastens throughout the song. After a few takes, he was able to swing the time perfectly.

The other session musicians just waited and watched from the bench as each one got up and hit a home run. After the drummer had played on four of the songs and now created an overall feel for each song, I wanted the piano player to just do fills, arpeggios and comping (chord inversions as accompaniments) on two songs. To be honest, he was decent, but I think I could have done some better fills myself with more time. He did, however, really help the song *My Country* get a country piano flavour to it by using the Hammond B3 keyboard and its great background ambience.

After the pianist had played on his songs, it was time for the "Saxophone God". This student will always go down as one of my favourite people to work with. Everything he plays on, he makes sound better. He is from Barbados, and plays the saxophone from his heart, with a mean background in music theory. His sax stole the show to be honest. He played on *Burning Dido* and *My Country* first. I got him to do four passes on each song. This took a while, but it was worth every minute and penny. I got him to do pads first (long drawn out, one note sax parts that kind of compliment the rhythm guitar and vocals). Next, I got him to do shots (single note blasts that can be placed in stacks on top of each other to create a chord from a sax). He did this by knowing his scales then playing chromatically all the notes in that scale for a certain part, so that I could edit them later in post-production and create beautiful shots that sounded like a whole horn section. Lastly, I got the brilliant Barbados player to just solo in certain parts, until I satisfactorily felt I had enough to work with in mixing. When he ended his turn, everyone was in awe. There was a high energy in the air and everyone knew we had all just witnessed something special.

Last up was the lead guitarist. Now, I play some decent slow hand lead, but I wanted someone who could play lead (Shredding) using multiple strings. The lead guitar player was wicked. He had a good theoretical foundation and technique, but he couldn't remember what he just played. I have experienced this too many times in my life, an amazing guitar player who can't repeat what he just played. To be honest, I would rather have a decent guitar player whom I can mould into my sound than a wicked guitar player who can't replicate anything. It takes too much energy trying to rein those types of musicians in. In this case, I didn't have a choice. I was restricted by time and capital. I am glad I took the time to really harness that guy's talent. The guitarist eventually played exceptionally well for the album, but it took many takes and a lot of frustration. In fact, by the third or fourth pass, when this blues style guitar player kept messing up scale changes in the song, the other session musicians were getting restless, so I decided to pay them well for their time and talents and send them home.

I then spent the next four hours going through the four songs with this lead guitar player who was from Toronto Island. Now, on all the lead guitar parts, this guy would absolutely crush every lead solo in two passes or less. I loved his lead solos, but when it came to playing a simple four note motif or fill in between lyrics that I had written, this guy would take forever to learn something and even longer to play it correctly even once for the recordings. I could see that his voicings and arpeggios were perfect and he really came up with parts that changed the songs to become more dynamic. As a result of that observation, I pushed on through with him. After we had the takes we needed, I introduced him to the song *Strength in Identity*, where he absolutely knocked it out of the park for a grand slam. He played that song so well that I swear it was like seeing Carlos Santana and Hendrix playing right in front of me, perfectly pairing with my vocals. I saw the light at the end of the tunnel and so did he. We had a blast on the last song and finished well. We looked at the audio engineer, who was exhausted. It was 11:00 p.m. I jam packed day.

By that time, I was a little frustrated at how late it was, because I planned to get an early night of rest, in order to be prepared for the vocally intensive fourth day. I went home and made a plan to do the easiest vocal songs the next day, stuff with low register harmonies and growling (*Burning Assholes*) and to save the hardest vocal songs (*My Country, Dreams* and *Into My World*) for day five.

While at home, I had a crazy idea.

Call your mom and ask if she would come out tomorrow and do vocal harmonies on a few of the songs.

I called. She actually picked up and agreed to come on short notice. Finally, what a champion!

The next day was fairly calm. The engineer set up two different micing techniques with the AKG 414 and a *Neumann* mic for airy soft vocals and my usual *SM7B* for boomy mid-range songs. The vocal takes worked out perfectly. I didn't feel rushed, and I was allowed to focus on multiple takes and multiple harmony variations. For the first vocal day, I had to adjust my singing pattern for the rhythm guitar change in *Emotional Retards*. Just as I was finishing the fourth song of the day, my mom walked in. She had never heard any of these songs, but she instantly loved *Burning Dido* and *My Country*. After a few takes, she had warmed her voice up and did some good harmonies. She added some nice harmonies on the chorus of *Dreams* as well.

Then it came to the song *Lies*. Now, I wrote this song about how shitty my parents had been to me growing up, and I didn't expect my mom to ever hear this song, let alone come to the studio to sing it. Being pre-occupied by so many other things, I had forgotten how serious the lyrics were in *Lies*. When she heard the song *Lies* for the first time in the mixing room, I glanced up and could see the shock and pain in her eyes. I did not want to choke there under the pressure, so I also asked her if she was able to do this last song. Surprisingly and ironically, this is the song that she had the best harmonies on. In fact, her harmonies kind of made this song. Thanks, mom, for the comeback!

The next day, I did all the harder songs, as my voice was rested. I had my chamomile tea going and the perfect mic set up for great high register singing. That concluded the two days of vocals. The last day of recording is what I call the extra day. It is where you do all the extras, bongos, acoustic guitar fills, extra percussion things and so much more if needed. We added synthesizers and the automaton to the hidden song *The Citadel*. I even had a soda Sprite can appearance in the song *Emotional Retards*.

We Missed the Bass in a Song!

Just as we were about to wrap up recording, the audio engineer, who often got songs mixed up, because he had been recording too much, noticed that one of the songs was missing a bass line. We all laughed and then scrambled to get the bass rigged up for a final take. It was to the metal song *Waiting on a Train*. I had never played bass on this song or even thought about a bassline for it. For some reason this all had escaped my mind, since I had a lot on my plate already. Every bass note you hear in this song was made up on the spot, and I am proud of that. Word to the wise: When in the studio, have an eraser board with all the parts to do and then check them off as you go. Don't wing anything at the end because of an omission.

The owner told me that his team and him were all in to get the best product for my album. On the other hand, when it came to the daily grind of the studio, the owner kept trying to weasel his way in, when I wasn't using the studio. He sought to finish his own album, clearly showing me he cared more about his album than mine. I later found out that the child star was bipolar. He had seriously dangerous depression issues stemming from being cast away from fame at a young age. In front, his run down house was actually home to about ten people. Every time I went inside to use the kitchen or bathroom, there were people already using it, or some music lesson was in progress and I had to step around on egg shells. Another weird thing was that the child star had his whole house curated by a creepy old man, who did obscure art (when not diddling the child star). He stressed that the house was a gala for both musicians to feel "comfortable" while recording and possibly selling artwork on the side. Well, I did not feel comfortable walking by a fiddler's weird art all day. I was glad to finally have my finished product in hand and the next step, mastering, ahead of me now.

I knew I wanted to go to Noah Mintz at Lacquer Channel Mastering in Toronto. It is debatable if he is the best mastering engineer in Toronto, but one thing is not debatable: he has been doing exceptional work for over twenty years, has mixed some very famous albums and is very established in Toronto. In fact, other than his studio being in the middle of nowhere in Toronto's East End, he was very welcoming. He made me coffee, had me come sit down in the mastering room for an hour to double check the levels and was prompt on the couple adjustments I emailed to him later. In all, Lacquer Channel did not disappoint. Many other studios talk shit about Lacquer Channel, saying they over-compress or "mess with" the original sound too much. But I, as you will later read, also went to these other mastering labs for other albums and I now know why they talk shit...because they're jealous.

In hindsight, I can see, after listening to the final mastered album versions that *Burning Jerusalem* is an attempt to be like the band *Chicago* or *Supertramp*. I have learned that distracting guitar leads and saxophone parts can leave the listener disorientated and disinterested, thinking about other things other than the song. It is not impactful if it is overly complicated. Some great advice I can bestow upon you is this: there are two types of fans. You've got people who don't know anything about music creation and just want the feeling. Then, you've got musicians who listen to other musicians. That kind of fan enjoys listening to the players rather than the music.

It is not staying simple that makes a song great, it is placement. What I mean is this. Today as I write this chapter, I just asked two different people from completely different spectrums of the musical universe to rate if my music was too busy. The first guy was a basketball student who obviously listened to hip hop and the other was a middle-aged white guy who obviously listened to blues. You don't get more diverse than that.

I got the basketball student to listen to the song *New Legacy*, and I asked him if it sounded too busy. He hears the rapping, the beat in the background, the horn shots, then a little lead guitar and then back to the vocals of the chorus. He liked the chorus piano, then back to the verse. He can easily hear the vocals, then when he starts to get bored, it goes to a lead guitar solo, then back to the chorus ending with a little more horns.

"That was awesome!" the basketball student delivered his verdict.

"Well, was it too busy?" I asked him.

"No, I liked it!"

"You're sure the guitar and vocals weren't too busy?"

"No, at any point I heard one instrument and the beat, then the horn perfectly filled a void spot and then back to the vocals. As soon as a certain part got boring, a new little part would come up, either guitar or horns and just when I was like what's next...the chorus. It perfectly kept the momentum going and kept me motivated to listen to the whole song. It felt like every instrument was in its perfect section, not intruding on other parts. No matter how many parts there were, or instruments, they were all in their perfect section."

Then I waited about ten minutes for the basketball student to leave, as to not create bias. Afterwards, I went over to the blues player and showed him the song *Burning Dido* from the *Burning Jerusalem* rock album. It should be noted that both *New Legacy* and *Burning Dido* have the exact same instruments playing on them.

"Instead of these nice instruments coming out at little feature parts to add to the overall song," the blues player chimed in, "they're all kind of played together. Too close. So, one overlaps the other. It was kind of distracting."

"What about the beginning of the song?"

"I liked the marching drum and rain FX at the beginning," he elaborated. "Then when the horns first came in, I liked where the song was going. The vocals of the verse came in, and I liked following the story; the guitar and horns weren't too distracting. Then it went to the pre-chorus, and I started to feel lost. The horns came in too much, I was trying to stay focused on what the vocals were still saying. Then, all of a sudden, this lead part came in. Then, it went back into the chorus, when my brain wasn't really ready for it, and I was expecting the same type of chorus as your intro chorus. But then, the horns were playing something slightly different. It got really confusing."

"I see. The amount of instruments is not confusing; it is where they are placed."

This was my first lesson in the art of "less is more". My album *Burning Jerusalem* was somewhat overly complicated, because I feared my first album would be considered simple or stupid. In conclusion, the album *Burning Jerusalem* is a masterpiece that was not delivered properly. Most of the songs are great, a few are legendary, but I would prefer to have the entire album slightly less loud, less busy and mixed better. Nevertheless, it is still good for a first album and much better than the cannon fodder on the radio today. In hindsight, I gave too many people too much money ahead of time, thinking it was a deposit for great results. I made a few small music video for YouTube for this album, the best being for the song *My Country*.

Lastly, the time came to design the album artwork. For the album art, we first got a graphic artist from OCAD (Ontario College of Art & Design), which was one of the best decisions for this process. I sat down with the album artist and explained the design concept in a busy mall food court. I thought it would be a disaster, but she was surprisingly good. What the album artist did with the lyrics page, much like my next *FunHole* album, is spectacular. Without it, I don't know if the *Burning Jerusalem* album would have the same personality. I love anime, because I love watching people's fantasies come to life. Like my fantasy of becoming a rock star finally came to life! I am not a sell out, but I had to sell out, or else none of you would ever know who I was!

Chapter 18: Shadows and Machines

The album *Shadows and Machines* is my pride and joy. I almost named my band *Shadows and Machines*, but people kept either forgetting the name, or thinking we were a metal band. When picking a name for a band, some bands claim it is an easy process and their name fell from the sky or came to them in some spiritual moment. In my case, I loved the name "Close Encounter", but because I struggled through life and it took me too long to create a band, the name was heavily saturated by other bands and the movie *Close Encounters of The Third Kind*. I was going to work with the name Shadows and Machines, since it came to me in an intense dream about the end of the world, but everyone I told the name to couldn't remember the name to search me up later.

Remember, we live in the generation of ADHD scatterbrain attention. If a name is not easy and convenient, no one cares.

After all this debate about the name, I stuck with my original plan and named my first album *Shadows and Machines*. This album took me about a decade to write. In fact, it started as noodling, and I don't mean fishing barehanded for catfish. I mean, I wrote it over the years of playing riffs on the guitar at a young age. I started making songs a young age as a way to express myself. Besides, I wrote some of the songs, including *Dive* and *Find it for Yourself*, at a very young age, before I knew I wanted to be a musician for life. Then, in high school, when I got a band together, the night before the battle of the bands competition, we surprised everyone and won the next day. That was all the incentive I needed to continue in music.

I will never forget my childhood and how music inspired me. I was not a music prodigy at a young age, that is for sure. What I did have though, was a keen ear and sense of what a crowd wanted. I guess I had performer in my genes. However, I never expected or wanted to do music. I saw my mother struggle in the music industry and, quite frankly, I was sick and tired of hearing terrible blown out bass guitars at small venues, since I was a baby. My parents played in a rock'n'roll band, so I was always surrounded by scum bag potheads, acid weirdoes and that one virtuoso guy who doesn't realize that everyone is holding him down because of his talent. I have heard terrible bands and flat singers my whole life.

What turned me on to music was my four octave vocal range.

I liked music early in life for the energy it brought. I liked hip hop and dance because of their well-produced beats. I actually thought rock music was for poor, uneducated people. In primary school, I excelled in music class because of my soprano register. During choir practices, I had a great memory and work ethic to get things perfect for performances. There were usually one or two better Asian players in my class, but they did not have the versatility I had. I was able to sing, dance, and play an instrument, while also excelling in academics and sports. To be honest, I am rare. Most children are groomed by their parents to excel in one particular thing. I excelled in four.

In grade school, I usually got the lead solo for all theatre productions. I was chosen for all choir solos and acting gigs. I just felt comfortable performing in front of older people,because I felt like kids my age were dirty, stupid and mean. I was constantly fighting with bullies, and the only way I could get even with them was with crushing them in sports or making such a great impact in music that it made them realize that they looked like failures to their own parents.

Fast forward ten years later:I am living at some *DIVE* in Toronto. I am slightly depressed after working two years at the summer camp and not going to post secondary yet. I remember having ten guitars in the house at any given time. These guitars were all dusty, broken, and had too high of an action to play. In a nutshell, they were damaged goods with old strings that made my fingers bleed. It was like my mom and her demonic boyfriend who owned the house were trying to discourage me from music, by putting thousands of guitars around me, all unplayable. I started not wanting to play the guitar, and I felt guilty for it. Then one day, I had a dream that I was in a desert with a thousand broken old guitars.Then, when I woke up, I knew it was all a setup. So I got my guitar back from the pawn shop that I had recently sold, re-stringed it and started playing like a mad man. In fact, the bass line to the hidden song on the *Shadows and Machines* album, *Quest*, has one of the hardest basslines I have ever come up with. It is epic and intense. Like a sports team rallying back from a deep hole.

When it came to writing the songs for the *Shadows and Machines* album, the process was very organic. I had a few songs that I had pieced together and played at parties. People enjoyed those songs so much they would randomly request them. One of those songs was *Meet Again*, which has a beautiful guitar intro. More intricate songs, such as *Close Encounter, Indoctrination* and *Band-Aids over Bullet Holes*, were pieced together from random guitar parts not placed in a song yet, but that people loved when I played them. I would actually be creating songs at parties, while everyone was getting drunk. If I would play a part and people would stop and listen, then I knew I had a "keeper".

For the more intricate, progressive songs, I would remember the parts that people liked and file them away in my memory bank or on a cell phone recording. Then, I would work on transitions from those parts to the next part. Sometimes I would have moments when I would shout "eureka" like Archimedes, the Greek scientist. During those moments, I would notice that a bridge of one song worked better as a pre-chorus for another song, and I would, by process of elimination, play parts next to each other, until I found the perfect fit. I guess this is how my young music mind worked, since I lacked the theoretic principles of transposing and key changes. It worked out pretty well for me. In fact, although it might have taken a little longer, I came up with parts such as the *SmokeStop* bridge that even seasoned veterans admire. I didn't force myself to be limited by structure, rules or key signatures.

Some people had a hand in creating a few sections for this album. My brother for instance. Before I got famous, he would always show me some band that was doing similar things to my music, but that was famous already. To him, it is like somehow I am in competition with these nameless bands. Sometimes I really don't care what other bands are doing, because they have already made their millions. Now is my turn to make a killing. Even though my brother does these mind games, I have to give him credit for having a great ear for fending off boring sequences in songs. He helped me improve the basslines to both *SmokeStop* and *Indoctrination* by altering their time signature and accents. My brother also helped me come up with a better walk down bassline into the bridges for numerous songs. For that, I give my brother credit. Sometimes a composer has heard a song so many times in his head that he cannot feel how it must feel for a first time listener.

For the entire Shadows and Machines album, I wrote the music first and then the lyrics, It was easier for my mind to "feel" a song when it was finished then come up with words. I may have had an idea for a theme of what I wanted to say, but I waited until the songs were finished before writing the lyrics. Now, however, I have a better grasp of theory and better technical chops. I know where I will progress with a chord progression, so I can start writing lyrics at any time. In fact, every now and then, I will write a whole song as a poem and then compose the music afterwards. I will expound on this idea later.

So there I was, at age twenty, with twelve fully written songs under my belt, which took me about a decade to finish. I had no direction in my life, other than seeking to be a rock star. The next five years would be like a roller coaster, with the highest moments and most gut-wrenching disasters. I screwed my chances at any athletic scholarship by smoking weed in Grade twelve, when I was a few credits short of my high school diploma. I couldn't even apply to a college with my grades. See what happens when you try to be cool in high school? I went from being a straight "A" student to pulling in 50's. The losers and idiots graduated and moved on before me. I felt like I was in a waiting room of life, just waiting for my chance to explode, like an Olympic sprinter who has to wait a second behind everyone else and then runs his ass off to catch up.

I am twenty years old, with an album in my mind, that I had written in parks while I was homeless or at parties while others were trying to get laid. I worked a lot of dead end jobs around that time. I became a good cook working in a bunch of restaurants. I became very articulate in my speech from a lot of call center jobs. I remember it became so bad one job, when I was working in a meat factory and all I could think about was that my chance to become a rock star had passed me by. I had a whole album, *Shadows and Machines*, in my mind. All I could do was compose and rehearse vocals in my head at a dead end job. I almost committed suicide at this point.

It was so hard to keep playing guitar when I was living in a youth shelter. I couldn't sleep, I had no money along with no family support. Nonetheless, everyone kept telling me how great my music was, but no one was paying my fucking rent. In fact, it was around this time that a close friend of mine committed suicide because of poverty. I write about this in both the songs *Close Encounter* and *Best Ones.* I felt like I was in the waiting room of life for far too long.

Then the unthinkable happened. I met a man in a local park, who would change my life. He was playing basketball and was the same age as me. He didn't judge me like everyone else. I had just confronted my father, whom I hadn't seen in almost a decade, then the next day I met a man, who changed my life. He helped me become a *White Rabbit Ninja.* This is how the epic story goes.

One day, I was leaving the church youth group that I used to attend. I randomly saw my dad, whom I hadn't seen in a long time. He was across the street at the subway station waiting for a bus. My dad was also talking to another shady-looking man.

"You can't be serious!" I assessed the scene in my mind.

I snuck up on my dad. When I was within striking distance, I grabbed him and slammed him up against the wall.

"Hey, dad," I blared while holding him against a wall, "it's your son. Remember me? You were never there. You call yourself a father, you talk shit about my family, smoke crack and left me."

My dad's friend tried to intervene.

"Hey man," the drug dealer warned me, "leave him alone."

"Fuck off," I threatened the drug dealer, "or I swear I will beat you so bad, your ugly mother won't even come to your funeral. I bet you sell him your shit."

The drug dealer looked away.

"You sent me away to get help and look at you," I said, while looking again at my dad.

"You left your shit at my house," my dad finally said while spitefully spitting. "Come pick up your junk."

I pushed him on the ground and held him up by the collar, ready to punch him. Suddenly, I remember stopping, looking up and seeing a crowd of people watching in awe. I looked at them all.

"This is what you call a no good dad," I laconically stated.

A lady started to cry.

I walked away into the subway and down the stairs to the trains. I started to cry to myself, as I waited for the train. I heard some yelling up the stairs, so I took off my blue jacket and hat. I was then wearing a white shirt underneath and I pretended to read my textbook. Two police officers ran down the stairs on the other side of the platform, as the train going the opposite direction pulled in. The police thought I was on that train and got on it. The train then pulled up going the other way and I safely got on.

Around that time, I became a loner. My parents and grandparents thought I was a criminal. I ended up homeless, living in a giant box in the forest beside my high school. It was embarrassing and shocking. I was running every day and playing basketball to stay in shape. One day, when I was running by a basketball court, I noticed a short Asian guy doing basketball warm-up drills. The Asian guy had a shaved head and was about twenty years old. I remember being impressed with his dribbling speed and explosive drive. I walked up to him and extended my hand. "I'm Digger."

"I'm Han," he replied prior to shaking my hand. "Digger? That's a weird name."

"Yeah, it's my nickname. My parents called me Digger since birth."

"You live around here?"

"Ah yeah, I'm staying with friends just over there, you?"

"I live with my parents in a condo," he pointing at the horizon behind the school. "You went to this school?"

"Yeah. A couple years ago."

"What do you do now?"

"Survive!"

"Ha! OK...I'm trying to get on the university basketball team, but you know I'm vertically challenged."

"Yeah, but you got wheels and a great shot."

"No man, not good enough."

"We should play more often. I'm trying to get back into shape, and...you're good."

"Thanks."

"Do you mind?" I asked for the ball.

I started shooting and hit a nice shot. "Yep, still got it," I exuberated.

"You got a nice stroke, man, you play?"

"I used to."

"In high school?"

"Yeah, something like that. Hey? Care to play a one-on-one?"

"Oh no, I just came to warm up."

I finally missed a shot and Han grabbed the rebound. "Come on man," I sent Han my invitation for a one-on-one again. "What do you say a quick game up to ten points? I'm really rusty."

"Well, okay," Han finally accepted my invitation with reluctance.

We started our duel. Both of us were great at dribbling and both had sweet moves to the rim. I was a better shooter, but Han had a faster cross-over. A man in a business suit walked by and stopped to take notice. Then a married couple walking their baby also stopped. I was playing serious defence on Han, who kept trying to shake me. I rejected the ball and ran to seize the rebound. "Score check," I said.

"It's eight to seven for you," Han confirmed the score.

I checked the ball, then drove right and crossed over left. As I saw Han coming back left, I tried to spin back right, but Han stripped the ball. Han bounced it at the perimeter. I was winded. Han drove past me and reversed a nice layup in. Han checked the ball.

"Tie game," Han exhaled.

A small group of people were now watching with impressed looks on their faces.

Han drove right, put the ball behind his back and pulled up for a jump shot. He missed and went in for the rebound, as I grabbed it over him. I ran to the bassline and jacked up a long three, while Han was chasing me. The ball hit the rim and went in.

"Wow," Han congratulated me, "what a shot, man."

"Wow, I'm tired." I said while holding in my vomit.

Everyone started laughing and cheering. The crowd dispersed. I won the game.

"We should have asked for donations," I proposed.

Han laughed.

"So, you come here a lot?" I asked Han.

"Yeah, I live in the condo right beside the school."

Han grabbed some water and started drinking. He noticed me looking at his water. Han handed me the water.

"Thanks," I expressed my gratitude to Han.

"You play chess?" asked Han.

"A little... in jail."

Han looked at me and started laughing. He walked over to his gym bag and pulled out a towel along with a bag of chess pieces.

"There's a board right on the table," Han informed me.

I noticed the tables had ranks and files painted on them.

"I never noticed that before, and I always come here."

"The teacher appears when the student is ready."

We both laughed.

"Wanna play?" Han asked.

"Sure." I replied reluctantly.

Han started setting up the pieces. I played white and Han, black. As we started playing, it was obvious that Han was a much more advanced player.

"You might not want to move there," Han warned me.

Han looked at me and then pointed to a bishop in the corner.

"I didn't even see that," I admitted. "Wow, you're good at this."

"You see, you should use your pawns strategically as pieces that funnel your opponent into moves, where you have an attacker positioned, but hidden, like this queen, (points to the queen) or this bishop (points to the bishop)."

"I didn't even see the queen, either. Okay, new game."

Han started to laugh.

"This one's not over. It is never too late to turn things around."

Han paused, the wind blew, like what he just said could mean turning one's life around, as well. I felt like I was in a surreal moment.

"You're Korean?" I asked.

"Yeah, I came here in Grade eleven and learned English on my own."

"Grade eleven? I thought you were born here."

"Yeah, now I speak better English then most of my white friends."

"Well, I'm Native and white, and I barely speak English."

We laughed and continued to play. While I was planning a move, Han was sizing me up. He noticed I was hairy, smelly and wearing rags.

"Where are you living?" Han asked in order to seek a final clarification.

"Ah, you know, with some friends."

"Listen, Digger, I know your living conditions might not be the best."

I laughed. "Yeah," I went along his statement, "you could say that. You can tell from the stains on my shirt."

"Yeah, and you smelled before the game even started."

We laughed.

"Say, my parents are going to Korea for the summer. How would you like to stay at my place for a while?" Han proposed.

"But you barely know me!"

"I know it's crazy," Han conceded, "but you seem like a nice guy who just needs a leg up. Plus, if you're a psycho, I can always just kick your ass and kick you out!"

We both laughed!

"You better hurry before I change my mind," said Han.

"Yes."

Han moved a chess piece. "Good. Checkmate," Han announced.

We laughed.

I followed Han into his condo. The condo was clean and spacious. There was a grand piano in the condo, Korean artwork on the wall and a moderate-sized television. Han showed me his room. It was a big room, filled with books, an exercise area, a couch and a computer desk. I was amazed by Han's library and computer. "You have a library in your room?"

"Yeah," he replied."I like to read."

"And your computer is like from the future."

"I built it myself."

"Is that a baby grand I saw when we came in?"

"Yeah, my dad bought it for me, since I told him I was going to drop out of university to pursue a career as a musician."

"Oh, you play music. I also play a mean guitar and can sing. Heck I ain't a bad drummer, either."

"Really? Here, check this out."

Han went into his closet and pulled out a case. Inside was a brass trumpet. Han started to play a military marching tune. He played it flawlessly. At the end of the song, I clapped and congratulated him. "That was awesome."

"No, I'm still learning," he said with modesty. "But I do play the piano."

Han opened his room's door and went out into the living room. He sat at the piano, as I sat on the couch. Han played a classical Mozart's *Symphony No. 40in G minor*, a musical composition completed in 1788.

"Yeah, I know that!" I prepared myself to venture a guess."That's from Beethoven, right?"

"Mozart."

"I knew that!" I said, before we both start laughing.

"Here's something I think might be a little more up your alley."

Han starts to play *In the End,* by the American band Linkin Park.

"What!!!! Ewwwwwwwwwwwwww!" I blurted while snapping my fingers approvingly. "So do you study music or something?"

"I am a university student who was studying physics. Then, I dropped out to pursue a career in music."

"Yeah," I said with a grin, "what did your parents do when you dropped that bomb?"

"They were OK with it... after they kicked me out for a night and almost disowned me."

That memory of Han killed us.

"So what do you wanna do?" Han asked.

"You mean, with life?"

"Yeah, do you like your life?"

"Wow, slow down, partner," I advised him. "That is a pretty personal question."

"Do you like your life?"

"No," I admitted.

"Wanna change it?"

"Yeah, but how? I'm broke, hate my family and only have drug dealers as friends."

"Have you ever seen the movie *The Matrix*?"

"Yeah."

"Do you remember the scene when Morpheus is training Neo by plugging him into the computer?" Han asked by pretending, with his hand, to plug a wire in the back of his head.

"Yeah!" I said with excitement.

"Well, that's what we're *gonna* do with you."

Everything happened so fast after that. I spent the summer training with Han in a place where I actually felt safe. Han started to train me, each day by teaching a new thing.

1) Han taught me new languages like Spanish and Mandarin using a Bristol board and audio books. He gave me homework and children's books in each language.

2) Han showed me a vocabulary building program.

"Did you know there is a direct correlation between the amount of words you know and the amount of money you make in your life?" Han asked."That's the conclusion of a study from Harvard University!"

"Really, then teach me everything!"

Han quizzed me on the new words I was learning every day. I absorbed words like "penchant", "nebulous", "conspicuous", "audacious" or "circumvent".

3) Han and I exercised on a daily basis. We were stretching, doing push-ups, sit-ups, barrel walking on our hands, skipping and running on the tread mill.

4) Han taught me about computers, how to install programs, run software and how to type faster. Han put a paper over the keyboard and I typed to a timer.

Finally, Han asked: "What was the one thing you always wanted to do in your life? I mean that one thing you've wanted to do since you were a child?"

"I have always wanted to be a rock star! To play my music in front of millions of fans, on the radio, concerts, everywhere. Both my parents are great musicians who never made it."

"Well, are you good?"

"You have a guitar?" I offered to prove my talent.

"Yeah, my dad keeps one in the closet."

While Han got the guitar, I looked at his DJ equipment set up beside his computer. Han came back in the room.

"You DJ, too?" I asked him.

"Do everything with a beginner's mindset, and you can achieve a lot."

I took the guitar and quickly tuned it.

"I wrote the this song," I informed him before playing *CarBones - Funhole.*

Han was amazed and got excited.

"Here, follow me," he invited me.

Han headed to the living room and sat by the piano. I followed him with the guitar.

"Here, maybe we can jam to this," Han assumed.

He handed me a musical sheet. As soon as his finger hit a key on the piano, I looked at the music with a sad look on my face.

"What?" Han asked.

"I can't read this."

"You don't know how to read music?"

"No!"

"Well, that's the first thing we have to work on if you're *gonna* be a rock star."

Han began to teach me music theory. Using a Bristol board, Han went through the treble clef and staff.

"Why does E not have a sharp?"

"Why does one plus one equal two?" Han quipped interrogatively.

"It just is!"

We both laughed.

I spent four hours a day that summer learning music theory and practicing the guitar. I started to practice with musical sheets on the guitar. Han walked into the room. "I think you're ready. We are going to write a music theory exam together next month."

"I am not ready for that," I told him.

"You will be."

Han continued to teach me more advanced music theories, like scales, sequences, chords, modes and harmony on the Bristol board.

Han and I wrote a music theory exam in a local school's gym. We were surrounded by children. I was focused. Then, the bell rang, which meant the exam was over.

"You know, Han," I initiated our conversation as we walked home. "I just wanted to say thanks for everything. For teaching me this stuff and going with me to the exam."

"No worries, Digger. You can buy lunch (pause)... forever."

We laughed.

As Han and I were walking through the park, I saw one of my old drug dealers. The drug dealer looked like a white trash with a shaved head. He was walking with an Arabic-looking gangster. As they got closer, I became spooked and turned my back pretending not to notice and trying to hide my face. Han noticed my gesture and so did the dealer.

"Diggy," the druggy trumpeted. "You owe me money."

"No, I don't," I said upon turning my back around."I paid your brother, and he went and drank your money away. That's not my problem."

"So what are you saying?" the drug dealer returned on the offensive. "You trying to rob me?"

"Hey man," Han stepped in, "he ain't trying anything. He paid you."

"Yo, mind your business, Chink," the hoodlum shot back at Han while sticking his chest out.

"Leave him alone," I told the drug dealer.

"Or what!" the drug dealer said provocatively.

"You know what?" I yelled."I'm sick of being intimidated by drug dealers and uneducated creeps still trying to be cool. I am not going to give you another cent of my money. We are *gonna* walk away, and if I get so much as a scratch, I will make sure that the only drugs you can sell is what you can stuff up your ass when you're in jail."

The drug dealer stepped back in awe and looked confused. As Han and I walked away, the dealer responded: "Yeah, we'll see!"

"Yeah, we will!" I declared.

After the drug dealer was out of range, Han was taken aback. "Wow man, you really handled that. Weren't you scared?"

"Yeah," I replied. "But I knew if shit went down, I could easily outrun you."

"Hey!"

And we both laughed.

Later that summer, Han threw a party in his condo, during which we both acted as DJs. The condo was full of people. All of my old friends showed up, as did Han's friends from his ESL days. The lights were dim. People were drinking and dancing.

"We want to thank you all for coming," I announced on the microphone during the interlude."Now let us take you on a little journey with DJ Digger and MC Buddha."A little rocker chick kept taking pictures of Han and then giggling with her friends.

Upon laying the microphone down, I told Han: "She is only harassing you, because she likes you."

Han looked shocked at this truth, then happy. He got up, walked towards the girl and whispered something into her ear. I saw both of them vanish into the back room. Then, I slowly but surely lowered the music's volume.

"OK, we're gonna change it up a bit," I announced to the guests. "I am *gonna* play a song for you that I wrote."

I grabbed the guitar and a friend stood beside me with a bass. Another friend had a bongo, which is a pair of drums originating from the black community of Eastern Cuba. When everyone was ready, I played and sang *Launchpads - Shadows and Machines*.

To say the least, that summer my friend Han saved my life. I would have probably ended up dead or in jail if he had never opened his home to me. Furthermore, Han didn't just stop there. He taught me music theory, vocabulary building and helped me get back into shape. He also showed me that I could get into university through a backdoor bridging program. I will always credit Han for helping launch my career.

Chapter 19: Burning Jobs

Summer Camp

Like I mentioned at the beginning of this book, I worked at a summer camp for three years just before entering university. At this camp, I made friends from around the world. Those teenagers looked up to me and they could tell that I was going to be a star. They didn't have the pre-conceived notions like some of the haters in North America. I will never forget the bond I had with the group composed of people from Spain and Taiwan. I cried when members of that cohort left by bus for the airport. I still stay in contact with some of them decades later, and they keep asking when I will tour in their countries.

Yeah, music industry record labels... when will I tour in their countries?

Working at the ESL camp, I felt like a rock star. In fact, I later wrote the song *Burning Jobs* as an assignment to describe my joy working at that camp. My song *Burning Jobs* refers to realizing you should never work to make another man rich, not to burn Steve Jobs.

After the job at the camp, which I held for three years, I got a great job at a hotel. The money was great, in fact, much more than the camp, but it came at a cost. I was often exhausted and miserable. I started smoking weed again, and ironically spent more money than I did at the camp on stuff like food, shelter and weed, because everything was accommodated for at the camp. While working for the hotel, I saved a little money and started planning to get my foot in the door of the music industry. Since then I have had a taste of what the industry looks like, and I have an old saying:

I got my foot in the door of the music industry, only to find out there were Rottweilers on the other side of the door, trying to rip my leg off. So I slammed the door and kicked in the back window.

While working at the hotel, I didn't like the rooming house where I lived. I put up with a crazy old landlady. I became so fed up and decided to upgrade my last two high school credits through online correspondence courses. My end goal was to apply to every college and university that had denied me the first time I applied after high school. To make a long story short, I wanted to go to music school so badly, and I would have, if I had any family support whatsoever. In fact, I had the opposite. I had applied to three colleges for music and two universities for a general BA. To this day, I regret not applying to the faculty of music programs, because I didn't think I was good enough. I thought you had to be Beethoven to learn how to play Beethoven. Ironically, in university, I eventually met people in the music programs who sucked, and I quickly switched my minors to music ensemble to salvage whatever I could get in music training while I was there.

In my music history class, I would listen at home to amazing audio books titled the *TTC course* in a class called "Understanding and Appreciating Western Music". This audio course changed my life and it was the only class I took with Han. What is so funny about this actual class is that our teacher got all his information from the TTC course and he would spit it out verbatim. Stupidly, I asked about this once and the teacher got very reserved before changing the subject. I went from an A- to a C+ by the end of the year. Trust me: it wasn't due to a lack of effort.

Never question where a teacher is getting his source material.

While studying Politics, Cinema Studies and Music at the University of Toronto, I came across books such as *Talent is Overrated*, which made me re-think my God-given abilities. I also came to realize the overlap between Cinema and Music. Many of my assignments, while getting a specialist degree in Cinema Studies had to do with dissecting movie music, themed scores and the evolution of the medium of music technology. This made me even more interested in both acting and placing my music in my own movies. To say the least, I graduated from U of T with flying colours and wrote four feature film scripts for each one of my years there. I became a much better musician and dealt with some deeply rooted anger issues. This is because I sought to allow for maturity and patience to govern my life.

Thinking back, I am somewhat glad I did not get into the faculty of music, because I have seen many musicians lose their ambition and love for music, when a teacher is loudly faulting them and assignments are piling up. This is hard for music students, especially if all some musician want to do is gigging. I didn't want to become some singer who only sings for rich people in operas, in other languages. I like pop rock too much. The theory on modes and scales would have been nice, but I can do that on YouTube now. The network connections are what I missed, but I am pretty outgoing, and with a few online posts and audition posters in the hallway of a music school, you can get the same crowd.

This whole condescending music teacher phenomenon is rampant in our schools today.

I remember being a gifted music student in primary school, but when we moved to Ontario, things changed. I had never been formally trained in an instrument or theory, so when the teacher gave me a trombone and told me to catch up to the class, I was lost. He screamed theory at us and showed obvious favouritism to his goofy-looking drummer and hordes of Asian violinists. To make matters worse, this teacher hated any of the boys who played sports. I used to dread going to his class, and I barely passed. In hindsight, if it were a different teacher, I knew I would have gotten into orchestral music sooner, because I love the arrangements of Beethoven, Mahler and Sibelius. Instead, I rejected the corny high school band class and jumped into the world of rock'n'roll.

While I was applying for all these colleges and universities a second time, I made a profound error. I still had a need to seek my parents' approval.

By this point, I had barely spoken to my mother in about a year due to the fact that she never helped me complete any of a typical adolescence's stages: prom, obtaining a driver's license, getting braces, first job, applying to college and so on. I was so happy I had found a college that offered exactly what I wanted: a curriculum on performance skills, audio engineering and the business side of the music industry. It sounded like a perfect program.

The day I was applying online, I was looking at a booklet of advanced music theory that had gathered dust. It was my mother's course booklet from Humber Music College. It dated back from twenty years earlier. As I flipped through it, I could tell by the notes and doodles the time my mom dropped out in order to give birth to me. There were side ledgers showing frustration with some of the advanced inversions and transpositions. I knew back then, my grandma was no help to her, either. While looking through the course outline of the college I had just applied to, I made a foolish error. I called my mom to celebrate.

"Hi, mom."

"Yeah," she blandly replied.

"I got good news."

"About time."

"I know which school I would like to attend. It has an excellent music college program with..."

"Hey listen," my mother interrupted me. "I'm proud of you and all, but I'm cooking dinner. So call me later (hang up)."

I was stunned and so viciously angry that I threw the phone against the wall. What had just happened had been a general idea of my whole relationship with my mother, a microcosm of my whole life. With my family, when I did something great or shared something that was deeply meaningful, my mother would love to make whatever she was doing seem more important and cut me off, stealing all the energy and momentum of the moment. I phoned back to chew her out, and of course, the answering machine welcomed me. Needless to say, I left a nasty message. I sat on my bed in painful disbelief. That is when the operating system of the world teamed up with my mother to try to kill me. I swear everything I say next is true. This is what happened five minutes later and is the exact story of what happened that day.

I get a phone call from my grandmother asking if I have enough to pay rent. I ask for a little bit more money to make sure, since I had just paid first and last on a new apartment. I was with my Grandma in front of a bank machine, trying to get some money from her in order to cover my rent. We drove together to the address of my residence. I unloaded my belongings down the stairs of my new basement apartment in a rooming house. The house was located in a seedy neighbourhood of Toronto. As I unloaded my furniture, we heard *Bad to the Bone*, by George Thorogood, playing loudly out of one of the upstairs windows. There is an old man standing at the doorway.

"Hi, are you the landlord?" I asked the old man.

"Yes, I'm Carmen," the old man replied. He spoke with an Italian accent.

"Is it always like this?"

"No, it's always quiet."

My grandma and I voiced our parting words. "So what are you doing now?" my grandma asked.

"I *gotta* work," I explained to her.

"Keep in touch," my grandma said as she was pulling away from me.

"Yeah..." I said to myself, walking to work.

Later that night, I reached for my keys in my pocket. I was in front of my door. It was late and I had just come back from work. After a few minutes, I exited my shower and swung by my computer while drying off. I sat down at the computer and looked at my college application. I turned to look at a binder on my desk. It was a binder with a label that read "music theory" on it. I picked it up and opened it. The binder also had a sticky note on it that read: "To Dig from Mom, here is all my music theory homework from when I once studied music. I hope it helps." That binder was the one my mother used twenty years earlier as a student. Upon leaving the book on the desk, I picked my cell phone up and dialled her number. "Hi, Mom. I want to go to school for music."

"That's good," she rejoiced. "Listen, Dig, I'm busy right now. We're gonna have dinner. I gotta go."

"Hi, did you hear me?" I asked before witnessing a brief silence.

"Are you ignoring me?" I broke the ice again.

"Listen," she replied."I don't like your attitude. I told you I'm busy."

"You're always busy. I just told you something that means a lot to me and all you can do is prepare to eat your dinner."

"I'm hanging up," she announced her intention.

"All you know how to do is hang up and go cook. You're a terrible mother that takes your children's power."

"I don't want to talk to you," she insisted again before hanging up.

I hung the phone up, turned the lights off and crawled in bed. Then, all hell broke loose.

All of a sudden, the neighbour next door turned his Spanish music up real loud. I lied in bed trying to sleep, tossing and turning. I got up and banged my fist on the wall. The neighbour banged back and laughed loudly like a hyena. I sighed. Then, suddenly, the neighbours above me turned up their music too, with a very loud bass pumping.

I climbed up the stairs, out to the driveway. I locked my door and looked up at the neighbours' window with a towering anger. Bad to the bone.

In order to blow some steam, I strolled to the park with my skipping rope. I skipped in the park across the street. Twenty minutes later, I was covered in sweat. As I walked back to my house, a beautiful brunette girl walking towards me caught my attention. Once we were less than an arm's length near me, she winked at me. I stopped and contemplated greeting her. But I was still in an angry mood.

"She doesn't want some angry guy," I spoke in my head. What a missed opportunity to make the best of a bad night.

Instead, I turned and marched straight towards the Spanish guy's door. Initially, I gently knocked. Receiving no answer, I loudly knocked again on his door. Still no answer. I looked in the window and saw a small Spanish guy walking around drunk in his apartment. I noticed pictures of the Virgin Mary all over his apartment."This guy's a nutjob," I said to myself.

As I was leaving, the Spanish guy suddenly swung his door open. "Hola," he screamed.

"Hey man, could you turn down your music?" I told him.

"Que musica? No!"

"Listen man, I know you speak English. I will call the police."

"Fuck off, pendejo," he replied while laughing.

"What? No, you fuck off. Some of us have work, asshole."

"Fuck you!"

"Come outside and put your money where your mouth is."

The Spanish guy's eyes went wide with fear. He turned to his stereo and turned his music down.

"Thanks!" I told him.

I went back inside my apartment. I was about to go back to sleep, when I heard the bass from upstairs turning up again. I got up and put on my black sweater. I looked like a boxer now.

I walked out of my door and noticed a group of people standing by the door next to mine. That door led upstairs. A guy wearing a white tank top and a bandanna was standing at the door, holding a bag of weed that he was selling to some teenagers. They all looked at me.

"Hi," I greeted them."I'm a university student who just moved in. I have to work in the morning. Is there any way you could turn your music down?"

"Oh, yeah man, for sure," said the gangster.

I walked back downstairs. The music was off. I thought I had reasoned with people for once. Suddenly, the music got turned up to the loudest volume I had heard so far. Obviously, the neighbours saw this as a power struggle. I walked over to my phone and dialled the landlord's number. "Hi, Carmen," I announced. "Sorry to bother you so late, but can you tell the neighbours to turn their music down?"

"Oh no, don't worry, you can tell them yourself. They are all nice boys. Bye!"

After that conversation, I stood there in disbelief. I threw the phone on my bed, since I had cracked it a bit throwing against the wall earlier that day. I stormed up the stairs. As I exited my apartment, I noticed that the neighbour's door was shut. I was about to bang on the door, when I saw a lady smoking at the picnic bench in the backyard. I walked across a small parking lot, with two cars parked, one red, one black, over to the lady. The parking lot and backyard were very dark and it was hard to see. I walked up to the smoking lady. The lady was older, a little attractive, but looked like a biker's wife. "Can't sleep, eh?" the Tomato Sauce Lady opened the small talk. "You're that university student who just moved in? Boy, did you move into the wrong house."

"What! Why?"

"Landlord didn't tell you, it was a halfway house for people coming out of jail and rehab, did he?"

"Oh my God!" I gasped.

"I heard you knocked on a couple doors tonight, you must have big balls or just be really stupid."

"Maybe you can tell me if it's big balls?"

We both laughed.

"I'm just lucky," I said. "I don't know...Am I lucky tonight?"

I winked at the lady. She smiled and offered me a cigarette.

"No thanks," I declined.

Then, the lady stood up. "I'm just *gonna* go get another glass of wine, be back in a sec."

The lady and I both started walking towards our doors, when suddenly the party neighbours stumbled out of their door. As the lady and I passed, I commented.

"Hey, thanks for turning the music down," I said sarcastically.

I noticed what the lady had in her hand, before she went downstairs. It was a plastic cup that looked like it had something with a red residue in it.

I thought nothing of it, except that it was her wine from before.

I went back downstairs. I was exhausted. I fell onto my bed and fell asleep. Some time passed, then suddenly I was rudely awakened by banging and kicking at my door.

"Get the fuck out here," ordered a gangster. "You pussy. I'm gonna fucking kill you."

I got up and walked over to the door. I saw someone looking through the peep hole and another through the kitchen window. The window had bars on it. There was no escape. I stepped back into the middle of the kitchen trying to think fast.

"They can't be that angry because I was sarcastic?" I asked myself.

I looked out the peep hole again and saw five people standing in front of my door.

"Why you pour shit on my car, asshole?" asked the gangster.

"What are they talking about?" I asked myself."These people are fucking nuts, too."

I looked around in a panic and saw a table leg from the dining room table that had not been assembled yet. I picked it up and slowed to the door.

"Who's there?" I asked through the door.

"Get out here," the gangster shouted at me.

"Leave me alone," I replied."I don't know what you're talking about."

"Bullshit!"

The gangsters kept kicking in the door and I knew it would give way soon. The door swung open and I emerged onto the street with a table leg in my hands, armed.

"Listen, I didn't fuck with your car. I just asked you to turn your music down, 'cause I have to work in the morning."

"So why you pour shit on my car?" the gangster asked again.

"What? I don't even know which one is your car."

"Then why you have a weapon?" he raised his voice.

"Because ten people are kicking in my door. Now, we can go to the park and settle this like men, one on one, but I didn't do anything to your ride."

"Need a weapon, eh?" he asked before casting a glance at his friend. "Frankie, get the bat from the trunk."

One of the other goons started inching his way to my blind side. Suddenly, one of the gangsters grabbed the table leg, while another rushed and punched me in the face. I panicked, ripped the table leg from the goon's hand and started to swing. I connected with a bald guy's head. Then the goon that punched me first, with his long greased-back hair, tried to grab the table leg. I swung again and connected with his arm, breaking it. Another guy seemed scared, hesitated, then screamed while running forward, so I hit him right in the crown of his head. The table leg stuck in this goon's head, because I didn't know there was a nail attached to the end. I pulled it out. I remember looking at the bloody nail and shrugging. The goon dropped immediately. The same guy that I hit in the temple came back to attack me, and I had to hit him again in the face. Again he dropped.

"They're like zombies that just keep coming," I told myself.

I started screaming for help, swinging wildly now to keep the gang at a distance.

"Help!" I yelled.

One of the attackers pushed a very large woman at me, and I raised the table leg to hit her and had to stop mid-swing.

"You shouldn't be here," I told the woman.

"You shouldn't be here," the female hoodlum screamed at me.

I looked around. I saw everyone occupied with injuries, and suddenly, I ran through a break in the crowd. I ran down the busy street late at night, wearing only boxers, flip flops and a bloody white tank top, yelling for help. I must have looked nuts.

"Help!" I howled again.

I realized that I was still holding the table leg, so I stopped, turned around and snuck back into the driveway in front of the rooming house. I peered around the corner and saw it was empty with my door still wide open. I was so scared, but knew I had to phone the cops.

"Come on, Digger," I encouraged myself. "Pull yourself together. Get your phone and call the cops."

I quickly ran downstairs into my apartment. Downstairs, I quickly grabbed my black jacket that had a work knife in my pocket, my keys and my cell phone. As I was fumbling in the drawer for my keys, I heard the goons.

"Hey," the gangster spoke. "The guy's downstairs."

The gang started to run down their own stairs, as I ran out of the basement apartment. I immediately phoned the cops, while running down the street.

"Hello," I told the police department's dispatcher on the phone."I have just fought five people who tried to B&E (break and enter) my house. Please send police officers. I'm being followed."

"Is this on Murray Street?" the dispatcher asked.

"Yeah!"

"Police are already on their way, so just hold on."

I had to jog back and wait safely across the street in the park. I then saw four police cruisers coming. When the police arrived, I approached their cars wearing my bloody shirt. One cop pulled out his gun and yelled...

"Get the fuck on the ground," the first police officer loudly and tensely ordered me.

"No, I called you," I sought to clarify.

"Get down!" the police officer yelled again.

I lied on the street pavement, the police came up in a group, put their knees on my neck, handcuffed me, and took me beside the cruiser. I leaned against the car. Three cops approached me. It was two skinny nerd-looking cops and one really butch female cop that the two skinny cops seemed to be trying to impress. The cops surrounded me.

"What happened here?" asked a second police officer.

"Five guys tried to break into my house, screaming they were going to kill me," I explained. "So I defended myself."

"Don't you think this was a bit excessive?" the third police officer scolded me.

"What would you do, if it happened to you?"

"Call the police."

The cop who originally told me to lie on the ground with my face down walked over. "So what happened?" he asked.

"Five guys tried to break into..." I started before being cut off.

"Actually, I don't care," the first police officer confirmed every cop's disinterest out loud. "Tell it to the detectives at the station. I'm *gonna* get their story (pointing towards the goons)."

As the cop went over to question the goons, the skinny cops continued: "You may be telling the truth, but this looks bad, man."

The goons were now pointing at me while they are talking to the cops. They started pretending to swing wildly. An ambulance pulled up and two paramedics got out. The first cop walked back to me. "Why did you hit the guy?" the police officer asked. "The guy says they came to your door to ask you to turn down your music."

As the paramedic tended to one of the goons, he looked over to me and used his hand to describe a slicing trajectory near his throat in order to threaten me.

"He said you poured tomato sauce on his car, and when they came to ask you about it, you just came out swinging," the first police officer told me.

"Why would you pour the sauce on his car?" asked the second police officer.

I was confused and did not remember the smoking lady with the glass of red residue. One of the cops snapped pictures of the indented door with shoe prints on it. The butch cop approached, holding a half full jar of tomato sauce I had left in my fridge from the night before. "How do you explain this?" the third cop asked.

"I knew I should have thrown that out when I was moving," I admitted. "Great, this looks terrible. Is this a conspiracy or something? I bet if you run that shit through forensic analysis, it's a different brand of sauce."

"Plus we found a knife in your jacket," the third police officer added.

"That's my work knife," I told him.

"Yeah right, buddy," the third police officer voiced his disbelief. "You're going in."

"Wow," I said to myself.

Down at the police station, officers sent me in a questioning room for hours. Time passed. It was getting cold in the cell, and my patience was wearing thin, as I was waiting for my phone call. I started to shiver. Then, I screamed at the cell's door. "I didn't do anything illegal! Those guys are fucking crazy! How many times do I fucking have to tell you? I want to talk to my lawyer. I want my fucking phone call!"

Suddenly a pig-looking detective named Hickson came storming in. "You make another sound, I'm gonna stomp your teeth in," he warned me.

The detective threw the phone on the ground. I went to pick it up and as I did it, the detective stomped on my hand. "One call, bud!" he ordered."What you think this is a hotel or something?"

The detective left and slammed the door. I held my hand in pain. Then, I picked the phone up, and struggled to make a call with my hand. The answering machine came on: "Hi, sorry, we missed your call. We'll be in Europe for the next couple of weeks, so please leave a message, and we'll get back as soon as possible. If this is an emergency, you can call my sister at...."

I quickly hung up and tried to dial the number I knew already. As I was dialing the number, the detective stormed into the concrete room, grabbed the phone and slammed the receiver to hang it up. "I said one call, buddy," Detective Hickson barked. He slammed the door behind him. While in a state of panic and desperation, I began kicking the door. "Give me my phone call, you fat fucking pig," I shouted.

Just then, the detective opened the door, entered with a phone book and started slapping me in the face.

"Help!!!!!" I screamed.

Although the detective kept beating me with the phone book, I managed to grab his tie and pull myself up while dodging a strike. Once up, I connected my knee to the detective's nose. I could feel that I was in real trouble now. Another cop came into the room and started beating me, which made me scream. "You may kill me, but I will make sure you both get fired."

The two detectives stopped. My nose and lip was bleeding and my head felt like a football.

"Fucking punk," Detective Hickson vociferated, while plugging his bleeding nose with his hand. "See if you get another phone call."

The two cops left and threw the phone back into the interrogation cell, maybe out of fear of being investigated. I continued bleeding from my nose and lips. I struggled to phone my aunt, but succeeded in placing the phone's receiver by my ear. "Hello."

"Dig," my aunt greeted me.

"I'm in jail. I need you to bail me out. The cops keep beating me here."

"Oh my God," she cried."I'm calling the lawyer."

While on the phone, I got dizzy and everything faded to black. I passed out.

I lied unconscious on the floor of the interrogation cell. I slowly awakened to hear a knocking sound at the door. A suspiciously shady lawyer, wearing an ugly plaid brown suit and sun glasses, walked in. The lawyer was an East Indian and spoke with a thick accent. "What happened to you?" the lawyer asked me.

I was bleeding from the nose. Even though I initially struggled to get up, I headed to the corner of the waiting cell and started pissing blood in the toilet.

"What are you doing?" the lawyer asked me.

"I'm fucking pissing blood," I informed him with a slight slur.

"What happened?"

"What does it look like? I got assaulted by the shit head cops."

"Oh, come on. They said you looked like this before they brought you in. They said you were in some sort of fight. I heard you put some guys in the hospital."

"I think I have a concussion."

"Listen, Dig, just plead guilty and get out tonight."

I looked up dead serious. "No," I declared. "I will wait till bail from my official lawyer, not some legal aid."

I got released with bail papers a week later, and I was in rough shape. I need a lawyer. I week later, I started my first year of university. I was wearing a nice tailored suit, standing outside a lawyer's office. I peeked at a piece of paper then at the office listings on the outside wall. I finally entered the building.

The first lawyer was a fat guy, who walked with a cane and had a feather in his hat. He walked around his office and sat in his chair.

"You don't have a chance, kid," the lawyer analyzed. "You hit them excessively, and they caught you with the weapon."

I get pissed. "You know," I replied. "You look like the detective, who assaulted me. I will win this case, with someone more competent."

Before I exited the office, I turned around and said: "And this is not a fucking Western film. What's with the feathered hat? "

I finally walked out of the first lawyer's office and slammed the door.

At a second lawyer's office, I sat in a room surrounded by law books. The room was made of glass and looked very elegant. The lawyer I was to meet was a young rookie. He did not know the criminal code well.

"So you think you could be covered under self-defence," the second lawyer tried to find the angle of my case in a law book. "Hang on, let me just check what code that is."

"I have to go to the washroom," I lied to him.

"Yeah," he replied while looking up towards me."It's down the hall to the right."

The surveillance camera followed me as I left the office, walked down the hall, shook my head and turned left towards the exit doors. Strike two.

The next week my family came back from a vacation in Europe. At my grandmother's apartment, I was tired and distraught. Suddenly, the phone rang. I picked up the phone. "Hello."

"Hi, I'm Tony. I heard you told off one of my associates a few days ago."

"Yeah," I replied.

"Well, I think you have a case," Tony the lawyer pitched. "It will not be easy, but you have evidence of a break and entry, and you called the police for help. I may be able to justify the assaults as self-defence. Are you interested?"

"Yes, when can we meet?"

The day after our phone conversation, Tony the Lawyer and I sat in his office. I explained the events, using pictures and body movements.

On my day in court, I sat with a suit, as one of the gangsters was on the witness stand. Lawyer Tony paced in front of the gangster.

"Repeat what you just said, so everyone can hear you," my lawyer told the gangster on the witness stand.

"We were just trying to get the guy to turn down his music," the gangster began."Then we walked outside and saw the damage to the car, so we knocked on his door, and he came out swinging. I now have permanent brain damage from him, attacking me with a metal pole and hitting the crown of my head."

My lawyer, who looked like an Amish Mennonite with his white beard and old school swagger, interjected: "Well, we can all agree that you are not dumb...just from this incident."

The court's stenographer started to laugh. The gangster didn't get it. Everyone knew he was bluffing about brain damage caused by me. Maybe he had brain damage from his parents dropping him on the floor, but not by me.

I was next on the witness stand.

"So you asked them politely to turndown their music?" Tony asked. "Did they?"

"No," I said. "They turned it up."

"And you're sure that you saw the lady holding an empty cup with red residue in it?" my lawyer continued his examination.

"Yeah. I thought it was wine. Then, when I was sleeping, I heard people trying to break into my house. There was no other exit. All I could do was walk out into it and defend myself."

"And you do not think you were too excessive?"

"Doesn't the criminal code say, 'whatever means necessary to preserve life'?"

Lawyer Tony smiled, looked at the judge, and shrugged.

"No further questions, Your Honour," my lawyer declared.

"Oh, and don't forget I was assaulted by Detective Hickson at the station, when he wouldn't give me my phone call," I almost forgot to add.

In the courtroom, members of my family sat on the right side. A few older ladies sat on the left side beside the two skinny cops and Detective Hickson. The latter looked down in shame. Next, the lawyer of the prosecuting party walked up towards me, while I was at the witness stand.

Lawyer Tony looked at me from behind the prosecutor with a big smile. He gave me both thumbs up. I thought this part was going to be so hard, but I just kept repeating the truth and the prosecutor started to reach for connections that were not there.

"No further questions, Your Honour," the prosecutor stated.

I got down from the witness stand and I sat beside Lawyer Tony, who then leaned over. "Way to go," he congratulated me. "You nailed that one, kid."

As I was about to be released, I looked back at my family members, who were either crying or smiling. My brother gave me the thumbs up. Then, the judge delivered his final verdict: "Under section 37B of the Criminal Code, I find, considering the context of your situation, and the eminent danger, your actions were not excessive and you are covered under the umbrella of self-defence. All charges withdrawn."

My family cheered and I sobbed.

"Furthermore," the judge added, "the actions and conduct of Detective Hickson are appalling and unfathomable, especially at that exact time of confusion and vulnerability (looking at Detective Hickson). An internal investigation will be conducted, and frankly, you should be ashamed of yourself. (Looking at the gangsters) For the so-called victims, I would advise you all to get out of my sight, trying to pervert the justice system, as I could very well convict you all of assault and break and entry."

They quickly left the courtroom in shame. As my family and I prepared to leave the courtroom, I slowly looked back, and the judge gave me the thumbs up.

My parents were so ashamed of me before that court date, yet so proud when I got into university.

I learned that when a child fails, it is the system's fault, but when a child succeeds, it reflects upon his/her parents. "We're such great parents!" That's insane!

HICKSON FIRED

Detective Hickson reclined on his chair in his office. He talked some shit to his fellow co-workers, as he laid both of his hands on his head and interlocked his fingers. Suddenly, his phone rang and he picked it up. "Hickson!"

"[...]."

"What? No! Who said that?"

"[...]."

"Well, that's just bullshit. I didn't do that."

"[...]."

"Yes!" Detective Hickson exclaimed while sitting with his back up straight and boiling with anger. "Well, listen here. I have been a detective for over twenty years. This doesn't scare me. And...."

"[...]."

"Oh, sorry. Ah...yeah."

"[...]."

"Number 32415," he added while rolling his eyes.

Detective Hickson hung up the phone. He sat there thinking for a second. "Who was that, your mother telling you she should have had an abortion?" one detective asked.

Everyone in the office guffawed.

"Remember that annoying kid that kept kicking the door a couple of weeks ago?" Detective Hickson asked.

"Yeah, the one who broke your nose."

Everyone, except Hickson, died of laughter.

"The one I fucked up with the phonebook," Detective Hickson attempted to brush a more positive portrait of himself.

"Yeah? What about him?" asked the fellow detective of Hickson.

"He filed a report with Internal Affairs and now they're investigating me," Hickson lamented.

"Didn't this happen last year to you as well?"

"Yeah."

"I hope they throw the book at you," Dickson's co-worker quipped.

Everyone laughed, except Hickson, who just sat there thinking in fear.

Chapter 20: Hidden Acceptance Letter

Due to the hectic mess I was in, I just wanted to end this bad part of my life and get into any post-secondary school. I thought that the music college, which I had wanted so badly to get into, had rejected my application. But lo and behold, I found a piece of mail that made me never trust my mother again.

While applying to all the schools again, I got into a backdoor, part-time program with the University of Toronto. I studied history for a year and got 90s. As a result of my hard work, I was accepted full time with a partial scholarship and the rest is history.

During my second year in university, when I was really struggling with my political science classes that I hated, I was questioning how my life had gotten to this point. I went up north to visit my brothers. At the time, I was really still angry about how I wasn't doing music and how the whole court case at the beginning of my post-secondary adventure kind of sent me on the wrong trajectory. Then, while visiting up north, I was helping clean some desk drawers and I came across an acceptance letter from Seneca College. They had accepted me for the 2009 music program, two years earlier, after I had just applied and gotten into that life-threatening fight with the neighbours. I stood there reading the letter in shock. Like in a movie, my mom walked in on cue, saw this and tried her hardest to pretend she didn't know what I was talking about. "You knew all along?" I asked her.

"Knew what..." she tried to defend herself. "Why are you staring at me like that? I don't like your tone of voice."

"You knew I got into Seneca College and you purposely hid the letter, because you never want anyone to go further than you in music."

"Watch your mouth, I..."

"You have done everything you can to ruin my life. You blame me for getting pregnant and for you never finishing Humber music and never making it. It was you, you lazy washed up drunk. You knew I got into music school and you were jealous of your own child, so you hid the letter."

"Oh, you don't mean that," she said while turning away. "No, I'm pretty sure you saw that years ago, I don't know what..."

"Shut up!" I ordered her. "Shut Up! You provide only for your retarded children that sit around getting high all day, but not for your true hard working child. I would have finished music school by now, but you forced me to go to U of T by hiding all the other acceptance letters."

"So what! You will graduate from the best university in the country because of me."

"No, because of me, you don't help me pay tuition, remember. In fact, you don't help me with anything, but criticism."

I left that day and did not speak to my mom until I phoned her to sing harmonies on my album titled Burning Jerusalem years later.

Reality Sports Check

While playing basketball as a red shirt for UofT, I almost made the varsity basketball team. When I was the last cut, I was a little disappointed, until something I will never forget happened that changed the way I look at sports. I was approached by Carter, the best player on the varsity team, and I will never forget what he said to me:

"Hey, Digger, I heard some of your music online and I couldn't believe it was you. Damn you're good! What are you doing here, man?"

"Huh?"

"I mean, look at me, man. I'm better than you at ball, and this is all I got. You are a talented musician and most of these guys around here could never do what you do outside the ball court.

"So?"

"In fact, some of us would give all this up for the talent you got. Why are you here wasting your energy on a pipe dream for basketball, when you have a dream waiting for you out there?"

I was stunned and almost started to cry.

Why didn't someone tell me this a decade ago. I wasted so much time.

I just looked at him and said "thank you" and walked off the court to never play professional ball again. I took music seriously for the rest of my life after that day.

YouTube Teachers

While studying in university, I made an effort to really improve my lead guitar playing by studying my favourite guitar teachers on YouTube. I have to give credit to the under-rated virtuosos, who give free lessons. They are so ahead of their time. Marty Schwartz and Andrew Wassen not only made lead guitar achievable for me, but they made me realize the importance of progressing with baby steps. Their respective approaches allowed me to not get discouraged. To put it simply, I honed my skills by adding simple building blocks onto each other little by little. Eventually, I went onto playing riffs, which I thought would take me ten years to learn. Please go and subscribe to those guys' channels and donate. They do their job for the sheer love of music; not money. So give them your money.

You may notice that the song *SmokeStop* has some Spanish character. Organically, without conscious intention, I started noticing the Spanish influence on the *Shadows and Machines* album. That Spanish influence stems from my experience working at the ESL camp and all those Spanish language courses I took in university. Yes, my classes were similar to the first season of *Community* with Childish Gambino. You can especially notice the Spanish tint in the songs *Indoctrination* and *SmokeStop*.

Speaking of Spanish, I hired a band of Spanish tool musicians during my second year in university. I call them tools because in hindsight, they only came around to fuck around and take my money. To be honest, I would have preferred meeting a few friends and creating an organic band for free, with everyone contributing time, energy and funds. Unfortunately, this never happened. If you remember in the previous chapter, throughout high school, I knew phenomenal church musicians, who were already engaged in twenty other bands. I couldn't start a band with them, so they were out. I then met a few potheads, who liked to play my music, however, they honestly sucked, had tempo problems and couldn't remember songs I taught them the week before. So in university, I thought about hiring a band of "professionals" or "music students" as a safer, faster bet. Again, some priceless advice:

Just because people go to music school does not mean they will be good band mates.

A band is a tightly knit family, a creative conduit for expression, pain, love and one's ego. Do you see yourself travelling in a van across the country with someone? Do you see yourself enjoying orgies with that same person? Did you answer "no" to both questions? Then, don't start anything with that person. Find someone else. You have to feel comfortable with your band mates even to death. Listen to how disorganized this motley crew was.

When I was in university, I hired a friend to play drums for me. I had known him since high school. He wasn't a bad drummer and had a great memory. Unfortunately, he had no groove, no swing and no soul. I remember we once tried to give a "soca" dance feel to the bridge of my song *Indoctrination*, and it took this guy all day to play a non-rock beat. I even remember him saying: "I'm the whitest-sounding drummer in the world." When I listen back to recordings of him, all the beats sound the same. He was able to transition between parts well, which is often an Achilles' heel for average drummers, however, he seemed to always sound robotic. Nonetheless, to do a unique beat would take him countless hours of analysis. This was detrimental when the band was in a groove and just wanted to keep going.

I learned a valuable lesson when auditioning band members. If someone does not take music as their career, that means they take it as their hobby. Besides, if it ever gets hard or tedious, a hobbyist will quit, because no one likes to associate pain and work with their hobby. It does not become a labour of love.

In this case, my band mates only cared about having fun and taking my money. Now, I am all for having fun, but you must earn the right to have fun in music, with a tight set list and great sound. Otherwise, you're just another band of children wanting to have fun and put their burdens of life into the music, which trust me, will take decades.

Mexican Musicians

I met an incredible guitar player, busking on the street corner in Toronto. His soaring guitar riffs caught my attention from blocks away. I saw him shred and go back to slow hand so gracefully and artistically that I fell in love with his sound. Sadly, he lived a shady underworld lifestyle. His friends were gang members, and he could only play when he was high. He was so unreliable. I found myself waiting for him at coffee shops and rehearsal rooms for hours. One time, I almost punched him out, and instead told him to fuck off and fired him.

Now, I jammed with this motley crew for an entire summer, and we still didn't get through the entire album. I did, however, pay all the musicians for their time every day and told them, that if they play something I like and I decide to keep it and we for some reason part ways, I will own all riffs and will freely use them on my album. They reluctantly agreed and I got them to sign a waiver.

For some reason, the song *Sixteen* always showed me who was serious and who was a *noodler*. Maybe it was a sign that I was playing with a bunch of guys, who had the mental capacity of a sixteen year old, I don't know. Guys didn't like that the intro changed so much, and I told them it was the hardest song on the album and to just plough through it and the rest would be a walk in the park.

This Mexican guitarist sounded like Carlos Santana meets Buckethead. Such a unique, Latin sound mixed with metal. It was so nice to hear a blues player mix metal and jazz fusion together. Plus he enjoyed my music. Regrettably, like the other band members, he only cared about coming to practice high, messing around, forgetting what he did the week before, taking my money and blowing it on whores. I did, however, like his playing so much on *SmokeStop, Indoctriantion* and *Launchpads*. That is why I kept some of the riffs for the album. I either played them myself or hired a session musician to play the more complex patterns that I couldn't, when I recorded it in the studio two years later.

The Spanish bass player was a poverty case. He would often not show up to practice and later text me he had no bus fare. Wow! I remember one time we jammed a whole song perfectly but something sounded off. I singled out the bass player and asked him to play his part so I could hear something. He played and we all started laughing. He had played the whole song on the wrong fucking string. Fired!

The piano player was the only person, who was actually musically better than me. Needless to say, the other band members didn't like him. The piano player preferred playing classical music and went off to study at Julliard, a prestigious academy in New York City. So there you have it, the most unprofessional "student musicians" I have ever wasted time and money on, hated me, along with the most professional one of us. I had lost the band.

After all this, I found out the guitar player went to Vancouver, because he hated Toronto's music scene. At some point, I even contemplated going to Vancouver to find this guy and just start something new with him again. That's how much I loved just practicing, creating and playing with him. I ended up meeting this Mexican musician again in Vancouver. I watched

him play with his trio band. Truth be said, he was great to watch improvising on stage. Sadly, he couldn't sing, didn't have original songs, played long-winded solos that lost the audience's attention and frankly was still an asshole. In fact, he was using and exploiting the musicians he worked with. Even after demanding his share of the money, he never paid his own musicians what they deserved. Fuck Blues Assholes! Typical!

Chapter 21: FunHole

While I was writing my first album, *Shadows and Machines*, I had a lot of musical ideas coming to me with new song titles, chord progressions and awesome lyrics. At a certain point, I realized that I could not fit all this in one album. Therefore, I started to write more material, knowing there would be another album someday. The *FunHole* album started. I was listening to a lot of the Dave Matthews Band, Jamiroquai and Oasis at the time. When you hear the *FunHole* album, you will hear those bands' influence all over it. In comparison with *Shadows and Machines*, the album is more mellow and intellectual sounding. The lyrics are more esoteric, and the chords are simpler with much more sophisticated melody lines over top, that I am very proud of. I was studying a lot of different things in university, and much of my research inspired those songs. Additionally, I would not be surprised if this album is the most conducive to smoking a joint and getting high while listening to. It is very smooth jazz, rock and pop. Thus, my album *FunHole* is perfect for relaxation, maybe even getting some of that FunHole.

I wrote the song *Fed Up*, when I was sick and tired of school getting in the way of living a healthy life. Let's face it, when writing essays all day, studying for exams and reviewing PowerPoint slides, one does not have much time to hit the gym, go for long walks, or even eat a healthy diet, when everything is a timed opportunity cost (economics term) for something else. Even with all the sports facilities at a student's disposal, if one chooses to get good grades, then it is ramen noodles and hours of studying, no exceptions.

When one truly dives deep into studying, it often takes a toll on one's physical health.

So here I was, writing the most intellectual material I had ever written, while still trying to get good grades and remain healthy. Looking back, all of the lyrics in this album symbolize something very profound. At the same time, they may seem like rubbish to anyone but me, since no one knows what the fuck I am talking about.

For example, in *Fed Up*, I say: "Watch out for the flying dead, they try to get in your head." This may just seem like a nice play on words that rhymes. But to me, it was indicative of rich assholes, who fly around cities and look down spying on people. I used to give the finger to low flying planes, back when I was very paranoid and did not trust any government. In fact, Political science and history classes will sow the seeds of your distrust towards the government. One time while giving the finger to a small private plane, I saw it actually shift its wings side to side just as it was going over my head as a way of waving HELLO. I would not have thought anything of it, until the same plane flew ahead of me, did a full circle and then came back right behind me at a very low altitude and did the exact same thing. The rest of the lyric phrase to Fed Up says: "Try to get in your head." See how much more a lyric has meaning to the writer then to the audience. Afterwards, see how much it means more to a listener once he or she knows the story behind the lyrics. Maybe you have your own interpretation of what the line means to you? That is the beauty and what I love about writing lyrics. They mean different things to different people.

So here I was, with one album under my belt (*Shadows and Machines*) and another in the making (FunHole). I had a few choruses matched with chord progressions, but I did not have a finished concept of an album until my second year of university. Then, with all this well-earned knowledge, I started writing songs that were either politically charged to change the world or esoteric in meaning because I felt like I had too much knowledge.

For example, the song *CarBones*, which I have to admit was heavily influenced by the song *The Masterplan* by Oasis, is an intellectual cry for help against pollution from oil companies. I watched a documentary called *Who killed the Electric Car?* and it made me very angry and sad. I was angry that people were so stupid and passive to allow our world to be raped by car manufacturers, who make combustible engines when they don't have to. I was sad to see that the ones who cared about this issue were so outnumbered and out-powered. I was shocked to learn that the car could have been running on water since the beginning of its creation, but no one would have made obscene amounts of money off that. I hated what I was learning, that scientists had created engines years ago that ran on water, having their departments shut down by Big Oil.

Did everyone stop caring about the environment? Was Al Gore, the former Democratic Vice President of the United States from 1993 to 2001, right? Here I was in North America, the supposedly best continent in the world, being lied to by my own government that had connections with oil companies, to start wars across the seas and to sabotage projects like the *EV1*. All people want is a healthier future. I was so angry and sad that all I could do was write a song. I put my heart and soul into *CarBones* and honestly, the song felt bigger than me. The song wrote itself, and I just came along for the ride. My favourite lines in the song will always be "graveyards for abandoned cars" and "surrounding the big glass dick, meanwhile black oil and smoke spew out of it." (*GM Motors, Detroit*)

Another environmental song on this album is *Change*. I wrote the lyrics for this song while living in a youth shelter while still attending university. Just imagine, studying for your exams while a gangster screams and beats the shit out of his girlfriend in the room next to you. I was going a bit crazy, having gangsters constantly trying to steal my laptop, cell phone and even textbooks, so they could pawn them for drugs. Like the story of my life, I endured everything and kept battling through. I was pretty proud of the chorus to this wonderful piano song *Change*. It seemed to subtly challenge society to be mindful of the poor along with homeless and to stop allowing environmental degradation.

Two other songs on the album *FunHole* that I really enjoyed making were *One Day in June* and *Good Knight*. Both songs have a very Dave Matthews feel. When I wrote those songs, I wanted something I could play effortlessly anytime on stage with only my acoustic guitar. Both the songs are somewhat quieter, so I didn't think much about their finished concepts. The lyrics of both songs didn't take an eon to write either. They are both a kind of storytelling that worked well with the chord progressions. To be maybe a little too honest, I thought those songs were just going to be either filler songs that would never make it to the studio or on the album. Then, I listened to them and realized they are very catchy.

When making a song, sometimes it all start with a killer part. You mould the lyrics around that main part. Other songs start as a simple acoustic ballad and transform into a wicked masterpiece, when the bassline and lead guitar motifs are added. What transpired for the *FunHole* album was very different, however. Now that I had time to actually compose music in between school homework, I started jamming to my own music. I would watch YouTube videos of my favourite guitar teachers, start practicing and warming up. Then, I would put on a recording of me playing the rhythm guitar to one of the songs and just start improvising over it. I came up with some of the coolest radio-ready basslines and lead guitar melodies for this album. In fact, while writing and playing these motifs back, I would get goose bumps, realizing that these riffs would someday be iconic. For example, the song *One Day in June* is melodic at the beginning. However, the bassline for the chorus suddenly busts out into a dance vibe. As for *Good Knight*, it goes from a folk feel to a *Third Eye Blind* feel with the iconic lead guitar line over every verse.

Recording this album proved to be one of my hardest tests and greatest accomplishments. I graduated from university and knew I finally wanted to get into the music program at Seneca College. I literally left university that summer and was enrolled in music school the next fall. Before entering Seneca College, I had rented a large three-bedroom, three-bathroom townhouse down the street from campus. I was renting a few rooms in the townhouse to international students. I could never afford it all myself, so I started a home stay house that basically gave me free rent for the year. This was a smart move, I know. I set up a studio in the garage and would record what I was composing down there, just so I wouldn't forget.

At the time, I did not know about audio recording programs. I thought they were all the same. Boy, was I wrong! Programs like Pro Tools, LogicPro, Abelton and FL Studio, are all unique in their own ways. Moreover, they all specialize in different aspects of recording and/or mixing. Different studios use different programs. Now, I can honestly say Pro Tools is best for recording and mixing, whereas *LogicPro, Abelton* and *FL Studio* are better for composing, producing and making beats. Before audio engineering school, I thought they all were the same. That is why I just downloaded some free software and started recording my sessions in the garage. I am glad I did this, because many of my most iconic riffs were created when I was in the mood. They could never be re-created if I didn't have the initial recording reference, even if it was bad quality.

So there I was, recording the whole *FunHole* album, which I had created during my years at the University of Toronto, with a free recording software in my garage. I was finalizing drum parts, SFX, basslines and wicked lead guitar parts to improve the songs before going into music school. This would later come in handy. I was so excited to get into music school, because I had heard that the recording capabilities were dynamite. The summer before I entered music school, I had to spend countless hours listening to the recordings and editing parts using the free software I had downloaded.

Please take this advice:

Do not use anything that does not have the imprimatur of the music industry's professionals. You will start to form bad mixing habits and worse yet, if you do not have a proper

I did not know about this, so I stupidly would listen to my songs and practice to them using this free software. One day, I woke up with my ears ringing. When I went to play my bass in the garage, I could sense my left ear was hearing the sonic waves at a diminished volume. It was like my left ear was in water. I got scared and went to see an otolaryngologist. He said that I had a slight hearing loss in my left ear that seemed to be caused by long term listening to high register buzzing. After hearing this news, I fell into a depression. I also thought I could never be a musician, especially if I played loud rock music on a stage for my career. I took about a month off playing and noticed a significant improvement. Even to this day, I still get a slight airy sound on my left side, when something is way too loud. Hopefully, it does not affect my live performances, thank God. I worked too hard to have to do music like Beethoven, I thought. I still didn't know what was causing the hearing loss, but I knew it was from countless hours listening to the bad audio quality recordings. I would eventually only put my right headphone in my ear to finish composing the album.

On the first day of class in music school, I found out what was happening. If you asked the right question at the right time, the teachers were very knowledgeable. The teacher started the class suggesting that we all buy Pro Tools HD. He also shamelessly plugged in his sponsorship from AVID. The teacher was explaining how some programs work better for different things and I raised my hand. "Yeah, I have been experiencing some annoying high pitch buzzing on my recordings that I think it's hurting my ears," I chimed in.

"Well, what program are you using?" the teacher asked.

"A free one I downloaded."

"Well," the teacher replied with a laugh, "there is your problem! I bet you don't even have a microphone, either."

"Yeah...no!"

"That high pitch buzzing that is hurting your ears is from your own computer fan."

There you have it, folks, I experienced slight hearing damage, because of the high frequency buzzing in my recordings from my own computer fan. Once I knew this, I immediately started re-recording everything into Pro Tools sessions, using some of the nicest microphones I had ever seen from the audio department of our school. Those were microphones such as the Neumann U87, AKG 414 and my favourite, the Sony C800GPAC Studio Condenser Microphone.

After evaluating the music program and finishing all my assignments, I would spend countless hours in the main studio room in order to record my albums. In fact, I spent so much time in those rooms that I basically lived there. On weekends, I would take my lunch there and spend roughly between ten to fourteen hours in the studio, and then I'd get kicked out by either the janitor or a security guard. Eventually, the janitor and security guards all became my friends. Security guards and janitors would wait and listen to me record sometimes. Up until then, I had fully composed, arranged and somewhat recorded two albums of material, but then the truth hit me. I would have to start from scratch and re-record every part of every song. This is because anything created with the free software was not reusable. Therefore, I spent hundreds of hours, throughout the year, re-recording the *Shadows and Machines* and *FunHole* albums.

To make matters worse, the teachers were not really professional musicians and didn't like the fact that I was a university graduate making them look bad. It felt like I had a target on my forehead. Even one of the teachers at Seneca knew one of the terrible teachers at University of Toronto's Cinema Studies Department. The dog director of the music program, who was also one of my teachers, tried everything he could to ruin my experience and stall anything I did that was fun. I didn't want to leave the program though. I had dreamt about this for years, prepared in university for it and now I wasn't going to let some old men block me.

I used to hand assignments in via email and spend all day in the studio. The teachers couldn't do anything about it, either, because my assignments were head and shoulders above the retards they were used to teaching. If a teacher needed me for something, they would just peek into one of the studio rooms that I basically owned by then, and ask the question. I got straight A's in the program. Although I hated the teachers, students and program, I loved the facilities.

When you get burned a few times from so-called expensive professionals, and your product doesn't turn out the way you anticipated, then you will eventually do it yourself or give up. I am not one for giving up. Whatever I do myself may take longer, but in the long run, it will always be of high quality.

Every note, every word and every drum beat is all done by Digger Jones. For the album *Shadows and Machines*, it was pretty straightforward. I had practiced my parts so many times that I recorded the whole album in the first month. I knew I would mix everything later, so I just left the Protool sessions in their raw audio format and continued on.

Recording *FunHole,* however, was a different animal. All the rhythm guitar parts were easy, but that was it. All other parts were very complicated, time-consuming and tedious. Ironically, this album may be the softest of all my albums, but musically, it was one of the hardest to accomplish and finish. Remember that it had been about six months since I had graduated University of Toronto and had practiced the parts for *FunHole*. I thought I could just listen a few times to the recordings from the free software and re-record it all in the new studio. It was not that simple.

First of all, my lead guitar playing is significantly better when I warm up and when I am in the mood. One song in particular took me almost a week to just get the lead guitar finished, because it seemed even too advanced for me, although I had written it (*Squirrels and Sparrows*).

I had to strain to hear the parts I wanted to replicate on the high pitched terrible audio recordings. I then had to sit in the studio with the bass or guitar humming, trying to figure out what I had played. I spent literally a week per song for the *FunHole* album. I would remember the basslines and play them, then do the same for the drum takes. The lead guitar parts took me the longest time, since I had to section off parts, re-learn them, play them perfectly and then move on. Finally, I got to the vocal takes and realized my voice wasn't up to par as I had practiced months before, and some of the harmonies in this album were the highest my voice register had ever reached. So again, I spent weeks warming up and perfecting the vocals.

Now thinking back, I am glad I did it that way. I am glad I didn't rush anything that I would later have to go back and correct. I am also glad I did it all myself, because all experiences with session musicians can be fun and sound new, but they are still not what you had originally created your song to sound like. I wanted my first two albums to be exactly what was playing in my head.

Like most of my albums, I do all the composing, arranging, recording, editing and mixing myself. The reason is this. I used to say,

Why would I waste all my time doing things that others have spent their entire lives doing better and faster than me? I'll just hire them.

Only at the project's end, do I do a final touch up with the "professionals". For *FunHole*, I edited and mixed everything myself. It took me about a year, after Seneca College, but it was worth it. I got all the sounds and embellishments I wanted to feature at exactly the right spot. This was the feeling of complete creative freedom and control. I knew that after I got famous, all the egos in the industry would not let me have the same creative liberties, so I squeezed whatever I could out of the time I had. When I was satisfied with my mix, I still knew I would have to go to a professional mixer, who would add his "secret sauce" of EQs, Compressions, Plug-Ins and Gates, all things that only twenty years of fiddling with mixing boards will bring you. In the end, the overall sound and style of the album would still be mine and would not change. BINGO!

Chapter 22: Album Art

When I finished recording all the parts for the *FunHole* album, I was exhausted. I didn't want to have anything to do with instruments for a while. I had almost completed the music program at Seneca, and now I focused on art. When I say art, I am referring to the album artwork. I take that process of the album artwork very seriously. Too many times, I see famous bands, with an album that sounds great, incorporate some of the worst and most generic album art I have ever seen. For me, the album's artwork is the way bands connect to their fans. I remember as a child loving to read albums, such as Green Day's *Dookie* album, for all its fun random artwork. A child, or even a pothead, could spend hours enjoying that art. Other albums that tickled my fancy were Our Lady Peace's *Spiritual Machines* for all its intellectual symbolism and bright colours. Of course, I will also add anything created by Hugh Syme for his outstanding work with Dream Theatre and Rush, some of the most iconic graphic designs the rock/metal world has ever seen.

If I had never found weed in grade school, I would have been an illustrator for a living. I always loved the freedom to create my own world on a page. Whatever I lacked in technique, I made up for it in creativity. Somehow, I thought my window had closed in becoming an artist, when I saw some international students doing what I could only dream of doing. Growing up, I always excelled in arts, sports, acting and music, in that order. Somehow, by high school, I found myself not in art classes, because I thought I was not good enough. Instead, I found myself in drama, music and videographer classes. Still in arts, but my skills as an illustrator started to gather rust, while my eye for cinema, acting and music started to thrive. I will always be creative and passionate about the arts, but whenever I walked past the Art Department I would get a sad, lonely feeling. I guess this is how Hitler must have felt when he wasn't accepted into arts school and instead tried to kill half the world. All throughout school, I knew I wasn't as good an illustrator as the Art Department's students. Nevertheless, I would always try to incorporate art and drawing into whatever art medium I was involved with. For example, I helped in the creation of storyboarding for script and short films, costume design for theatre, elaborate title pages for assignments and then amazing album art for my music albums.

To this day, I am still not an amazing artist, but I have amazing ideas that I can now communicate with artists, because I have done enough work on illustration to know what steps they will take after me. The album cover of *Shadows and Machines*, with the robots, was drawn by me, very roughly and then given to an amazing OCAD student, who specialized in digital design. We paid eight hundred dollars for my drawings to be drawn better and have a great background digitally designed. When I got the final proofs back, I was amazed. There is no way I could have produced a work as detailed as the OCAD student did, and I wouldn't even know where to start to digitize it. That is the downside of missing your calling at a young age, because of a broken home, and a dysfunctional family. I had emotional problems and a terrible group of friends, who always ruined good things by peer pressuring vulnerable poor students like me.

By the time I had finished university, done some storyboarding, and created my first album cover, I was adamant to do the second album artwork myself. No more people trying to stick their hands in my pot of gold. I knew I needed some practice, but with some of the terrible artwork I had seen on famous albums already, I knew it didn't have to be perfect. (*Rise Against - The Sufferer*) Ironically, when I went down to OCAD to see if there were some students I could hire, I noticed that even some of OCAD's students were not as creative or artistic as me. Maybe I still had a chance. I knew I didn't want to join an art school in my thirties, but seeing people that I bested gave me confidence that I could design my own branding image, logos, one sheets and album covers. So, while finishing music school, I started seriously developing my artistic hand again.

It was time to get serious with art again. I started watching tutorial videos on YouTube, bought *The Illustrator's Bible*, a book that is considered an industry standard, and started drawing cartoons along with limbs of humans, because those aspects of art were my weaknesses. I then got really into MechWarrior machines, since I found metallic objects easier to draw than landscapes. I liked sketching comics, but my proportions were always a little off, because of the lack of fundamental principles learned in art school. Eventually, I started going into the local park and drawing for hours, getting better, but it was still far from an artist's caliber. When I was comfortable with my proportions, I started the concept art to the second album *FunHole*. I knew I wanted a hilarious album, full of random people crawling through lyrics, random cartoons on the front cover and of course a women spreading her legs with the CD hole in the middle. Hence, the title *FunHole* for my album.

Classic! The front cover of *FunHole* is of a house I used to live in called the *DIVE*, and the old creepy drunk wizard, is the guy, who lived in the basement with his dog. For this album art, I wanted animals, Mech Warriors, landscapes and stained glass images of butterflies all throughout the album. I even started adding little cartoons throughout the lyrics page that added to the story of the songs themselves. I drew all the art myself about two or three times. When I was satisfied with the sizes, I coloured the cartoons as brightly as I could, labelled everything and scanned the pictures into Photoshop. Finally, I did some tweaking and made everything ready to be digitized for the final product. I am very proud of the artwork on the *FunHole* album, a real throwback to *Dookie*.

Chapter 23: False Profits

The Great Obfuscation

As I write this novel, Donald Trump is the President of the United States. When he was about to be inaugurated, he claimed to finally acknowledge that "Jerusalem would be recognized as the capital city of Israel". I was about a month away from releasing the *Burning Jerusalem* album, and I could feel the tension in the air regarding the name. It was like what *Rage Against the Machine* had to endure, being blocked by the cops, corporations and even the government to not let them speak or release music that would help spur a revolution. There is even footage of *Rage* playing outside the Stock Exchange, while cops were waiting for their set to finish, so they could arrest them.

Here is another word to the wise:

If you toe the party line, you will be played on the radio, as a gimmicky, fun, fake rebellious (Blink-182) act. On the other hand, if you actually have something important to say, you will be the musicians relegated to side stages in unknown folk festivals. Do not let the people with money know your political, ideological and spiritual aspirations, because what you say will be held against you in the court of popular opinion.

When I write this book, everyone and their dad is debating about Trump. I feel like he is an asshole for taking people's attention away from real life issues, such as deforestation, starvation in Africa, and community civic disengagement. I am a political scientist by merit, who frankly hates politics. I see everything so simply. If people could for once put down their hatred, greed and egos in order to work together, we could accomplish more than any boardroom of rich people. In fact, we can accomplish more than any generation ever in history. All those fake political scientists keep talking about what Trump said or didn't say as a cheap way to avoid real Earth problems like global warming, food shortages and unprecedented murder rates. It is all one great obfuscation by the false profits.

False Prophets

Speaking of False Prophets, I played in another person's band once for about a week. It was a terrible experience.

When I was still writing some songs for *FunHole*, I met a couple of guys I saw playing in a bar one night. They were both playing acoustic guitars and seemed to gel perfectly together. They also had a really catchy song called *False Profits*. I approached them and asked if they had a bass player and if I could jam with them. We exchanged numbers and to my surprise, they were really prompt at getting back to me. I invited them to my house, and we jammed a few times, always playing their material. I studied six of their songs for an upcoming show. To be honest, I crushed those basslines, as I came up with some of my best material for them. I later took one of my own basslines from one of their whimsical songs and made it the bassline for the verses of *CarBones - FunHole*.

I started doubting the idea of playing for them, however, when I realized I only liked one of their songs, and they were not very open to allowing some of my more catchy songs into their set lists. I asked if we could share some of our music, or collaborate, thinking it would be a great experience to expand.

This is where most bands breakup. One guy wants the music to be all his, while others do not fully want to be sidemen. Two guys try to share responsibilities and one keeps trying to squeeze the others' material out, claiming it is a clash of styles.

The singer of this *False Prophet* project told me straight to my face that this was his project, and that my songs would be on the back burner. I told him straight to his face to find another bass player, and to not steal my awesome basslines. The singer of the band also happened to be somewhat cross-eyed, and I would sometimes not know if he was looking at me or the person behind me when he was talking.

The last time I ever saw the crossed-eyed prophet was when I actually went to their show about a month later. When I walked in, I saw a bass player playing the awesome bassline that is now the bassline to *CarBones*. The singer looked at him on stage halfway through the song, and the guy actually changed the bassline right on stage, as not to be caught copying me. I just walked out of the bar to never see any of them again, or so I thought.

Busking For Quarters

Upon leaving the music program, I had met the same space cadet guitar player, whom I had met in the band that had the one hit *False Prophets*. I did not like the crossed-eyed Prima Donna singer of the group, but I did enjoy some of the beautiful riffs his lead guitar player would play. I actually jammed with this guitar nut job for about a month. He used to talk to himself in front of my bathroom mirror for ten minutes before coming out to jam. He started scarring my other band mates. I have learned that some of the best musicians, who never make it, never make it because they have serious mental issues.

All of my work and frustration culminated to one hectic day. The nutjob guitarist and I decided to test the waters and try busking downtown. We left the northern part of the city (Seneca College's area) with a few posters and our guitars. Our first stop was Yorkdale Mall. I don't mean inside the mall, because busking in malls is illegal now. No, I mean the bridge that connects the TTC to the mall is where we posted up. When we arrived, we saw some black guy sitting in the usual busking area, eating his lunch with his saxophone lying on the ground. I politely walked up to him and asked if my friend and I could play a couple songs while he ate lunch. He abruptly told me to fuck off and screamed that this was his area. I waited for him to pick up his sax again and start playing to scare us off, but instead, he went back to eating. I was a little surprised and pissed off at his reaction, so I decided to start playing anyway.

At first, he started yelling that he would phone the police. Then, he started yelling just to be heard over our music. Then, he got tired of yelling and went back to eating. What happened next will forever remind me of why I hate Toronto and scrub musicians. A fat black lady (of course) walked by, reached into my guitar case, took out a five dollar bill that another lady had just dropped in there and then proceeded to hand it to the saxophone player on break. I was shocked and then started laughing at the absurdity of this "busking wars". Even the asshole sax player started laughing at me in shock. I was about to pack up and storm off, when a group of teenagers came up, started hanging around me while I played some hip hop acoustic songs and started taking pictures. They really started liking my rock rap song *Indoctrination,* and they all dropped money in my case. Obviously, they didn't like the esoteric jazz played by the other musician and preferred something with a little more energy and relevance.

The sax asshole got so angry that he came over to try to steal the money. When I pushed him away and told him to fuck off, the same fat black lady came running over with a security guard to protect him. I just explained to the security guard that no one could monopolize a busking area and I went on my peaceful way. The worst part about all of this is that the nutjob lead guitar player, whom I was busking with, kept trying to stop songs halfway through playing them to keep complaining that the sax asshole was in the right. I literally turned to him, while he was about 6 foot 5, 250 pounds and asked him: "Whose side are you on? Do you want assholes like him ruining our busking experience? Even the security guard didn't like him. He is there every day, with no license, and few people enjoy his music, and we can't stop and play for twenty minutes, fuck that guy."Suddenly, it seemed this little argument became a racial thing, like all things in Canada nowadays. I decided to find a new place to jam.

I immediately jumped on the TTC's subway train and was off to my next destination. When things start going bad, I have an uncanny ability to just disappear like a ghost or like Nightcrawler from *X-Men*. Before we knew it, we were at the Spadina Station underpass. Now, this is a hotspot for buskers, since it always has a steady flow of pedestrians walking by. It is never vacant. To my outmost surprise, nobody was busking there that day. The nutjob guitarist and I just looked at each other in amazement, started laughing and then ran over to set up before someone else came. We started playing songs, while I was on rhythm and vocals and he played arpeggios and lead solos. It was pretty good for the first few songs when I wasn't really noticing what he was actually doing. I was more feeling out the crowd. We made a few bucks and then I got a great idea. "Hey," I began, "we can actually practice our material here while getting paid."

"Yeah."

We started practicing some of the *Burning Jerusalem* material that I was in the process of teaching him, when I noticed that he couldn't remember what he had just played. I noticed that people started seeing the miscommunication between us, as I would go to a chorus and this guy would be noodling still, not aware of which part of the song we were on. I had taught this guy my songs for countless hours, but nothing was getting through. We started to get large crowds of people ignoring us, and this bothered me.

I immediately turned and put my hip hop backing tracks on, and started rapping and playing guitar on my own. Instantly, young crowds started to stop, take pictures and drop money again. I turned around and saw the nutjob pouting and packing up his guitar to leave. All of a sudden, it became a one-man band. I stopped playing, turned to him and said: "What the fuck, man? You pout all day, come here, can't remember any of the riffs we've practiced so many times and then pack up and go home. Just because I improvised and got us some attention again. Here take all the money, too."

I started throwing the change from my guitar case at him, and I actually thought he was going to beat me up. But instead, he looked scared of my intensity and backed away to never be seen again. Busking has always been a fear of mine. Not the fact that I am playing in public or in front of people, I relish that role, no, I fear it, because I am playing with no protection at the mercy of the streets that, let's face it, can be pretty hostile these days. I also have a stigma of playing for change on the street, since my mom was a busker when she was young.

My mother told me she often met weirdo men trying to pick her up. She did, however, meet a Native Indian guy once. He was pretty nice to her and helped raise her children. He ended up becoming my step father, and they had a relationship for years. He also blessed her with the name Yellow Butterfly.

Chapter 24: Yellow Butterflop

By this time, you may have an impression of who my mother is, from the previous chapters, stories and dialogues. Truth be told, my mother is a very dynamic person, with multiple dimensions and maybe even multiple personalities. At a young age, my mother was a very innocent girl who just wanted attention via music. She could write great social commentary lyrics and melodies. She was perfect with my nerd dad on the bass and her as the front women.

Later on in life, when I was older, my mother changed into a control freak with a talent for music. She would often make bizarre and questionable decisions when it came to working with certain musicians. Before I tell you the next story, I want you to understand something. Maybe you come from a great loving family and have a strong relationship with your mother. Maybe you come from a family that isn't perfect, but has love between its members. Well, some people come from a family that is so dysfunctional and abusive that not all mothers want or know what is best for their children. Moreover, some children are actually better being very far away from their mothers.

Twice I got punked by my mother while auditioning for her makeshift band.

The first time, I learned a whole set perfectly and was excited to play bass for her band. Then, without warning my mother and her demonic boyfriend came up with a plan to sabotage me right before I went on stage. About an hour before the concert, my mother ran over to me and said that her boyfriend had broken his sitar strings. He needed to buy new strings and we had to transpose everything up four semitones. While for her, she just used a capo. For me on bass, I scrambled around trying to re-program all the runs I had learned in different keys. I had not yet mastered on-sight transposition. I was panicking. Then I realized it was all a lie.

When her boyfriend showed up and I asked to go over some songs with him in the new key. My mom came over and tried to stop us. WOW! I got on stage and knew I would bomb, but good, fuck her. She kept looking at me on stage with this disgusted look every time I hit the wrong note. I had enough. Right there on stage, I just told her to fuck off and walked off. It felt like an insurmountable test and a musician's worst nightmare. The worst part: it came from my mother and other musicians who are worse than me. Of course, as soon as I walked off stage, some hillbilly friend of my mother "randomly" came on stage and played the songs perfectly. He only played the tonic of every chord, because he just knew that this type of music has the same chord progression in every song, regardless of the key. The music is so generic, that E, G, C and D are their life source. No artistic value! Ironically, it was the same day as I had an audition for stand-up comedy school. I walked right off stage, hopped in my car, went to the audition and was accepted into comedy school. What a joke!

The second time I got punked was when I had just graduated from university and was preparing for Seneca College. Around this time, I auditioned for my mom's makeshift folk band again. Insanity is doing the same thing expecting different results. I went with my mom to her band's practice and had the most sincere intention. I thought I could heal our broken relationship by pleasing her with my bass lines. I aimed to improve her songs. That day, I realized my mother was always trying to sabotage my music career. She made things so hard for me in her band, because of her fragile ego. It felt like this time was another one of her impossible tasks. That night my mother was so hard to work with. She always pushed the pace, constantly getting frustrated with all her musicians. She expected me to learn ten songs in one night. It was not a fun experience. I can understand if someone had a gig coming up and was paying for serious session musicians, but even then, you need to give them time and lead sheets, and maybe some MP3's.

My mom is old-school. She didn't realize that I wanted to make her songs actually better with nice basslines. Being her son, and she could have shown me those songs anytime. Therefore, when I got there, I was expected to learn ten songs that all sounded the same. To add insult to injury, none of my embellishments were appreciated. I had no time to come up with real basslines, and my mom just wanted me to play the tonic. I wanted to shoot my brains out after three or four songs. I wanted to help my mom and I felt sorry for her. However, rushing ten songs, all of which could be substantially better with an extra night of bass work, seemed ludicrous to me. I had been there for five hours and was getting tired. My mother kept drilling those terrible songs at me like a drill sergeant. That is why I started an argument, walked out and waited in the car. Of course, for the show that came next week, she got the same tool to play the tonics that had weaseled his way in at the other festival.

It took me all this time to realize that this bass curse that I had experienced in my life is actually obviously my mother's bass curse. She beefed my father, who was her bass player when I was born; she beefed me being her bass player; and after I chose not to be a bass player for life, I have had nothing but problems finding reliable bass players. "C'est la vie."

Coma Toast

Coma Toast was the name of my mother's partially successful band growing up. It actually is a cool play on words and the name for a dead beat, *DeadHead* band of drug addicts. Before my mother's bass curse, there was her band Coma Toast. That band had one decent album. Unfortunately, as soon as they started achieving any real success, half the band's members got cold feet. My mom left this band behind in Toronto, while she tried to better herself in Vancouver. Obviously, one day on my walk back from school, I walked onto our property to see the whole band camped out on our driveway waiting for my mom to come back from work. She allowed those scumbags back into our lives, and we had to move again.

My mother then went on a fluttering solo career, which could have been so much better, if she just had worked with level-headed musicians. She had a few really catchy songs, such as *Stay Wild, The Circle, Plastic Fantastic* and *Shaking the Mystery*. In fact, after my mom went solo, I would come home from school and hear some pleasant music playing. One day I heard a song from the back room and I thought it was the radio, because it sounded so professional. I then walked into my mom's home studio and noticed it was her playing back her song *Stay Wild*. It was such an honour to know that my mom was about to make the radio. I was so proud of her I thought she was going to make it. She had changed her stage name to Yellow Butterfly after a Native medicine man had given her the name. I don't know what happened, however, where it all went wrong. She got pregnant with my youngest brother, stopped doing studio work and started hanging around dead beat musicians again. She turned into *Yellow Butterflop*.

Chapter 25: Vocal Lessons & Choirs

Vocal Lessons

I also studied vocal lessons with a few private teachers while in university. I did this for one summer, and it started to get expensive. I noticed my range, tone and power improving, but I knew there must be a cheaper, more schedule-convenient way to keep up with my vocal pedigree. I found the most wonderful teacher on YouTube. His name is Eric Arceneaux. He is a great singer, teacher and coach. In fact, I have a playlist of ten of his videos that comprise about an hour of vocal workouts, making up my favourite vocal class of all time. I will never have to go spend another penny on a single vocal lesson again. This is the exact perfect lesson and timeframe for my voice type. Thanks, *AApproach.com*.

Those vocal workshops have helped me heal from the vocal damage caused by excessive marijuana smoking and coughing. You may ask why someone gifted in vocals would want to smoke weed. The answer is that when you have family problems, no indication of vocal success, no money, and constant heartbreak while pursuing your passions, weed is the only thing that is reliable to help a person feel good again. Even if it is all a lie, one could end up regarding weed as an outlet. When I failed to make various varsity sports teams by being the last cut, I was devastated and smoked. When I had my high school sweetheart cheating on me, I smoked. When my band started falling through my fingertips, I smoked. It took some serious will power to quit each time. But when I quit, I would quit for three to five years. Then, I would try so hard to achieve something else. In the event of a failure, I would throw in the towel and relapse into the consumption of weed. To be honest, with a good upbringing and a little financial support, I would have been an Olympic runner, a Varsity star athlete, and a famous actor with a side band, all before I was the age of thirty-five. I write this book when I am thirty three. I almost made the Olympics, but didn't. I almost made Varsity, but was injured by a jealous opponent. My life up until thirty-three had been all about "almosts". I am a star actor that was kicked out of acting school, and an amazing musician who nobody knew about. That all changed when I moved to Vancouver to reset my life. I found a proper publicist for my music as well as a good acting agent in order to start to show the world what I had to offer.

I still keep doing my vocal exercises though, waiting for my big break. People say you can't wait for your big break, you must go out there and find it. Well, I got news for them: given how the system is rigged, you will exhaust yourself like I did going everywhere and trying to break in. The gatekeepers already know when I'm coming and try to block me. Maybe you will have it easier, but remember they may know you're coming and rig it against you. Therefore, either keep trying to gain access or pause in order to find a smarter way in. You will spend countless hours of time and money trying to reach fan bases that don't care about anyone not ordained by the conspiracy. Then, you will stop, like I did and realize, they find you, they don't let you find them, so keep touring, keep pushing, maybe someone will recognize you, or not!

I personally like doing vocal lessons in the steam room, when it is not too hot. It is like singing in the shower, which most people like because it is moist on the throat and quickly clears it. As a result of that, your voice becomes strong without much force.

I've had to do vocal warm-ups in basement washrooms of clubs before a gig, because that was the only place available in winter. In warmer weather, I will usually go for a jog a couple hours before a show, then drink some tea, and then do a few lip rolls and trills to get warmed up, but never over worked.

Notwithstanding the circumstances, always find a place to prep your voice. I don't care if you have to sing into a damp towel in the stall of the dirty bathroom. Your show will be better if your voice does not crack on stage.

University Choirs

In university, I sang in two choirs. One was the U of T's jazz choir. I had the highest male register, like an alto (counter tenor), but the conductor had "friends" in the choir, and I knew that in order for me to get a lead role, I would have to endure hardship for more than two years. Not worth it! I was a much better singer on my own studio albums, something that surprisingly a lot of music students do not have for some reason. To put it simply, the better they get at music, the more self-conscious they all become. For some reason, there were assholes in every choir I was part of. They were usually bass singers, who always sang too loud. In fact, it is commonly known in music school that singers have something stuck up their asses. In the U of T's jazz choir, it was a group of Jewish kids, who felt that the choir was an extension of their home synagogue and families' rich connections. They strutted around like they owned the Cinema Department and the choir. Ironically, the other tenor singers didn't like them too much and instead would challenge me to beat them for our group. The tenors admired my tone, power and range. I would always try to make our section the best.

There is a video of me in that choir on YouTube. It shows me hitting a high A from the female range. It is the highest note I can hit, and I am very proud that I hit that note during the final song of the final show of the U of T's Jazz choir. Most importantly, we got it on tape for eternity. I once even got a group of Asian guys from that choir to do a special performance with me to NSYNC's song *Tearin' Up My Heart*. Of course, I was Timberlake, and they were the rest of the band. We were actually pretty good. We had the dance moves down pat, good harmonies and a little Asian flare. We performed at the end of the year's show, and it was well received. I knew, however, I would never join a choir again. To be honest, choirs do not help people become better singers. They usually exploit free talent and push singers to over-sing, because someone in the group keeps going flat. You have to constantly repeat parts and after long-term choir membership, you will also notice that your voice starts becoming less powerful, more airy and even raspy. The only reason I joined the U of T's choir is to prove to myself that I could.

Another tip for vocalists: don't let the world force you to talk. When the world knows that you want to be a singer, it seems that it will put you in a predicament to get you to always talk. If you don't talk, people will seem offended or try to make you seem weird or rude. Ironically, when you really start talking, nobody cares and they will start ignoring you. Take care of your voice on the downtimes. Do not get into arguments or yelling matches, and don't cheer too loud for your favourite sports team. Lastly, don't smoke weed or get into lengthy debates about politics.

Chapter 26: New Legacy

For my second attempt at releasing an album, I actually did this next album in a rushed panic, and it worked out better than the first album. I got great musicians, who knew theory and were gifted music students. However, that came at a price. They were emotional retards, who cringed at the fact of toiling. They still didn't remember parts, and seemed to only come around for the money.

The other albums I have mentioned in this book are mostly rock with a bit of hip hop. *New Legacy,* on the other hand, is mostly hip hop with a bit of rock. Being at Seneca around so many hip hop artists inspired me to get back to my hip hop roots, which I loved as a child. I always loved the energy and style of hip hop far more than the dusty heaviness of rock. Sports and hip hop go hand in hand, just like the ebb and flow of a sports game and performing a concert.

I always knew that I would do a hip hop album. I have written a few killer freestyles and raps throughout my days, but being at Seneca was the first time I felt that it was not a waste of time. I would have used a few of my raps for some of the songs on other albums, such as *Dive* and *Indoctrination*, if I never attended a school full of rappers. When I studied at Seneca College, however, I knew I would be able to write new material, so I went to the art supply and book store, got a nice new notebook and started writing new raps.

That means I was recording two albums, however, and I started experiencing a conflict of time, interest and genres, when I started writing new rap material around my Seneca friends. I always felt like it was a waste of time, because I had other albums to record. I see now, it was never a waste. I just had a lot on my plate. I had to juggle doing assignments for class, writing new material that would later go on the *Burning Jerusalem* album and then have fun with my friends writing new rap material. I would get high, write new rhymes and then record them in the studio. I became like a producer, audio engineer and rapper during those sessions.

I met a pretty good rapper named Tre Blaze at Seneca. Blaze's problem was that he had wicked lines that he could rap well in the vocal booth, if alone. Sadly, because of his shy personality and quiet voice, he was a nightmare to perform with in front of larger crowds. During class projects, he could never be heard. Later that night, however, he would write the funniest line I have ever heard and I would just put it in a song. To be honest, Blaze had lines for days, and he started inspiring me to get back to my raps. Blaze is featured on a few songs on the *FunHole* album, but he really has some of his best lines on the *New Legacy* album.

Eventually, I noticed that I would have a full album of hip hop material. This idea excited me. I was kind of sick and tired of rock and all the dusty rock fans. I wanted to just wild out with some hip hop. I also found hip hop a lot easier for me to perform, since it was more about memorizing lines than conducting a band. I can honestly say that the music part of hip hop is easier. It is the world of hip hop and the streets that are difficult. Ironically, the "musicians" in hip hop are tougher and more dangerous to work with.

I composed and produced most of *New Legacy*'s material while at Seneca College. I loved using FL Studio and LogicPro for making beats. As for recording vocals, Pro Tools is my software of choice. I wrote and recorded a lot of the initial lyrics and basslines at Seneca College, but I knew that I would have to take the semi-finished album to a professional for the next steps. When getting the band together for the *New Legacy* studio sessions and eventual show, I knew I wanted to work with the saxophone player from the *Burning Jerusalem* album and his friend from Barbados. The latter played a fusion style of guitar that reminded me of Guthrie Govan, a talented English guitarist.

In fact, I never wanted to fall out of touch with this Barbadian guitar player. He was comical and compassionate and played guitar not as an instrument, but as a method of communication. He literally spoke out the notes of his guitar like someone speaking in musical phrases. It was awesome watching him come up with improved jazz fusion riffs on the spot or learning how to play my guitar motifs that I had spent years creating. He could play those in five minutes. Unfortunately, what is epically ironic and disturbing is that on the night of the show, this guitar player was barely heard, because the sound guy kept trying to sabotage us and when he was heard, he made mistakes because he was really high. I explain more in an earlier chapter.

Chapter 27: Bass Player Fiasco

Imagine you meet a bass player trolling the hallways of the studio building you just moved into. He says that he is available to play bass. You notice that he doesn't have the best timing, but he is one of the hardest working guys that is committed to learning the parts. Up to now, I had only worked with musicians, who didn't put a lot of work into learning my material. In short, he was a pleasant surprise.

Of course, both types of musicians – meaning a dilettante and an assiduous artist –can be hard to work with.

Those are either musicians, who have attitudes and believe they can wing everything on raw talent, or hard-working tool musicians with fragile egos, because they know that they are not that good. The latter obsessively work on something until all the joy is sucked out of it and then quit in frustration. I had a bass player quit one week before the gig. How convenient!

So there I was with a bass player, who thought my studio was his playground. He didn't even knock when entering my studio room. This guy once caught me getting a blowjob, because he stormed in without knocking. He then left the door open and walked away. To make matters worse, he often forgot parts, had no rhythm. He complained and passively-aggressively sulked all the time that my songs were too complicated. I could tell that he was waiting to throw a wrench in things, because he probably knew I would fire him after the show. He gladly took all my money for rehearsal time, practice time and even rehearsal space, all while just waiting to get even. It all started with a response to a comment on social media.

I had made a small little rant on how someone I was dealing with in the music industry was incompetently trying to hustle my money. This bass player immediately jumped in defending the incompetent person in the industry. He then told me that I should hire a manager to do all this, when he knew I obviously concur. However, things were almost done, and I was running out of money. The show was in a week. At that moment, I got pissed off, because this guy had never offered to do any of the work. As for the one mission I did ask him to fulfill, he fucked it up. I asked him to get our show on the website *Ticketfly* to sell tickets or at least *Eventbrite*, and he said that it was all done. A weeks later, I saw nothing had gone through on the systems.

Now, this guy seemed to be chiming in his two cents at the worst time. I got so angry. I then declared that maybe people, who don't commit time and money, should not try to correct the ones doing all the work. I posted that maybe what someone thinks is a suggestion is actually a subtle insult. It was not helpful. So I deleted the post and went on to block him.

What happened next will forever show me how a hurt ego can go to insane lengths to try to get even. This guy actually tried to contact me on Twitter, Instagram, FB and even email, all in an hour. I could tell that he was pissed, and it started to feel like he was stalking me. I thought I could just ignore him for the night and talk to him the next day at band practice, when everything had blown over. Well, the next day I showed up to my studio and Bass Buffoon, as I will call him from now on, walked in without knocking, trying to punch above his weight. "So I'm fired?" Bass Buffoon fired his first salvo.

"What?" I asked him.

"You blocked me?"

"Well, you're not fired at all. I just blocked you for the night, because you were kind of getting annoying. But I knew we'd talk about it today."

"Oh shit," Bass Buffoon gasped.

"What?"

"You didn't get the message, did you?"

"What? The one you said I should get a manager, after I had just spent a month doing everything for free. I was a little pissed, and I just wanted to vent, and I felt you were defending the wrong people, ya know?"

"No," Bass Buffoon interjected. "Not that message. The one about me leaving for the military."

"What?"

"Yeah, I got assigned last night. I leave on Monday. I'm going to the military."

"The show's on Thursday."

"Hey man," Bass Buffoon tried to tug my heart's strings. "I told you I would be going to the military. I just didn't know it would be so soon."

"No," I corrected him. "What you did was lying to us all, getting salty because I ignored a stupid comment of yours and now trying to throw a wrench into our whole plan. Are you gonna give back the thousands of dollars I gave you to learn this music? Of course not! Well, at least I can officially say I had to redo all your basslines for *New Legacy*, and you are a terrible bass player, who is fired. Why don't you stop taking all my time and energy re-teaching basslines and offer some real help, instead of coming late, demanding money and only coming around after I have done all the hard work. Fuck, you won't even let me vent a little, without trying to correct me or suggest something to me, learn the fucking basslines and keep time, you tool..."

(Pause)

"You asked me why don't I get a manager to do this stuff?" I broke the ice. "DAH, I would, if we had the time and money, idiot... Why don't you lend some time and money to do this.... Didn't think so... Anyways, you were a terrible bass player, and should just stick to being a roadie. Oh, and Fort York's reserve is still in Toronto, you idiot. Yo, enough comments from the peanut gallery. Get the fuck out of my studio. (Turning towards the band) Yo guys, let's get practicing."

When I first met him, I should have known that Bass Buffoon had some weird card up his sleeve. When I mentioned that I had lost two bass players to the military earlier, he looked down and his mind went blank in space. It was bizarre and kind of scary. While my band ended up going on a tour and I noticed on this guy's social media that he got shot in the military and came back for recovery. There are some weird people trying to ride the coat tails of any successful musician. Luckily, I can play bass too in the studio.

Fixing a Bass...Easy Enough?

To start the *New Legacy* studio sessions off right, I wanted the best equipment I could find. I had auditioned a few musicians, whom I knew would possibly be on the album for one or two songs. A few of the session musicians were legit but most of the guys were "wastemen", people who do nothing with their lives. They had too many family, drug or work commitments. By that time, I was running on fumes going into the studio.

My first experience with incompetent people for this album started during the simple task of trying to get my instruments ready for the studio. Three weeks earlier, I had sent my bass and electric guitars to be repaired at a guitar shop. I needed the action lowered on both guitars and the active pickups on the bass to be fixed. I brought my guitars into Demonic Guitar Shop (I should have known it would be a lemon by the name). The guy was pretty nice and assured me that my guitars would be ready in a week. I remember, the night I went to hand the guitars in, I was running late. When I left my studio near the downtown beach of Toronto, I phoned "the Demon" and apologized about running a couple of minutes late. The Demon was not impressed and told me that the shop closed at 5:30p.m. I mean what kind of store opens at noon and closes at 5:30p.m.? I said I would be there at 5:40p.m. and beseeched him to wait.

Of course, when you are late, the world only sends idiots to make you more late. I had a cab driver pick me up. He might have been the stupidest, most dangerous person I had ever seen behind the wheel. He picked me up almost half an hour late, took the wrong highway, then turned onto a one way street and almost got us killed. We pulled up to The Demonic Guitar Shop around 6:00p.m. and I thought for sure the Demon had gone home. To my surprise, he was just walking back to the store with a pizza in his hand, a little annoyed, but grateful for my business. I told him to charge whatever it took to get my instruments in tip top shape.

About a week later, I phoned again and was told that they were running behind, and it would be ready the following week. I waited and waited and waited to the point that my hired military bass player had to buy his own cheap bass for rehearsals. Finally, I phoned The Demonic Guitar Shop and inquired about my order. They told me that it was all ready. I went to the store early in the afternoon this time with high hopes.

When I walked into the store, there were weirdo pothead musicians lingering around not buying anything, seemingly wanting to eavesdrop on my conversation. I went to the Demon and handed my order slip. He went in the back, brought out a guitar that wasn't mine and then went on to say, he couldn't fix the bass, because he didn't know it had active pickups. He complained that he would have to order the parts but didn't want to spend his own money. Therefore, he had to wait for me to give another deposit. I was so furious, but hid it well, because I wanted to see if the electric guitar he accidently gave me was worth all the mistakes. It wasn't. Sure enough, the guitar was worth less than my Fender Telecaster, so I immediately flipped out. "This is the wrong guitar!"

"What, no?" the Demon stood his ground.

"I gave you an Epiphone Thunderbird bass and a Fender Telecaster. Pretty simple."

"Oh damn! Let me look in the back. I hope it's done!"

"You mean I could have waited two weeks for nothing?"

The Demon came out from the back with my guitars and a sad look on his face.

"I'm sorry. I don't know what happened but I can have these..."

"For fuck's sake!" I exploded.

"Huh!"

"I can't believe this," I yelled. "I have spent weeks renting equipment while my guitars sit in your basement and have not even been touched. Now, you bring out some shitty guitar and try to pawn it off on me as mine, when my guitars are still unfixed, and I am in the studio tomorrow. WOW!"

I was about to stomp out, when the Demon said: "Man, I am sorry. I can lend you any bass we have for your studio sessions."

"Oh really!" I replied, while regaining my composure.

"Yeah, my apologies, man. Our orders got misinterpreted. Your guitars should have been done last week. So yes, I can give you any bass you like for the next couple of days, until we fix your bass."

"Hold on. Wait on fixing the bass until I bring this bass back," I said while pointing at a nice red Fender P Bass.

"Okay," the Demon agreed. "I can give you that one for a couple of days, and sorry about everything, Digger."

"Ok, I will give you another chance," I stated, because I was now a little reassured. "I'll use this bass well for the studio and take care of it and bring it back as soon as I am done."

Just like that, I had a new bass for the studio. I did finish the studio sessions using that bass, and it had a nice bite to it: perfect for the funky hip hop rock I was recording. This bass can really be heard on the song *Fly With Me*. When I returned the bass, I was not surprised that my electric guitar had not been fixed. I just laughed and left the store with my equipment and never did business there again.

La Music Store Mal

After recording in the studio, I still wanted to fix my guitars for the upcoming show. I had to find a new trustworthy store. I found a guitar shop that specialized in fixing guitars. I had gone to the place and offered to pay top dollar for an intonation setup. The guy at the front desk was so underwhelmed and aloof that I thought he didn't speak English. As I was about to walk out of the store, he asked: "How can I help you?"

"I need to fix the pickup in an active pick-up bass and I need the intonation, action and pickup fixed in my Telecaster," I responded with a slightly grouchy tone.

"Easy enough!"

"Oh, okay. How long will this take?"

"About four days."

"Oh, that's great."

"But we need a deposit of one hundred dollars now to."

"For sure. Here you go," I replied, while handing him two fifty-dollar bills.

"We'll call you when it is done."

"Any idea how much more it would be after that?"

"Shouldn't be much more," the store's employee hazarded a guess. "Less than a hundred."

I wish I could say I went there four days later and everything was fixed at an affordable price. But the truth is, in the music industry, everything is crowded, slow and dusty. I got a phone call a week later, fairly close to the show's day. I went in, and the desk guy acted like he never saw me before. He then spent about an hour trying to find my guitars. He came back and dropped the bomb: "I thought it would be an easy fix," he lied. "But my repair guy said you needed a whole new pre-amp. So I went ahead and fixed it all up for you. Your total comes to $381.95."

"What?"

"Yeah, but I can knock five percent off for you."

"You mean four hundred dollars including the hundred I gave you deposit, right?"

"No," the employee said sheepishly.

"I could have bought a new bass for that price!" I roared.

"Well, actually..." he attempted to reply slightly churlishly.

"Do you have Interact?"

"Ah, yeah."

I paid and just left the store and never did business there again. The experience was overpriced, underwhelming and annoying. The guitars were barely fixed. It seemed like they had too many guitars to deal with as well. Then, when I plugged in my bass, it played for about ten minutes and then, it short circuited. On D-Day, I had to use my own equipment from my studio. I used my Fender Champion amp, because I love the pre-set options. I do like some guitar pedals, but I honestly think a lot of lead guitarists use pedals to over-compensate for their lack of chops. I ended up only using the electric guitar and amp at the show. I also got all new equipment rented from Long & McQuade. To be honest, L&M are the best for professional music equipment renting.

Long & McQuade Rentals

I rented all the percussions for the show from L&M. They had so many options. It was like a kid picking toys in a toy store. I already had the bass from The Demonic Guitar Shop, my electric guitars were top notch, and everything else would be DI (Direct Input).

One of the best decisions I made before the show was renting a drum kit, which all performers and bands could use. I walked into the L&M Toronto store and I saw so many drum kits, electric kits and percussion items. Finally, a store that knew what it was doing! I immediately saw a really nice Yamaha Kit, which was brand new and had a beautiful green and black design that worked perfectly with the *New Legacy*'s artwork. We got all the drum heads and extra cymbals that we needed and a Cuban drum, for the acoustic songs. The sales rep at the store was so helpful, even though I knew he was overworked and underpaid. I told him that I was probably going to buy the kit after I rented it.

To be honest, I would have if my band was not a bunch of cry-babies and I didn't have to flee for fear of death after my show. When I returned the drum kit to L&M, the same sales rep could see I was disappointed, and he was disappointed as well. He allowed us to take a brand new drum kit that was sitting in the show room. We were the first band to rent it and now he had to take it back and make this new kit a rental kit. I later went back a year later and bought the kit myself. Although it was a little banged up, I fixed it back to its original state, and I loved the sound and color of it. Sometimes we don't get things in the rush of the first attempt. In addition to that, we have to wait and be patient for it to come around full circle.

Chapter 28: Emotional Retards

A year earlier, I had heard this one drummer play at Seneca College's show, and I was amazed by his energy and ability to vary his drum rolls on different toms and cymbals. He could play different timings and never made his fills sound generic. In fact, he reminded me of the drummer from the Dave Matthews Band. I knew I wanted to work with him, but when I showed him the first album, *Burning Jerusalem*, he instantly became reluctant. When I met him, he said that his name was Culture, but I asked what his real name was, and he said Jay. I called him JCulture. The name stuck. I think he still uses the name to this day. I am usually good at branding and marketing people's images. If I have the financial backing along with the ideas, I can come up with catchy names for anyone.

JCulture was reluctant to play with me, because he was a church drummer. He played in so many churches that it started to conflict with our schedule of band practice. We often would not have a drummer for practice times, because JCulture would be playing with some church band on the other side of the city. Being a good little church boy meant that he hated the album name *Burning Jerusalem*. JCulture phoned me up one day asking what *Burning Jerusalem* meant.

"I don't know about the name, man?"

"Let me guess," I replied, "you think it's racist."

"Why name it burning Jews?"

"What? I didn't name it Burning Jews! Did you even read the explanation on the album jacket?"

"I'm just saying it sounds bad."

"Yo, sometimes to get in the industry, you have to shock a few people at first."

"Well, I don't want to be associated with anything racist."

"It has nothing to do with race," I repeated for the umpteenth time with other words."You're a Christian, right? How many times has Jerusalem been burned or destroyed in the Bible? And how many times did it come back with endless resilience?"

"OK," JCulture said after a brief silence.

"And one last clarification: I named this album almost five years ago, far before Trump's decision to recognize Jerusalem as Israel's capital city and all this political offensive cry baby shit today."

"Yeah, but people won't care about that."

"I don't care what people think, because as soon as they look at the album, they will know it has nothing to do with a race, place or face. I wrote that as a cry for help, for people in power to stop destroying the most sacred places on Earth. With churches, synagogues and mosques being bombed every day, maybe they should just burn the Great Pyramid of Giza and Niagara Falls while they're at it. Just take away everything sacred from us, maybe then they will get their point across. *Burning Jerusalem* was a cry to defend what is sacred. Got it? Not a hyped up attempt to racially offend, and I'm sick of kids jumping on that bandwagon."

"Well," JCulture voiced his reluctance again. "My mom is worried how it's *gonna* make her look at church."

"Well, lucky your mom didn't write the album. Listen man, practice is on Saturday. We will do a few rock songs but most the set is from the *New Legacy* hip hop album anyways. So I hope I see you there, I gotta go," I responded prior to hanging my phone up.

It became a running joke that JCulture would love playing on my hip hop album, but despised the rock songs. That was because he thought they were all racist. I did, however, love his energy and snare ghost notes on the hip hop songs. He thoroughly enjoyed working in the studio for the *New Legacy* album. After bickering with JCulture to reassure him *Burning Jerusalem* wasn't a racist album and that he wouldn't be smitten by God for playing *Burning Dido* along with *My Country*, he agreed to play those two rock songs at the show.

A Dive Bomber Band

JCulture - I have spoken enough bad things about my band, so I will keep this section succinct. JCulture was a great hip hop drummer who looked like H, a character in the movie *Ready Player One*. However, he was always too busy with church bands to take any other band seriously. I noticed as well, during big performances, that he would often forget transitions. This was probably just from lack of proper rehearsal time. He was very fast at his drum fills. He was advanced with syncopated timings and paradiddles, a drumming basic principle all drummers must master. I was thankful, however, that anything I wanted to add with the snare, he could learn quickly, unlike the robotic drummer I had for the *Shadows and Machines* album.

JCulture had soul and groove. However, he was a bit of a jerk when it came to anything not germane to music. He didn't like to share, often forced people to clean up after him and was a prima donna. I had to pay for every cab ride, every rental and every dinner. I started to realize that JCulture thought he was so good, he expected everyone else to do things for him, never going the extra mile himself. I thought he was so pampered for someone who came from the sticks (rural farmland). Maybe this was his first rock star experience and he thought he would sit back and relax while I did all the promotions and work. He wanted all the money for himself and his friends, but never wanted to help me make money. I loved his drumming but not his lifestyle or friends.

Blazed - I knew Blazed from Seneca College, and honestly, the only reason I hung out with him is because he had one of the purest tones I have ever heard in a rapper's voice. He sounded like how an angel would have sounded if an angel decided to rap. The downsides were many. He expected me to do his homework, always did little work, was always late, lazy, unreliable, confusing, and had the worst gangster friend that we would bring to the studio. Of course, when I refused to pay him for his bombing at my show, he then trolled me so hard online to try to get paid. This is so typical of Toronto.

Waco - This is how I called the last bass player I auditioned. He tried to throw a wrench in my plans for my album release party. You may have heard me refer to him as Bass Buffoon, but really, he reminded me of David Koresh from the cult murders that occurred in Waco, Texas during the 1980s. I have already explained how we had an argument and how the Waco then trolled my social media accounts. I felt he was sticking up for idiots like him in the industry (*Now Magazine*'s terrible customer service, Torstar's ridiculous advertising prices, the worst Demon Guitar Shop, and CHIN Radio, who tried to hustle large amounts of my money for a terrible radio ad that was too busy sounding).

After having to do all the marketing, promotion, online work and paying everything myself, I was bothered by how bad this one particular radio station had tried to hustle me into paying for an ad that I could have honestly produced better in an hour. I was a little frustrated and posted online that I was sick of incompetent people in the music industry over-charging and providing sub-par results. Seems logical. Why would my own bass player go against me?

Waco was sticking up for the wrong side. When I first met him, I used to call him, during rehearsals, T-Dog .We had a cool sounding band of guys who all had nicknames that I gave them: Stone Free, T-Dog, JCulture, Sprout and me, Digger. I later changed the bass player's name to Waco and now you know why. This guy trolled me about getting a manager we couldn't afford. He couldn't even get us on Ticketfly properly. Like I mentioned before, I then ignored him and he magically went to the army the next day. Yeah right! What's funny is, I called him out about this a month before it happened, saying I had lost a bass player to the army. When I said this, he stared into space, got all weird.

Never hire a Hallway Troll.

They are people who troll/work in many music places in Toronto. People like Waco/T-Dog will hold a grudge forever. I didn't realize till much later that this guy felt angry at me for telling him off when he constantly walked into my studio, without knocking. I also told him off at the end before he left too, to leave my band mates alone, or I would complain that he was harassing us. I later found out he was gay as well. Not that I have a problem with that. After all, my grandmother is a lesbian. I just don't like people who never show their cards until something bad happens.

Imagine having a bass player, whom you are stuck with, try to stall us in rehearsal time knowing we didn't have much time. I swear he even tried to pretend that he couldn't remember parts. I would constantly have to take the time to re-teach Waco parts or overly simplify my bass sections so he could play them. All this came at the opportunity cost of getting tighter with the rest of the band. This idiot bass player even left his skateboard lying wheels down on the ground one day in the studio, and when I went to turn around, I tripped on the rolling skateboard, had to do some epic Bruce Lee basketball pivot to save my ankle from rolling, and landed like a cat. I was so pissed off, I just stared at him. His carelessness had almost broken my ankle a week before the show. All that, and then he quit before the show anyways, wow.

Amateur Film Editors

While I was still learning how chaotic the entertainment industry is within major cities, I asked an editor, whom I had met doing background work on a film, if I could hire him to edit my first music video. I needed someone to edit the footage for the hip hop song *Bright Lights*. I had seen some of his works on music videos online and I liked what I saw. He had a creative eye for creating tension in his shots through anticipation. Therefore, I thought my video would be easy for him. I had all the footage shot on good cameras and boom cranes. All I wanted to do is superimpose multiple shots of me performing on different instruments, in different coloured costumes, seemingly playing at the same time, like a one man band. For advanced film editors, this technique is easy.

I arranged to meet the editor at Yorkdale Mall. When I arrived, he expected me to give him the footage on a hard drive. I had already sent him two hundred dollars as a deposit, which was a mistake. I told him I had the footage on my computer and I could transfer it to him in about twenty minutes. He looked annoyed, like I was wasting his time. I felt a little uneasy around him, and I was starting to have reservation about my decision of hiring him. He suggested we drive to his house and get his computer, so we could transfer it quicker.

This creep offered me to come to his house. However, on the way to his house, things started to get weird. He started to talk about racism in Hollywood and how black people are not getting their credit in the industry. I agreed, but mentioned that no First Nations people were getting any credit for acting in their own country, either. This seemed to bother him, like I had trumped his argument. He immediately asked if I was a Trump supporter. I said his question made me feel uncomfortable, that I was part Native and sick of being wrongly accused of being racist.

Let's rewind a bit. I thought African Americans had a pretty strong proportion of star power in entertainment industries with Will Smith, Denzel Washington, Morgan Freeman and Idris Elba enjoying a lot of success on the big screen. Also, adding to the equation, the hip hop industry is replete with unskilled rappers getting rich and famous, while they are promoting gangs and questionable values. Yet, he thought I must have been racist. I guess with most athletes being paid crazy amounts of money, yet nobody donating that money back to starving African babies, that I must have been racist. He immediately stopped the car, which was a nice Jaguar, and told me to wait at the local Tim Horton's until he got his computer and came back. I asked him about his change of mind to let me come over to his house, since it would be easier and faster for us both. He responded that his wife was feeling sick or some excuse along those lines.

When he dropped me off, I was about to leave, but I was in the middle of nowhere in Vaughan, a suburb of Toronto. I was somewhat obligated to wait. When he showed up an hour later, I was pissed off and so was he. I thought we were going to fight, which I would have won in thirty seconds. I got very focused to just finish the task at hand, and I started to transfer the files. When he saw that it would take twenty-seven minutes, he started flipping out that I didn't have it ready for him on an external hard drive. I managed to calm him down and explained that I was not familiar with how film crews and editors did things and I would make sure it didn't happen again. At this time, I knew this guy had mental problems, but I just wanted to see what he would do with the footage. If it was anything like his previous work, it would be worth the hassle. While we waited, he explained that some people in Jay-Z's circle had watched his twelve minute short movie and were really interested in it. I felt like I was being sold lies by a used car salesman.

When the transfer was about to complete, an error message popped up saying the files were dirty and corrupted. He got up to leave, and I made a quick decision to give him the original footage I had on my only hard drive in my bag. I was scared to do this, but I knew I had another copy on my PC at home. I just didn't want to give my hard drive with all my music files and footage to a stranger I barely knew. He said he would transfer it that night and I could meet him the next day to pick it back up. He then got up quickly and said he would drop me off at a TTC station. At that moment, I felt that he judged me for being temporarily broke like I was beneath him for not owning a Jaguar. I left feeling that maybe he would actually steal or ruin the footage.

That night I received a disturbing message saying that my footage was garbage quality and a waste of his time. I wanted to get angry and demand my refund of the hundreds of dollars I deposited. However, I didn't want him to get vindictive and corrupt the whole hard drive, as it had an album of music material on it. I just asked if the files were readable and everything was still there. He answered yes, and I agreed to meet him at the TTC station where he had dropped me off the day earlier.

The next morning I called my Uber ninja and told him we needed to go get my hard drive back from an asshole. When we arrived near the location, I could tell this editor was trying to set me up to assault him, so he could get me in trouble with the police. What he didn't know was that I had been spying on him for a good ten minutes and followed him there. I got my chauffeur to approach him from one side and I knocked on his window from the other side, scaring the shit out of him. I grabbed the hard drive back, and told him that Jay-Z didn't give a fuck about his twelve-minute generic video. I screamed for him to give me back my deposit, and he got scared and drove off. Looking back on it now, I can tell the Illuminati and gate keepers of the music industry did everything they could to not let the *Bright Lights* music video and single get made or released. Maybe they feared that it would propel me to instant stardom. Almost immediately after it was made and released, I was signed to a major record label. Fucking amateur film editors can suck my rock star balls.

Chapter 29: New Legacy II

New Legacy Studio Sessions

So finally, it was recording day. The studio was in a garage of a really nice house. When you do not have a lot of money, you will have to do a lot of recording and mixing in home/garage studios. The reason is this:

A legit professional studio anywhere in the world is roughly a thousand dollars a day. I can do the exact same sound for five hundred dollars a day. There are some wicked audio engineers, who can do this exact same sound for free in their basements.

I could tell that this studio was made for mixing and less for performance, because the mixing console room was huge and the drum room beside it was tiny. Thankfully, there was a nice drum kit set up and the microphones were high-end. Therefore, the drum sound was pretty crisp. I knew that the main component of the project would be the drum recordings, since I had most of the beats and bass already done from my previous sessions at Seneca College. The mixing engineer, who was renting the studio space, agreed that I would only need two days of instrument recording and one day of vocals. After all, the rap parts already sounded professional from the Seneca recordings.

In the studio for *New Legacy,* just like for *Burning Jerusalem*, I only had to play rhythm guitar for five songs and I banged those out in two takes each, in under an hour. That is the benefit of practicing your music for years in the shadows of obscurity. As soon as you get into the studio, it is a cakewalk. All the other songs on the album either had all instrumentation recorded at Seneca or were just beats that I had made with the software FL Studio. Those songs with beats didn't need anything else, such as *Kush, Hollywood Harmony* and *The Truth*. They only needed lead guitar and bass added on top of the beats. The other more rock-sounding songs needed to be re-done from scratch. I adamantly wanted the rock rap stuff to fit in the same theme as the other more trap rap sounding songs.

After recording the rhythm guitar, it made sense to do the bass. This is before I knew the bass player was a flake. We spent an hour recording the bass takes for three songs that the bass player could only play the tonic notes to. I started to realize that bassist would be better for live shows only, and that I could do a better bassline for the studio recordings than him. I guess it was like how Billy Corgan must have felt recording with The Smashing Pumpkins.

Then we came to the song *Fly with Me,* which all the musicians loved. It is a funky hip hop song that sounds a bit like *Seven Days in Sunny June* by Jamiroquai. It has a vibe that automatically makes people feel happy. Anyways, it became a running joke that the bass player had no groove. The bass line that I had written was in a perfect counter-point to the rhythm guitar, and it worked perfectly to give the song a push forward. Unfortunately, the bass flake could never get one good take of that riff in the verses. We couldn't even cut and paste them into other sections. He literally got frustrated and handed me the bass to finish the fourth song. I did it in one take. Then he asked for his payment right away. So typical!

The other session musicians wanted to relax in the studio and really put their heart and soul into this song, as Waco just wanted to leave and go home. After Waco left, I redid all the bass parts and everyone found this so funny. I had wasted five hundred dollars and two hours of expensive studio time on this flake. I would have hired my dad instead to come play bass if he wasn't getting high in some crack house.

By the end of the month, I lost the band, because I was too afraid of firing the shitty bass player. I should have given the bass responsibilities to the other awesome guitar player. I didn't see the forest for the trees, because everyone was so disorganized and irresponsibly unreliable that I was afraid if I fired one for the other, none of them would show up. What I should have done was this.

"Hey flake," I said in this alternate narrative, "you're fired!"

"What?" asked Waco.

"Sprout, you're the bass player now."

"Finally, something that makes sense," Sprout stated, as if he had wanted to get a truth off his chest a long time ago.

"Oh, fuck you guys!" Waco swore.

"Don't worry," I took a pot-shot at Waco. "You can be our *roadie*!"

Everyone laughs.

So finally, we got to the fun part, watching JCulture crush the drums on every song. I had him play on half the album. I even had him play on some songs that already had a beat, because his drum fills were so quick and tastefully in different places. Everyone in the studio, including the audio engineer and studio owner, were in awe. This kid could play anything from any style. He excelled at hip hop beats and loved to use the ghost notes on the snare, but could also slide in a little jazz syncopation. JCulture played a cool hip hop beat for both the songs *New Legacy* and *Fly with Me*. Then, we turned to the rock songs *Note H* and *White Rabbit Ninja*. His off timing on *White Rabbit Ninja* was so awesome that we just watched as he played it flawlessly in only two takes. I will always appreciate what he did in the studio, especially when I asked him on the spot if he wanted to drum for the hidden song as well. He agreed and when he went to drum it, he stopped in the middle of a take and poked his head out the drum room."You do realize this song is not in timing," JCulture commented.

"What?" I asked him."I just played it to the click track."

"Yo, play it from the first verse and let me show you something."

Sure enough, when he went back in the room, we all listened and heard the beat actually slow down about 4bpm (beats per minute) and then speed back up two bars later. It was like watching a song get a slow motion replay for a part and then come back on timing. Talk about a swing timing. JCulture impressed us all, as he actually slowed down perfectly without missing a hit and then sped back up to catch the transition on the one. The piano player started laughing and commented that this could only be done by a professional. Good job, JCulture. Have a listen to *The Long Graveyard* (Hidden Song) as it goes off timing twice in the song.

It is heartbreaking to lose a good band, because there is so much glitching. I always had to pay them, when no one put in any time or money to help the band grow. I loved their sound when we were on. However, when their friends came around, they all wasted time, screwed my sound and only wanted to use me for money. I have never had such a talented band choke so hard when it counts.

It felt like LeBron James hating JR Smith in the 2018 NBA finals after botching a possession to win a game. I guess some people are better as session musicians and others thrive in front of people.

The next part of the *New Legacy* studio sessions were the fun guitar solos. I am a perfectionist when it comes to this, and I don't mean in the studio. In fact, I let guitar players play whatever they want. I will just perfectly edit different lead lines from different takes in post-production to make it sound like the best the guitarist has ever played.

I had two wicked guitar players come into the studio for *New Legacy*. They played completely different styles. One was like Allan Holdsworth meets B.B. King. He loved technical chromatic sweep picking and then would burst off into a crazy blues solo that usually incorporated many strings at the same time. His name was Sprout, and he was the same guy I had hired for the *Burning Jerusalem* album. This time, however, I was not so impressed with his blues style playing, since it didn't really fit with the hip hop album. He did, however, pull off one of the best lead lines I had ever heard for the song *White Rabbit Ninja*. I don't know how he did it, but it works perfectly with the crunchy sound of that song. It is rare that a lead guitar will work well with vocals in a verse, but in this case, it added such a cool high pitch, and it did not compete with the vocal frequency.

On the other hand, the song *Note H* is a little busy, because I added too much lead guitar on the verses. I did, however, love some of the transition phrases and the extra harmonics that Sprout recommended that we do. I told Sprout to play something Arabic-sounding in the harmonic minor, as a tip of the hat to my Arab friend that was in jail. My Arabic friend helped inspire this song *Note H*, which is about learning music theory, so I wanted to give him a part...shout outs, "Save George! I fear for Amir!"

On the other hand, the other guitarist was completely different. He did not like overly bluesy sounds and loved the melodic guitar playing that producers love. He looked like Jimi Hendrix and played like Guthrie Govan. He was so flowing and emotional, with a beautiful fusion style. We called him Stone Free, which is an allusion to a song by Jimi Hendrix. You can hear his beautiful fusion guitar in *Better Left Unsaid* and *Fly with Me*. It is like a hint of funk rock within a hip hop song. I joked with him that his whole purpose in life was to play on those two songs. I loved his ability to not only learn riffs that I had created, but then improvise and never make something boring.

In fact, a few of Stone Free's soaring riffs evoked some hidden emotions in me that would make me cry when I heard them. To me, that's a good guitar player: anyone that can evoke hidden emotions in people and make them tear up.

I loved jamming with this guy, but when other people came around, all my band members changed into assholes that just wanted to jam and not practice. They exhausted me and I had to let go of their talent for much more important things, such as my health and true route to fame.

After all the lead guitar parts were finished and everyone could really get a sense of what the overall songs would sound like, everyone got very excited. It was getting late and the mixer wanted to wrap it up, so we would have energy for the next day. The piano guy was a little disappointed that we didn't get to his parts, but I assured him that it would be better to wait, since he would have more time the next day to do whatever he wanted in the studio. I assured him that all we had to do the next day was piano and acoustic guitar overdubs.

The next day in the studio was very mellow. The audio engineer assured me that all the previous days' takes were final and that we would just need about four hours to do piano as well as acoustic guitar overdubs. We would then take an hour to double check everything and bounce the recordings. I would then have to spend the next week editing everything perfectly before he started mixing.

The second day in the studio saw the piano player struggle to find the right accompanying chords to support the rhythm guitar. To be honest, I thought the piano player was better than this, and I was expecting some nice piano arpeggio fills in between parts. Unfortunately, this only came with my much needed guidance. Things got better, however, when the piano guy found the right phrasing variations and inversions that started adding to the songs. There was a nice synthesizer in the corner and when he hopped on it, immediately we came up with nice swells and phrases for transition parts in the chorus of *Fly with Me* and *Note H.* Although the piano guy did play some nice background layer keyboards, especially when in the strings settings, in retrospect, I didn't really need him. When all the musicians left, I stayed for the last hour, quickly played the piano parts for *City of Bones* and fixed some of his parts.

The audio engineer and I sat for the last hour and listened to all the instrumentation to all the songs. Once we were happy, we saved the files and I went home early to get a good night's rest before the vocal session the next day. Vocals had to be done at another studio location, because the mixer didn't have access to the good studio and he wanted to save money. It was in a basement of one of his friends' house. I was a little reluctant to record there, until I heard the high-end microphones work with the small Neve recording console his friend had. It sounded better than the whole *Burning Jerusalem* album.

Before I started recording, I did my usual vocal warm up (more on that later). To be honest, all the lyrics for the *New Legacy* album are very well written. They took me a long time to write and speak about important issues. For example, *Bright Lights* is about poverty in Africa and Native American reserves. When recording and mixing the vocals, some of my rapping would make the audio engineer burst into laughter. I felt that I killed it on my vocal takes with some of my punch lines. I rap, sing and harmonize on this album. Moreover, I did a good job with the vocal sections. I liked a lot of my harmonies.

Blaze was awesome in the studio as well. His tone is so beautiful. It is like taking a completely undamaged voice and getting it to rap so smoothly. My audio engineer loved his voice and would use a boomy microphone for him (SM7B) and an airy microphone for me to increase the brightness above 5000Hz (Audio Frequency Spectrum).

After all the recording was finished, I spent about a week editing the sessions on Pro Tools. Unfortunately, I was also in the middle of teaching my session band the other songs for the upcoming concert set list at the time. I would have wished to edit a bit more thoroughly, but the songs were almost done by the time I was editing anyway, so it wasn't hard for the mixer to polish them up. I was impressed with all the session musicians' tracks. The drumming was so on point that I didn't have to edit much. The bass was easy so that was another time saver. It was the lead guitar choices that took the most time. I had a choice between a bluesy rap feel or a fusion rap feel. I took the fusion style, not to say I didn't use some awesome lines written by Sprout for such songs as *Note H* and *White Rabbit Ninja*. They all had a fun time in the studio and they should have, I paid them overly well.

The next step consisted in sending the sessions to the mixer and letting him work on one song a day. This time I was paying per song and not per day. Therefore, I preferred giving the mixer a day for an entire song. This avoids audio ear fatigue. After about a week, the mixer sent me back rough mixes. I went through all of them and made corrections, additions, omissions and suggestions for every song. I believe this made it very easy for the mixer to understand the direction I wanted to go with the album. In fact, I was so precise in my email back to him, here is an excerpt:

Hollywood Harmony -

Vox harmony @ 0:28 turn it up and fix the timing

Verse 1 vox are perfect, so are the lead volumes / Turn up bass a tiny at the end of verse one

Can you take off the SFX and reverb on my vox in the chorus, or at least make it a little dryer.

@2:28 turn the vocals down, they are booming because the beat goes soft here

@2:27 - 2:53, turn the bass down, it is also booming ...Great mixing with the vocals at the end

Better Left Unsaid -

Keep it non-busy with lead from 0:10-0:20 seconds, then I want it exactly the way the lead was edited from 0:20 - 0:47sec.

Then at 0:47sec, can you keep the lead lick that hits the same note like five times and the lick right after it into the breakdown before the chorus, I like that lick.

I like the non-busy chorus of little lead guitar, but can you add the licks at 1:00-1:04 and 1:08 - 1:19, 1:28-1:42, 2:12 -2:15, 2:17 -2:25

@ 0:48 I do a low bomb drop sound effect. Can you keep it in. It is kind of like a dubstep subwoofer.

@ 2:22 Little higher on the sex SFX lol

Mixing New Legacy

After receiving the song's revised versions, I was asked to come to the mixing studio with the mixer. This was a sketchy experience, as the studio was in the middle of the lower east end of Toronto. It was attached to the mastering studio that I was kind of coerced into mastering with. I knew I didn't want to go to Lacquer Channel for the second album, because I wanted a completely different sound. This album was more DJ Digger Jones and less *Close Encounter*. In the studio, the mixer had me basically mix the album myself. He may have used the plug-ins I hadn't mastered or the EQ, compressions and gates that would take me a while to do. But I told him exactly what sound I wanted. In terms of all the producing, volumes, panning, SFX and even instrument features, it was all me.

I did have to, however, get the mixer to stop panning all the harmonies to the left ear. After listening later, when I had a fresh ear, I noticed that all these audio engineers think they are being creative by adding echo vocals and spots of doubled vocals to one side. However, if it is not done masterfully, those additions are so unprofessional and distracting like a Frankenstein song. I caught this a few times and always had to adjust it myself. On everything else, the mixer did a very good job, but he was a bit of a greedy liar when it came to pricing and disorganized in general.

When everything was mixed to my liking, my album was held ransom. That is the best way I can describe the situation. I explained to the mixer that I only had two thousand dollars in my account until payday that Friday. After I had already given him about four thousand dollars, I was pretty sure he would let me pay him the last thousand dollars in a week. That was not the case. He said he needed all the money right there before he would give the finished versions to the mastering engineer, who was in the next room beside us. I assured him that I was going to pay for the mastering first, to get that ball rolling. The CD duplication manufacturer needed the material ASAP, in order to meet the deadline before the concert release. I begged the mixer to allow me to pay him the last portion on Friday. He refused and I got upset.

"I have spent countless hours on this project, and you have just been at it for a couple days," I vented.

"Everything has been confusing up to now, with changes in prices, hourly rates and even random studios. This is not what we agreed on when I decided to hire you. I have paid you well for recording and mixing. Now you are holding my album ransom, because you think I'm *gonna* rip you off the last thousand dollars, when you know I am in a crunch for the release date?"

Afterwards, the mixer met my rant with silence.

"I can either pay you everything now, get the product, never work with you again and even tell others that it was one of the most chaotic experiences of my life," I offered. "Or you can wait a couple of days, let me master with your friend next door and have me praise your work when I come back for the next album."

"Sorry bud," the mixer uttered, "I've been burned before. I need that money now."

"You were burned by poor asshole flake musicians, not by me. I have basically made this album easy for you. I always pay on time."

"Can't release the album until I am paid in full," the mixer reiterated his terms. "Sorry. Guess you are *gonna* have to push the release date back."

"Ok, I see how it is."

I immediately sent an e-transfer of a thousand dollars to him, got the final renditions, and never spoke to that greedy asshole again. Because of this, I had to wait a week to get things mastered and this put a heavy burden on trying to organize with the CD duplication manufacturing. I should have just done it all in USB. It may have cost more, but there would have been more excitement and hype surrounding the album release, especially through a new medium of USB. With a USB, you can put the logo of your band on the unit, a lanyard to carry it around and add a music video, album art and even extra pictures. The audience can even download everything and then have the USB for themselves. I planned to do this for my next album.

New Legacy Rating:

After listening to the mastered versions that are on the final album, here are some of my thoughts about each song:

In that mixing session, I really like what I was able to pull off with *City Of Bones*, since this song was the last to go on the album, and was kind of the "filler" song.

Better Left Unsaid has great vocals in the chorus, and the raps are so raw that it still gives me goose bumps. The reverb on the mix is perfect.

My engineer even said that he was able to replicate any song he wanted to, but *White Rabbit Ninja* would be impossible to duplicate. I took that as a compliment.

The beat for *Bright Lights* was made for me by a Nigerian friend, who gave me a perfect beat that he was going to release as an instrumental. Once he heard my guitar and vocals on it, he just gave it to me and asked that I add him on the credits for the album. So I did. Thanks, *Beaver Yino*.

Light up this Track was made in a day with a friend at Seneca, and may be the best song on the album.

Kush was the hype song. I played the bass for this, and people really liked the rap.

The Truth was done entirely by me out of sheer anger against Eminem.

Lonely West is one of the nicest songs I sang on, with a beautiful guitar arpeggio that I played. I really like the feel of this song.

Last but not least, *New Legacy*, is a masterpiece. The horns, the acoustic guitar and the raps are perfect. Everything on this song sounds good. I wouldn't change anything.

Oh, and by the way, there is a hidden song (usually is) called *The Long Graveyard* that talks about China's history and its disturbing progress in building the Great Wall. It is worth listening to.

All scratching is done by DJ Digger Jones, after all other parts were edited. So I knew what parts were a little empty and needed a scratch or a SFX. This all worked perfectly.

New Legacy Album Art:

The *New Legacy* album art was very fun to create. I always knew I wanted the front cover to be the street graffiti I had seen on vacation. This portrait of the evolution of man left me speechless. Of course, I had to edit the picture with new colour brightness, cropping and text to make it my original picture. Copyright infringement is a real thing. Obviously, if a million people take the same picture, make yours unique somehow. I knew I also had to leave space for a parental advisory logo. Then I had a genius thought: I could replace the stop sign on the front with the parental advisory sticker, making it a part of the scene itself. After I finalized the front cover, I knew the album would have a colour palette of green. I knew I didn't want a complex inside jacket. That is why I devised a plan to have as many random pictures as I could and as little album info along with lyrics as possible.

While creating the picture collage for the inside jacket, I tried to use pictures that appealed to nature, social commentary, Native arts and hip hop. While creating the random pictures for the tray card, I came across an old art piece that I had created. This piece worked with the history raps of some of my songs such as *City Of Bones, Lonely West*, and the hidden song *The Long Graveyard*. I put the lyrics of *Bright Lights* over the images and then, I wrote a little message to two people that really annoy me in the rap game. Read it and find out what I said!

What is the Next Step?

A great piece of advice is to have a producer in the studio with you, because a songwriter has heard his vocals too many times. Therefore, they assume the vocals will always be heard, but when guitar and saxophone parts start overwhelming the song, it may become lost. When I was recording *Burning Jerusalem*, I was so enamoured by the saxophone player that I put him in the song *Burning Dido* too much.

Please, never have lead guitar or horns play too much over vocals in a verse.

Seems easy to remember, right? I made sure not to repeat this for the *New Legacy* album. *New Legacy*, sounded like a style never heard before, like a new version of rock rap. Maybe I'm making my own genre. Sometimes when an album is near perfect, the studio, record company or band will just go with what they have anyway, because most fans will not catch the errors. Only the band will hear the errors. They must then accept and live with them. But if the entire album is all too busy, it must be re-mixed.

So there I was waiting to get paid, so I could pay the mixer for the final mixes. I had to get them to the master quick enough that the CD manufacturer would have the final DDP files (encoded with album info for iTunes) in time to meet the album's release deadline. Immediately after paying a ridiculous rush fee, the manufacturer stalled due to an error on their behalf, and I had to rush to pick the boxes up myself on the day of the show.

By the time I was picking up the album, I was broke. I had spent almost $70,000 up to this point for the two albums, merchandises and ancillary costs. Because I was poor, I didn't even have my own car. It stands to reason that I was either relying on my Uber driver or my grandma. Quite pathetic really! On the day of the show, I had to beg my grandmother to drive me to a random industrial warehouse that didn't even have any workers around it. I spent five minutes banging on doors and trying to find someone.

Finally, some old guy came out and said that the order had been dropped off a couple of minutes ago. He proceeded to open the garage door. I thought I was going to see the inside of the duplication company with workers, a printing press and boxes of orders. I saw only a van and my boxes. That is when I found out the headquarters were in the United States and I had been hustled. I furiously put the boxes into my grandmother's van. My grandmother was constantly yelling, complaining and trying to micromanage everything. She was in a terrible mood on the one day I needed her most. Of course, when we went to leave the industrial site, she couldn't ignite her van's engine. We had a breakdown with the van right there. I immediately got out of the van, phoned my Uber ninja and had to wait another precious hour to get out of there. When I was leaving in the cab, my grandmother looked at me with one of the most disgusted looks I had ever seen. If a stare could kill, I would have been nuked. At that point, when I saw that face, I just kept tight-lipped, because I knew that would be the last day I ever saw my so-called family again. That was the last time I ever saw my grandmother. I felt that it was all a conspiracy against my dream to be a rock star, trying to make it a nightmare. I felt that everything that day was a spiritual experience to free me from a shitty life. What a terrible memory.

As I jumped into my Uber ride, I knew I still had to head to my studio and retrieve some things for the dance video and concert. Out of nowhere, my mother showed up to my studio with my annoying brother. It felt like an attack. It wasn't like my loving family was trying to wish me good luck. It was more like they were coming around to pry, get their shots in, and then try to foil my plans at the worst possible time. I didn't want any help from anyone, who hadn't helped up to that point. I literally had to sneak out the back door of my studio to avoid a confrontation. My mother lives for confrontations, like a loser bully lives for fighting. It is better to let scum wander around than to give a target. Thank God my brother didn't snitch on me. He saw me. We gave each other the finger and started laughing. Then he led my mother to my studio, and I literally went out the back door into my Uber ninja's car. I didn't know that would be the last time I saw them as well.

I left my studio quickly with the snacks for the dance team, my outfit for the music video and the boxes of the *New Legacy* album.

Now, I was two hours late for my own music video. I thought the crew would just start with the shots as per the storyboard: the shots I wasn't in. Of course, they didn't. While I was flying to the studio around 2:00 p.m., (I planned to be at *The Mock Club* at noon) the traffic was like a video game. Many cars either came out of nowhere to try to create an accident, or they moved at a snail's pace. It was like the city of Toronto was subtly laughing at me. I felt like the music industry was terrified to allow me into it, because losers will stop at nothing to hog a piece of the pie.

They are afraid that they will stop making millions and I will bring music back to the musicians, not the corporate suits who take all the money. Just ask the infamous Sixto Rodriguez! He'll tell you that someone made millions off his first album, Cold Facts, and it wasn't him.

So there I was flying in downtown Toronto, with a municipal infrastructure built against me. My driver had to slam on his breaks multiple times, and it eventually became a running joke. They wanted me to get into a car accident on the way to the show. I then arrived in front of the venue, rushed my boxes of merchandises into the doors, and that's when a whole new nightmare began.

Chapter 30: Music Video Shenanigans

When I first walked into the front door of The Mock Club, I was taken aback by the fact that there were workers repainting the front door lobby. Not really a nice sight for people, who wanted to come check the music video out. This didn't help, since we were trying to get extra random people from the street to come into the club to make it look more crowded. I saw people coming in, seeing the paint crew along with guarded off entrance, turning around and leaving, thinking they were in the wrong place. It was like The Mock Club was mocking me by picking my important date to do what they could have done any other day.

The club was dark, stuffy and crowded with painting debris. I was already running late, so it felt like I couldn't prepare the way I wanted to. I soon realized that the owner of the club was a mob affiliate, who purposely tried to sabotage everything I did, maybe to show some cheap power tactic.

Remember, the music industry is a billion dollar enterprise and if you are not handpicked by them, you are taking their money and they will spend a few bucks to block you.

In fact, the club was so dingy for a supposedly nice venue that my friend thought she was at the wrong place when she walked in. She had to double check her GPS and was astonished that even an average venue like that one was so expensive to rent for a day. This is why large production companies and record labels rent the venues themselves and just fill them with their stock talent on a nightly basis. Very few artists do the booking and run the show themselves. Now I know why! If they did, a club owners and his grandma could do whatever they wanted to fuck with them.

As in the movie The Pursuit of Happyness, don't let anyone tell you that you can't do something, because people will always try to prevent you from doing something that they couldn't.

Music Video Meltdown

When it was time to do the music video, we had a music video meltdown. I had just walked into The Mock Club and seen the camera guy named Martin Clown. I had hired the latter for four thousand dollars, sitting around talking to one of the dancer girls. None of the dancers was on the stage practicing. The camera wasn't set up. None of the easy insert scene shots had been completed. On top of that, the place hadn't even really been cleaned.

You'd think that if the star of a show phones and says he is running late, the team would jump to their feet, ready to get to work, and make up for the slack the minute the star arrived. No! Artists think that rules don't apply to them. That day, I literally wore many hats. I became a director, cinematographer, dancer, manager, musician and dictator. I learned a valuable lesson that if you are not a rich star with power leverage over people, then people think that they do not have to respect you even if you are paying them. That is why big companies and star entourages always intimidate people to respect them, because they know that if they do not, people will slack to the point of disrespect. People always want to make someone else look like a failure, even if he is spending his life savings. Nobody does more than what he or she is paid for anymore.

I will never forget when I first came into the club and checked the front lobby, which was full of paint cans, I had to close the front door myself and signal to get the lighting and smoke machines ready. I even started sweeping the floor myself and brought the snack tray and drinks in myself for the dancers. I was the star of the show doing the grunt work. Of course, once everyone saw me doing everything, they jumped to their feet and started getting organized. I then went over to the cameraman. "Hey," I initiated the conversation with Camera Clown, "did you guys do any of the non-essential shots, while I was in traffic?"

"No, I thought we had to wait for you. I don't know how you want to do them."

"I gave you the storyboard and memo of every shot a month ago," I reminded Camera Clown. "You know exactly what I want for the insert shots."

"I don't know. Talk to the dance coordinator."

I was furious. They all knew the simple shots that I wanted ahead of time. With all of those people that I hired knowing each other, the dynamic of the room felt like there was a group conspiracy at hand. I walked over to the dance choreographer, whom I had hired to organize everything like a director, so I wouldn't have to. He could tell I was angry and sheepishly walked over to me. I had also paid him four thousand dollars in advance. He was supposed to be my dance coach for the video. Granted, the choreographer was very nice during the dance practices I attended as he was guiding me through the routine, but that was because I hadn't paid them yet. As soon as I paid them, they devolved into lazy bums. I walked up to my overpaid choreographer and ask: "Why has none of the shots been done to save time before I came?"

"Well," replied the lying choreographer, "we didn't know how you wanted them done."

"Why are you all treating me like a fool?"

"What?"

"I sent you the storyboard a month ago. In fact, you suggested a few of these scenes yourself. You have the script, don't you? I gave the green light for some shots, because I was stuck in traffic. You know that every minute is precious today."

"Yeah, hang on..."

I literally saw him run over to his bag and dig out the storyboard. That's when I knew this would be the most disorganized music video if I didn't do something drastic.

"Here you..." the choreographer mumbled.

"Okay, listen up everybody!" I interrupted the choreographer, while grabbing the papers."I am sorry I was late. We are going to start in ten minutes. So get your clothes on, get your cameras ready, stretch, go to the bathroom, whatever the fuck you have to do. Camera's on in ten."

That moment, I realized why all the directors on the movie sets, where I was involved as an extra, were such assholes. People are idiots unless you tell them what to do. And even then, you have to scream it into their dumb ears sometimes. Of course, the moment I shouted with some balls, a cute Asian girl came over to me and wanted to talk. She was the wardrobe witch I had met once during a dance rehearsal. I could tell she was a control freak. "Hi, Digger," the Wardrobe Witch said, "did you get the shirts I asked for?"

"Yeah," I replied without deigning to look at her."I got a few options, plus I already got my band mates to wear red and black, like you suggested."

"Okay, let's get you in costume. The wardrobe area is upstairs."

"Okay," I said to my dance team, "get the audio sound ready and get in position for the intro shot."

"Did you hear me?" the Wardrobe Witch came back at me."I said wardrobe is upstairs."

"Yes," I confirmed. "I heard you. I'm doing me for a second, relax. I'm getting my shirts and will be right up."

I turned to grab a Gatorade from the box that I had just brought in, and they were all gone. The film crew, dance team and even venue staff had already helped themselves to everything like a kindergarten class. I went downstairs and filled my water bottle up with tap water. I knew this was going to be a long night, because I was already feeling tired and I just got there. I got my sharp dress pants on and a nice red shirt like I was instructed and made my way up to the wardrobe.

A couple of weeks earlier, I had arranged to have the wardrobe team buy me a circus conductor's jacket and top hat. I had recently seen the movie *The Greatest Showman* with Hugh Jackman. The great costumes and mise-en-scène blew me away. I wanted a red circus conductor jacket, with a black top hat and shoes. That was the choice I was willing to go with it. A week earlier at dance rehearsals, the wardrobe team had gotten me a jacket that was way too small for my big shoulders. I specifically told them to get a much bigger size, preferably something not brand new, since it would only be worn once. I demanded to have multiple options just in case we needed different sizes. In retrospect, I realized that the wardrobe team was trying to make me feel self-conscious about my slightly chubby size. That was why they kept 'mistaking' the jacket's size. When I went up to wardrobe, the wardrobe witch walked over and said:

"Here, try this..."

"I can already tell that it's not going to fit," I told her."Look at how small the shoulders are. I told you to get me something a little larger, since I told you I have big shoulders."

I realized that they were spending a lot of money on brand new suit jackets when they could have just gotten five different options and sizes from a thrift store.

"Okay," the Wardrobe Witch conceded with a slightly huffy tone."I hope this fits."

That crazy lady went on trying to present me with one of the ugliest pink suit jackets I had ever seen. That is when I snapped.

"Is this all you have? I gave you all my measurements and all the money weeks ago. You came to me last week with a dinky little suit jacket, and I told you I'm a big guy. I need large shoulders for my red conductor uniform. How fucking hard is that? I bet you guys spent top dollar on this shit, when I could have just gone to Value Village, gotten a dozen different options for under fifty bucks and we wouldn't need a wardrobe department."

Then, I heard a radio silence from her.

Then, the makeup dude walked over and put his soft hand on my shoulder.

"What the fuck!" I bounced.

I turned away in disgust. The weak hand, the idiots staring, my dream vision crushed with no time to fix it, I just had to grit my teeth and keep going.

"Diggy," Makeup Meek called me, "do you want any makeup?"

"Of course I do," I blew my steam. "But not until I am in costume."

Feeling the tension from the silence, I regained my composure and tried to lighten the mood.

"Here," I said, "are there any other options?"

"No!" replied the Wardrobe Witch with a hint of embarrassment in her voice.

I am so lucky that I don't trust people. I always do everything with a contingency plan. I stormed down to my suitcase. I had brought my own black vest, green silk dress shirt, and a change of pants. I quickly changed into my new look, scraped the idea of a circus conductor and asked:

"Okay, is there at least a black top hat?"

They gave me the top hat. The hat was too big for my head and kept slipping down over my eyes while I was dancing, just like the *Green Lantern* mask in my indie music video for the song *Treemen*. I improvised with what I had. I put a pair of goggles over the top hat to make it look Steampunk. Furthermore, I got my dress shirt and open black vest to look like Usher's *My Way*.

Just then, all the extras I had hired walked in with their suitcases of costume options. To this day, I will say, they were the best part of that whole day. They came on time, had many good clothing options, waited around patiently for their turn, and performed so well when it was their chance to shine. I will explain how they saved the show later.

When I was happy with my look, I went back to the Makeup Meek and had makeup done. This is when I noticed that I was starting to stain my light green dress shirt with sweat stains. I knew they would be visible on camera. The stage area was even stuffier and it would only get worse. Therefore, I made a decision worthy of a chess virtuoso. I ran downstairs to the bathroom and soaked my dress shirt in cold water. The color of my shirt completely changed to a forest green, but it all looked glistening with the silk. It was now all one colour, hiding the sweat stains, and it actually looked cooler than before. The whole camera crew loved it, because they knew with my sweat, the shirt would retain that colour the whole day. Perfect...only because of me.

Finally, I was in uniform and the dance team was on the stage. I noticed that I was missing two of the "cultural dancers" for the bridge and last chorus scenes. When I say cultural dancers, I am alluding to four dancers from different cultures I instructed the choreographers to find prior to the video's shooting date. For example, I wanted a dancer from the First Nations in full head dress regalia, either a traditional Chinese dancer or a Japanese Komodo dancer, and maybe a couple of Brazilian Samba dancers in outfits. The choreographer was reluctant to do this because he said it was racist.

"What are you talking about?" I shot back."I am part Native and I love dances from other cultures. To make this video ultra-Western would be racist. I want a few random shots of people dancing to the song in their traditional attire. I think that makes the video so much more artistic and cross cultural, not racist. Heck it may even boost sales and interest."

"I think it is cultural appropriation," the choreographer parroted.

"Wow!" I exclaimed while rolling my eyes. "We live in Toronto, the most diverse place on Earth. I want my cultural dancers, whether you think I'm racist or not."

Well, it was time to start shooting, and I looked on the stage and didn't see my cultural dancers. As I looked over to the couches on the side, I noticed some carnival dresses for Brazilian parades, and I thought one of the present dancers was going to get into the costumes when that scene came up on the shot breakdown. "Is everyone ready?" I asked.

I looked around and saw the band ready in their black and red semi-casual wardrobe. I saw the instruments ready. The lights were bright. The smoke was on. The camera crew was ready behind their monitors, and I was walking up to the stage. Show Time!

"Okay," I announced, "cue the music. Let's do a couple of run-throughs, and then we'll go from the top."

"Oh sorry, Digger," said a crew member named Liam. "We don't have the music. We thought you were *gonna* bring your own speakers."

"It is a club," I responded while scoffing at him. "Why would I bring my own speakers? Do you even have a sound guy? Where is the sound guy?"

"I think he left before you came," the Camera Clown stepped in, "because I heard the owner tell him that he wasn't needed until the actual concert tonight."

"For fuck's sake!"I cursed.

Just then, the Italian grease ball owner heard us talking about him and came running out of his office. "Can I help you?" he asked us with a confrontational tone.

"Yeah," I said. "Where is the sound guy? We're ready to go."

"You said you didn't need a sound guy for the video."

"No. What I said was once he gets the sound for the video, he can leave until the concert tonight."

"Well, I..." the owner said while being at a loss for words.

"Does someone have the song on an iPhone or something? So we can just play it from an aux chord? The light guy can just press play each time for us or something."

I gave the light guy the thumbs up, and he gave me the finger. They didn't even have the songs ready on an iPod. I literally had to use my own aux chord that would eventually go missing by the end of the night. I had to use my own phone just to get my song playing on the house speakers, so we could dance and lip sync to it. I knew this should have been so simple, but people kept adding problems and making it so difficult. The light guy was inexperienced, and the club owner had gone for lunch, because he is an asshole. I got my own phone along with my own aux cable and walked it up the stairs to the sound area. Then, I had to spend another fifteen minutes searching for the right soundboard and speaker outlets, since I am not a sound guy. I did everything. By the time I was ready to go with my single *Better Left Unsaid* pumping out the speakers, the dance team's members were all slumbering on the couches again.

"Sorry about the delay," I shouted, "let's get going!"

Everyone jumped up and was back in their positions.

The Footage

The first shot of the day was of the entire band and dance team. Thankfully, I knew my dance routine moves were not that hard, seeing that I would have to sing while I was doing them. I already had experience dancing with the dance club in high school. Besides, I had danced a lot in many clubs I had attended or DJed drunk off my ass. When the song started, we were all in our starting poses. I had an East Coast/West Coast gang sign repping on my hands. The goal was to signify a unification between the Canadian East and West Coasts, stupid, I know. All the dancers were in their own stances with their hands at different heights for visual effect.

When *Better Left Unsaid* first starts it dives directly into a fast paced chorus. It starts almost like a sprint from the beginning, so everyone had to be on time. A simple two-step dance starts the song, as the dance team spins on different cues, crossing in front of me. During the run-through, we bumped into each other so many times, because the Mock Club stage was very small. We had to adjust our trajectory when walking across the stage and even shorten some of our dance moves. Once we were comfortable moving around each other in the tight space, we started shooting. As the chorus progressed, I really enjoyed the part where we all side to side together. By the end, I got to do a punching movement with my hands that acted as a cue for each dancer to do a little move before exiting for the first verse.

While we were shooting a few takes of the first and most important chorus, Blaze and his ugly Native girlfriend walked in about four hours late. I was not surprised, since that was his usual timing to all our studio sessions. We had done the dance routine about ten times from different camera angles, focusing on lead singing and different dancers. We even had a few takes in slow motion.

First Verse

The first verse does not have me rapping in it. Although I wrote the whole song, I got Blaze to rap this first verse. Since Blaze does not dance in the first chorus, we had to cue him perfectly to come on stage with the microphone in his hand, right when the chorus ended. Blaze was very shy on stage, and we had to do a few extra takes to get him comfortable rapping with full facial expressions. Blaze was constantly reminded to keep his head up, so the camera could capture his face. Everything had to be in time with my dance movements to synchronize to the lyrics. I could tell the dance team was getting tired because of the retakes.

This is probably why the dance team was so off with their timed cues, when coming back onto the stage for the second chorus. In fact, it was ridiculous. We had to cut and shoot the second chorus as its own stand-alone scene, because the dance team could not time it perfectly. One girl on the dance team just kept laughing like a hyena when someone made a mistake. It was getting annoying. I have to admit that the two male Filipino dancers, at the front of the video, did earn their money, and I would hire them again. Unfortunately, they always work with the rest of the group members.

When the second chorus came back in, Blaze threw me the microphone at the line "Like a Boss Man, I'm off this" (So appropriate). The dance team then went into the same dance as the first chorus, as I prepared for my upcoming verse. We had to re-take many good shots at this point, because the painters (remember them) kept opening the door during shooting and screwing up the lighting.

Second Verse

For my verse, the lyrics are very much like dating advice for men. At this point, the dance team did some very nice floor routines. It created a nice height dynamic with me standing and rapping, while the two best dancers were doing a break-dance routine on the floor directly to my left and right. Their break-dance routine came equipped with flares, hand stalls and even a windmill.

In post-production, I really enjoyed watching the footage of the second verse, when I was helping edit the video a couple of months later. For the end of my chorus, I did a little head swing with two girls on my shoulders for the line "I never show 'em all my dreams and hopes". When the cute girl broke through with a very sophisticated and sexy solo dance, "I never leak my surprises", I love how the camera zooms in on her. I also love how the camera then has me hunt her like a prey, as I angled to come back in from the side on my line "I don't stoop to spread the dirt, never show 'em when it hurts". This was my favourite part of the shoot.

Chaotic Bridge

At this point in the song, there is a big change in the direction, as the bass line turns chaotic, and the beat gets a little less swing. For this section, we had planned to do many cutaway shots. We were going to have a girl walk into the club, grab a drink from a random table and pick a random guy to dance with. We were also going to have all the extras dancing by the bar. I created a storyboard with a great sequence of shots that saw everything turn chaotic, like a couple kissing, while another couple fights on the dance floor, a guy drinks too much and pukes on the floor, and even a small food fight erupts. In all the confusion, during the bridge scene, I forgot to ask the best dancer to do the most hilarious scene. He was supposed to do a flip, fall on his back, and everyone was supposed to laugh at him, and then we would all jump up and do the last chorus dance together.

All of those shots could have been done, while I was running late and stuck in traffic. But the choreographer did not have a directing eye, like I did. Most annoyingly, when we got to this part, Camera Clown kept trying to be the director, and I had to literally have an ideological battle with him to get the shots I wanted. For example, one of the scenes has me come off stage to talk and kiss a girl, while her jealous cock-blocking friend pulls her away from me and slaps me. In this scene, Camera Clown thought it was funny to have the pretty girl slap me, while I was trying to pick up the ugly girl. "What's your problem man, huh?" I confronted Camera Clown. "What you consider a practical joke will be the first impression the world sees of me before I am famous. So quit trying to throw a wrench into my plan, man. I graduated from cinema school, not you. I call the shots, not you."

"Sure bud," Camera Clown uttered with a dismissive and defensive tone. "Whatever."

Great, now the camera guy was offended. Luckily, that's when the caterers showed up. We had been shooting for about three hours, and I knew I would be crunched for time to get the last shots of the band playing and Samba dancers. Those were all shots that could have been done when I wasn't there.

I had ordered Chinese food to be delivered. It cost me roughly two hundred dollars, and I got it at a discounted price. I had a variety of options, even for the vegetarians. And before I could even get unchanged for the half-an-hour break, all the food was almost gone. Those animals had not even taken the baking sheet off the food trays. They had just ripped a hole in the middle and scooped out food using a beer cup. I immediately lost my appetite. That's when I realized that I was working with emotionally retarded children. It was a motley crew, where everyone was lazy, late and disorganized before the shoot. Then, everyone complained and made mistakes during the shoot. However, when it was break time, everyone was quick to forget about the task at hand and rip into someone else's food, along with their bank account, like animals. All my other snacks, drinks and catering had been finished off. There was garbage everywhere, even some lying on my merchandise boxes. That's when I flipped out again. This was all getting too exhausting. "Clean up your garbage," I roared, "or you can go home for the last shots."

The crowd actually kind of ignored me when I said this, until I walked over to one of the dancers' outfits and literally put my plate of food on her dress, spilling some rice on it. Then when everyone looked up at me, like I had committed the biggest sin in the world, I repeated calmly:"Please clean up your garbage, so it's faster to transition to sound check for the show, thanks."

The black girl kissed her teeth, so I farted loudly, while looking at her. Everyone knew I meant business and started cleaning up for the last scene. I knew I would never hire any of those people again.

For the last couple of scenes, we were supposed to have the Samba dancers beside the band, as we were jamming out the last chorus. It was about 5:00 p.m. and the Samba dancers were already three hours late. All of a sudden, a fat East Indian couple walked in. I thought they were the most awkward Samba dancers I had ever seen. By this point, nothing would have surprised me though. They were not the Samba dancers. They walked up to me. "Hi, we're with *The Torch* magazine, and we are supposed to do some sort of article on a DJ Dicker Jones."

About two months earlier, when I was doing marketing and promotion for the album release party, I came across a magazine, which did local events and concerts for a decent price. The lead editor did an article on me, and we agreed to have him and his team come to both the music video and the concert. His magazine was to be the only media allowed in. They would do all photography, interviews and editing later on. Unfortunately, those two had been informed by that idiot that the show was on April 27th, 2018, even though I had told him a month earlier that The Church Club had screwed me and the venue had been changed to across the street a day earlier on April 26th, 2018. He had all the revised press kits and posters, so he knew the story. No excuses, bud! Those two wannabe journalists realized the morning of the show, they had the wrong date, and when they tried to call their boss, he was sleeping and unavailable.

"We're sorry we're late," the girl added an apology. "But it is our editor's fault."

"The video is almost over," I replied."You guys are like four hours late. Now you expect me to pay you the remaining four hundred dollars for a few photos of the concert? This is so unprofessional!"

I just walked away, back onstage for the final shoot. The two reporters looked so out of place, trying to walk around and take photos of the behind the scenes. The music video was all over, and those two hadn't seen or done anything. I could tell they felt hurt, and in about an hour, they discreetly left before the concert even started. Terrible!

With still no Samba dancers and the dance team assuring me that they couldn't wear the outfits due to size and a lack of Samba skills, I decided to do Plan B. Instead, I organized the camera crew to do close-ups of the band playing and me singing the last chorus by myself, kind of like *Get Lucky* by Daft Punk. We did this a few times, and the camera crew decided it was better to do those last shots in slow motion, because the top hat I was wearing kept falling down over my eyes. I could feel the end coming, and I was excited to finish. Or so I thought. I looked up during one of the shots and saw the opening band standing on the dance floor, waiting for us. Was it six o'clock already? I looked at the clock on the back wall. Sure enough, it read 6:10p.m. Wow, I was already infringing on other people's time. I asked the camera guy how long it would take, and he said another twenty minutes. I could see the frustration on the faces of the impatient opening band, but at that point, I could tell they were also bad people, so I didn't care. They stormed over to the couches, just as the extras got up to leave. I waved goodbye to the extras and gestured for the hot girl to call me. They laughed and gave me the thumbs up as they left. All the actors saved the music video from the mud that the dance team animals dragged it through. As we were finally finishing up the last chorus, Camera Clown asked for the shot list. I handed it to him, and he asked: "Do you still want to have the light bulb break at the end?"

I completely forgot the last scene I had storyboarded, because of all the confusion and disappointment up to that point. As per my plan for the last scene, viewers were to see a light bulb bursting on stage, while the camera zooms into it and fades to black to signify the end.

"Yes," I told Camera Clown, "of course. Do you have a light bulb?"

"What? You didn't bring one?"

"I have been so busy bringing everything. I thought I asked you to..."

"I'm just kidding," Camera Clown chuckled. "I brought it."

I hate that guy, I thought.

The camera crew took fifteen minutes assembling a light bulb onto a stand. They took another five minutes of precious time tapping a microphone to a stand that I would swing at the light bulb and shatter it. The opening band was furiously watching and waiting. I could feel the tension, but we were almost done. This shot would be in slow motion, so it had to be done perfectly. Everyone got off the stage and was about to pack it in, when suddenly in walked two Brazilian dancers. The Samba dancers had arrived five hours late. "Wow, you girls won't even be in the video," I imparted the bad news to them. "So I guess you won't even be getting paid."

The cultural dancers looked mortified, then immediately looked at Wardrobe Witch for support. But the damage had been done. The two semi-beautiful Brazilian girls walked over to where their outfits were on the couches, and grabbed them to leave. Wardrobe Witch ran over to them and started talking. I couldn't tell what they were saying, but I had a feeling that it was something along the lines of: "Listen, girls," Wardrobe Witch affected a rational tone."I know he is an asshole, but he's right. If you don't perform we don't get paid, and I already screwed up the wardrobe so we need you to dance for any chance to get out last payment."

All of a sudden, the Samba dancers were on the stage, and Camera Clown looked at me with his hands open asking what to do. "Alright, everyone," I shouted."I know we are about half-an-hour behind schedule, but if you could just wait patiently, we will get a few shots of these dancers and then move onto sound check."

Broken Glass / Shattered Dreams

My band, the dance team, and the cultural dancers had to come back onto the stage in full outfits again, and this obviously pissed them off. We had to do four more takes of the entire last half of the song to get any usable footage of the Samba dancers. I should add that those girls cost me another five hundred dollars. Finally, the song was finished, and I got ready to break the light bulb. When the coast was clear, and the camera was running in slow motion, I swung as directed and busted the light bulb. Glass shattered everywhere on stage. Suddenly the prick club owner, who had been absent the whole day, ran over to the stage screaming: "Who told you to break glass on my stage?"

"It's part of the video," I stated, "and we did it safely."

"No, you didn't! I just saw pieces of glass fly into the soundboard."

The Mock Club had a soundboard directly to the left of the stage, which is very convenient for live shows. For the entire music video, a curtain had been covering it, but without me noticing, one of the dancers had torn down the curtain doing his routine and not told anyone. The camera crew, who was supposed to be responsible for the safety protocol of the last scene, was oblivious to this. Of course, the real sound guy showed up just as this had happened, and he also ran over to his sound board, saw the ripped curtain and broken glass, and instantly gave me the finger. I tried to apologize, and he told me to "get the fuck off the stage", as they cleaned the mess. I was so furious at the dysfunction of the whole process that I almost left my own show and didn't return. As I stepped off the stage, the mob rushed me. "Hey, we need to do another broken bulb scene," Camera Clown rued. "My hand was a little shaky."

"Not a chance! I'll work with what we got!"

"Hey," Wardrobe Witch made her presence known, "can we get that last payment? The Samba dancers want to know."

"Sure," I said while suppressing my laughter. "Everyone will be paid for their last payment tomorrow night, as stipulated in the contract...when everything goes back to normal."

"Oh," Wardrobe Witch gasped.

"Oh, also," I added, "we want to have a live performance of *Better Left Unsaid* for the opening song tonight. If you can stay, I'd appreciate it, because this video will not be edited for months, and I want the audience to get a sneak peek. It doesn't have to be perfect. I would like you guys to do the first two choruses with me on stage and then throw shirts into the crowd, when you jump off the stage for the bridge. You can then literally just mingle with the crowd for the last minute of the song and then leave. Sound like a plan?"

Everyone groaned with agreement.

When I asked the dance team to stay and do a dance routine for the opening of the concert, they all groaned and demanded an extra five hundred dollars ($100/person). I had to give it. They knew I had come too far to fire them now, so they lazily exploited me. Yeah right, what else would they be doing at 9:00 p.m. on a Thursday night, making money, no, more like spending it at another club. When I hired this dance team I thought they were going to bring hot girls to dance. I know it is shallow, but hot girls are better promoters of the album, because sex sells. One of the girls in the video was hideous, and the other two were only decent-looking. Thank God I brought my own hot girls as actresses! You can see the *Better Left Unsaid* music video on YouTube now, and it should make this more vivid and hilarious to read. The most important advice I can give regarding all this is:

Don't do a music video on the same day as your concert, unless it is a live concert video. It gets too confusing and exhausting. Even if you are trying to save money by killing two birds with stone, at one venue, nothing goes according to plan.

Sound Check

It was almost 7:00 p.m., and finally time for sound check. I couldn't find the opening band that had been pouting in the corner for the last hour. When it came time at 7:00 p.m. for sound check, the opening act had already left to get dinner, so my band got on stage to do our sound check instead.

Musicians are very impatient, impulsive and childish. If you make them wait, it is like an attack on their egos, and they will find any way to rebel.

When my band *Close Encounter* got on stage, the sound guy already hated us because of the broken glass incident. We were about to start micing the drum kit, when the opening act walked back in with coffees. The sound guy went over to grab a coffee and started mingling with the other band. Forced coffee break, I thought. There I was, standing on stage like an idiot when the soundgoof shouted up:"We're gonna do sound check with you guys first then the opening band, so their pedals and sound is ready for the opening song."

"Remember," I instructed him, "we are doing a little dance routine as the first song."

"That's ok," the soundgoof said, "as long as no one touches the pedals or instruments, you can literally just push the stuff to the side to give yourselves more room. It will be to a backing track only, right?"

"Yeah," I confirmed.

"Give me a sec, I'll be up there shortly."

I turned to face the band in private and declared: "Great, more time wasting!"

"I think he's pissed about the glass," Stone Free, one of my band's members said.

"I think he doesn't like us before he has even heard us," I said.

"No," JCulture chimed in. "I think he likes us, he just doesn't like you."

"Well, that's good," I replied.

Everyone laughed.

The Soundgoof finally came back on stage and started adjusting the mics and volumes for the drum kit. When he walked over to the drums, he stumbled into my acoustic guitar, which was nicely placed on its holder. I had to channel my inner ninja to save it. That's when I smelled alcohol on this sound guy's breath. Great! A drunk sound guy. I was too far into this nightmare to scream something like, "That's it, shows cancelled, and I am suing you."

If I were Universal Music, I would have, but I am not.

"Ok," Soundgoof said, "sorry to let you guys know, but micing the drums and getting the right sound usually takes about twenty minutes. So the other musicians can relax and I'll call you up one by one. All the bands are sharing the same drum kit right?"

"Yeah!" I replied in a slightly grouchy tone.

"Perfect!" Soundgoof replied.

Well, that twenty minutes turned into an hour. When I looked at the clock and saw 8:00 p.m., I panicked. I rushed onto stage and literally cut the Soundgoof off mid-sentence: "Listen the show starts in an hour, and at this point, we are spending way too much time on the drums. We will have no time to get a good sound from the rest of the instruments. Can we move on?"

"Fine," Soundgoof voiced his annoyance. "It's your show…"

"Yes! Guitars now!"

We did a half-ass sound check for the bass, lead guitars and rhythm guitar, but it still sounded pretty good. I still noticed that the drums sounded too boomy, so I suggested we turn them down a little, and the Soundgoof turned them off. What a baby. I literally had to go over and turn the volumes to the perfect setting myself on his console. I guess I was also the sound guy that night. We did vocals and then the saxophone and finally we were ready.

I had planned to have an hour nap before the show started. In fact, I also planned to then warm up my vocals for twenty minutes. Everything was delayed and cramping my style. The opening band finally went up for their sound check, and they literally walked by me onto the stage, joking about how unprofessional I was.

All these rock 'n' roll creeps look the same, I thought.

They all have unusually long grey hair, black glasses and bad attitudes. I literally wanted to turn to this old band of wannabe rock stars and say: "Yo, don't even go onstage, you're suspect! You guys suck, and I'll do a better show myself. Here is some of the deposit. Hit the road!" I couldn't do that though, because I thought this band called Behind The Cage, had some pull in the Toronto indie scene. To think I actually thought this band had a fan base, and it would be detrimental to fire them.

The band went on stage, using the drums and amps that I had rented. Then, they set up their very large lead guitar pedal boards and specialized mic. I could tell that this was going to be problematic when the dance team and I went onstage for the grand opening of *Better Left Unsaid*.

It was about 8:30p.m. and, to my horror, I looked at the back of the club to where my merchandises table should have been set up already. I just saw open boxes. There was a mess everywhere. I was already exhausted and right then and there, I realized I should have waited a year to do this show. I should have spent twice the amount of money to get qualified people to departmentalize and delegate everything, so I would only have to sing. Instead, I elected to do it all myself, save a bunch of money and watch idiots struggle with the simplest tasks. Well, in the end, I had to save the day while being exhausted.

Merch Table Fiasco

I walked over to the merchandizes area and saw Angel Investor struggling. My angel investor was not very organized when it came to a small task like setting up a merchandize table. I thought all she had to do was put a few pricing signs up and display a few t-shirts along with CDs. I thought this would be a walk in the park for her, since she knew everything I had ordered and seen it all weeks in advance. Instead she panicked and asked for the DJ from the opening act to help her.

Big Mistake!

This big ape DJ literally rampaged through my boxes of clothing, looking for sizes that were already organized neatly, then crushed my float box and tip jar. Even important letterheads got thrown in the garbage because of this guy's "help". He literally did more damage than help, all because my merchandize table girl couldn't or wouldn't lift a box herself. She said it made her feel embarrassed trying to drag a box across the floor for five seconds, because she couldn't lift it with her weak arms. She instead asked the worst possible person to help her and he destroyed the merch area before we even had a chance to set it up.

I knew I had a choice. I could either let them struggle with the table, after the doors opened, which would allow me a small ten-minute nap and ten-minute vocal exercise, or I could plough on through, help them and only do a minimal vocal warm-up in the bathroom. I knew the opening act would be on stage for forty-five minutes, so I could rest then. This came at a cost though. I was not able to do my vocal practices and could not be at my own merch table or better yet, be at the entrance to greet the fans.

Not only was the merchandise in a disorganised mess, but I also noticed there was no merch table at all. I had been promised a table to set up an hour before the show by the venue owner. Another lie and another oversight. I hunted down the venue owner to ask for a table. "Excuse me," I said, "where is my merch table?"

"What, do you need me to run your merch table too?" asked the club's owner, sarcastically.

"I want to fight you right now for being an asshole and relishing in my agony, but instead I'll just politely ask for the merch table again, like you promised, since it is like ten minutes before opening."

"Huh," the owner chuckled."I don't know... find one behind the bar."

I had to go over to the bar, take a table myself, fold it open and set it up by myself, while everyone watched. Everyone knew I was on in ten minutes. I noticed all my boxes, which I had organized earlier, all in a mess. I asked my girlfriend what had happened. She just pointed at the big Ape DJ. I was fed up with fake musicians ruining everything they touched. "Excuse me, buddy," I approached the Ape DJ, "why are all my t-shirts boxes ripped apart and my organized paper work at the bottom of those boxes?"

"What!" Ape DJ exclaimed with his chest puffed out."I'm try'n help!"

"It's okay, I got it from here...oh where is my letterheads?"

"I dunno, homie," he replied with a smile."This is how I saw things when I came over."

My girlfriend shook her head behind him to signify he was lying.

"Ok," I huffed. "You guys fucking ruining things before they even get start. Why not go get ready for your set, hopefully thousands come to the show to see you guys, right?"

As soon as I said this, Ape DJ wiped the smile off his face and looked pissed. He stormed away and I felt a little better, cleaning up the mess. My girlfriend told me that this was all too much for her. I asked her to just make pricing signs. When she made a spelling error on the first sign, she got so frustrated that she just torn up the poster and started to cry. With everything she had seen me go through, she just snapped and broke down. I had to run over to her, hug her and assure her we would make it out of the night alive. The owner, who had not been helpful or even present all day, of course, just happened to be roaming nearby when I was consoling my girl.

What a coincidence? "Hey," the club's owner blared, "the show is *gonna* start soon. Do you have anyone to do the front door? You are *gonna* need a float and stamp or wristband beside security."

"Yeah," I coldly replied.

I motioned for my friend who had been upstairs having a drink for the last hour to come down and get into position. My friend was pretty reliable, so I asked the owner:"We have everything, but can I borrow an actual cash register tray so we don't have large amounts of money lying around in an envelope?"

"Now it's a tray!" the club's owner griped. "What's next? You need a guitarist too?"

By this point I didn't give a shit about my own concert, this venue, or anything anyone would say other than an apology. Not a good state of mind to be in before a show. I just ignored the owner's last comment and asked my girlfriend if she could help me run the front door as well as greet the fans when they came in. Little did I know that there were about twenty five underage fans waiting outside trying to find a way in.

I had handed out flyers for weeks at the Weed March and Raptor Nation, trying to gain random fans. On my D-Day, a lot of High School students were interested in coming. If I didn't have to do so much that night, I would have woken up from my nap, noticed them and made a deal with security guards to let them watch from the balconies. Of course, I didn't see the group of them pleading with security and they were hard blocked from coming in. It was another loss of some of my fan base.

Finally, with everyone in their positions, for what seemed like the first time all night, I had only five minutes to superhero a merch table together.

I will always remember that people are scum until the last five minutes. Then, everyone shows up and tries to make it look like they have been professional all night.

I stole a black table cloth from the bar, covered my table, re-wrote two pricing signs, with a discount SWAG BAG option on them, taped up some sample t-shirts and buttons, and got all the CDs organized on the table with *Burning Jerusalem* rock stuff on one side and the *New Legacy* hip hop stuff on the other. Lastly, I got a card holder full of free business cards, a tip cup and my cash register. I reorganized the shirts into boxes and slid the boxes under the table. I threw out garbage and looked around to see if everything was looking perfect again. I kissed my girlfriend. In fact, all the musicians and staff had been witnessing me doing this in a frenzy. They were completely amazed. I had not even noticed. In five minutes, I did what others struggled to do for an hour. Literally, as I put the last box under the table, the owner yelled: "Doors Open!"

The show had begun, on my cue!

I initially saw about twenty people rush in the door. I got excited thinking the show was going to be packed. Sadly, when no one followed behind them, I peeked out into the front lobby to see only one person in line outside. I got really sad. My girlfriend saw this and looked at me with sad eyes. We had both realized the show was a flop and we would have to endure embarrassment for the next four hours before we could escape. She just shrugged her shoulders and smiled at the next fan walking in. This lifted me up. The show must go on.

Chapter 31: The Show

During the show:

The show had started and the opening DJ was already playing some terrible Bollywood-type beat that was not from the playlist I had given him. I wanted some music prepping the crowd before the opening act. I hoped to give everyone fifteen minutes to get seated, order drinks and get ready. When I looked around, I saw the fifty people that did come were friends and family of the musicians, not fans. I immediately, ran up to the stage, pressed the button on the Pioneer DDJ Disc Jockey Turn Table and switched the beats to my top forty hip hop playlist. This annoyed DJ Ape. But because we were on stage, at my show, he had to bite a bullet. I had to be the DJ. I then grabbed the mic and started the show."Congratulations, everyone," I announced, "for making it out to be the first audience ever to see DJ Digger Jones. One day you will look back and say I saw that guy at a little show when no one knew him."

The crowd responded with a few claps.

"I want to thank you all for coming out!" I continued."We have a special show for you tonight, filled with dancing, singing, rapping, rock, and even some free swag bags. So please dance, grab a seat, Twitter and Snapchat your friends to get on over to the Mock Club for DDDDDDJ Digger Jones!"

This seemed to get the crowd lit, as they cheered and applauded. I have a real great ability to do that. I guess I had to be the MC at my own show as well.

The dance team came up the sides, ready to perform the opening song. I had to signal for DJ Ape to cue the song and he gave me the thumbs up. I then pushed the large pedal boards from the opening band out of the way to avoid injuring the dance team. To be honest, the first dance song and the last rap section of the night were easily the best part of the show, since I did it all myself. There was no chance for the Soundgoof to fuck it up.

We performed *Better Left Unsaid* almost perfectly. During the actual performance in front of the live audience, the chord from my microphone got caught in one of the female dancers' high heels. We had never practiced with a live microphone, because the one for the music video earlier that day was wireless. We were also supposed to throw T-shirts into the crowd for the live performance (as rehearsed), but of course, with everything going on, I forgot to remind everyone. As a result of my omission, not a single person remembered until we were already performing it. What a letdown. Otherwise, it was a pretty good opening, and the crowd loved it. Everyone started cheering.

The opening band, Behind the Cage, then took the floor and I could feel the energy change in the room to a dark, low energy feel. I could see a lot of the people, who came to see hip hop, were puzzled.

I will never, and advise to never, let a metal band into a hip hop show. Pick a genre and stick to it. If you do a little metal or rock in your set, then, leave it so only you do it; not any other bands.

Before I was going to lose these random fans that had just come in off the street, I ran to my merch table, grabbed a few swag bags along with t-shirts, ran over to the crowd of about thirty and threw some free merch into the crowd. Everyone loved it and starting cheering.

The show had started and was slowly getting better, or so I thought. The keyword is slowly. So slow, too slow, that anyone who came in, waited, got bored and left before I even got on stage. The opening band, which had assured me it would bring at least a hundred people, had brought about fifteen family members. Most of those family members were middle age parents whom I knew wouldn't stay till my set.

I should never have let the opening band have such a large forty-five minutes set, but I thought, when preparing the show, that they would attract a lot of fans. I thought their fans would be coming all night and that around 10:00 p.m., the time of my band's set, the crowd would be pumped up for the main event of the evening. It played out so different than what I expected. Instead, it was a Thursday night.

On Friday nights, people are prepared to not get going until 10:00or 11:00 p.m. But on a Thursday night, when people have work in the morning, it is better to do a show around 7:00 p.m. as a more mellow night that finishes at 11:00 p.m. Now I know, and now you know for your own shows!

The opening band played a decent set, but their overall sound was so bass heavy that everything sounded muffled. The Soundgoof was just terrible. I started noticing hip hop people, with their groups of friends, starting to look around, questioning if this would be a rock show. I had to do something, as I saw a few of them leave. There were only about fifty people in the audience, and I really didn't see anyone outside in the lobby. So I knew I had to work with what I had. I quickly got on my laptop and started making a slide show that I could put on the side projection screen to let people know what was coming next. I made a slide show introducing my band and DJ Digger Jones, the star closer. I knew if I could just get them to wait another half-an-hour, my show would be exciting.

Well, let's see if my plan worked.

Sure enough, after the opening set an hour later, the old parents started leaving. Not even one of them bought a single Swag Bag or even t-shirt. At the merch table, I had a SWAG BAG offer with any CD and t-shirt and a complimentary press kit, all in a free gift bag for twenty dollars. Still no one bought any. It should be noted that I later did the same promotion online and I made a fortune. It was now 10:00 p.m. I was supposed to be headlining at 10:30p.m.I had an opening act that was supposed to play a few hip hop songs with DJ Ape and my drummer JCulture before I came on to get the crowd warmed up for some hip hop. By this time, I saw a couple of my friends come into the club and grab a table.

MC Lazy

I started thinking that the show could still be a minor success, until DJ Ape and MC Lazy ruined what little hope was left. I thought those guys would definitely bring people. They talked the talk.

Well, folks, a hard lesson to learn in the industry is: very few musicians have any real pull, because most musicians are social outcasts or have very small niche markets. This is unless they're party musicians, then they bring the crowds, but also the prima donna attitudes.

I wouldn't have minded a prima donna here. At least, it would have meant ticket sales, but by the time DJ Ape and MC Lazy got on stage, the crowd was getting restless. I left the merch table, where one of the door people came to substitute, and I went on stage to introduce MC Lazy. The beat dropped and I thought his set was about to start. I timed it that I would go downstairs, rest on the toilet for five minutes, drink some tea, then, do ten minutes of vocal practice and his set would be near finished. What happened next will forever make me never trust rap artists again.

I am all a show needs. I rap, sing, play guitar, drum, do stand-up comedy and dance. What else do you need?

I went downstairs completely exhausted. I walked by Blaze making out with his Native girlfriend. I went into the washroom and set my phone alarm clock for a ten minute nap. I woke up seventeen minutes later, and jumped up. As I was washing my face, expecting someone to run into the washroom and say I was up next, I heard the same Bollywood beat that I had turned off earlier. I ran upstairs and saw MC Lazy talking to the DJ on stage, with half the crowd leaving. I ran on stage and as soon as I came on stage, MC Lazy started his set. Some of the crowd turned to stay but others just kept walking out. I was confused, I felt like I was in the twilight zone déjà vu or something. I looked at my girlfriend at the merch table and she gestured she didn't know. So I went behind the stage, snuck up behind my drummer and asked: "What the fuck happened? Why is Lazy not almost done his set? People are getting tired and leaving."

"I don't know, Digger," said JCulture. "I think he was just waiting for his family to show up."

"What!" I replied. "He fucking stalled his set twenty minutes to wait for his family?!? FUCK!"

I was so angry I looked at the clock and it was almost 11:00 p.m. I would not get on until 11:30p.m. and people would be exhausted or the place would be empty.

This is the last time I do a show with anyone, I thought. I am the star, not these fakes.

I went back downstairs and started doing my vocal exercises. I knew the songs in MC Lazy's set list and it should have been five songs, roughly twenty-five minutes. While I was doing my warm-ups, I saw Blaze out in the hall studying his lyrics on his phone. It was weird to see Blaze needing to look up lines that he had just recorded in the studio. I had to memorize fifteen songs verbatim, and he was only performing in three songs. WTF! At that moment, I heard a song I didn't recognize and I felt things were going awry again. I went back upstairs to the side of the stage to signal to hurry up. MC Lazy just looked at me with his googly eyes and then ignored me and kept playing for the ten people that were cheering for him. This guy thought he was a star or something, stealing my time. What an asshole! I let this guy into the show, and he upstages me. I literally walked on stage, and MC Lazy then said to the audience: "Ok, folks, this is my last song."

Better be a banger, I thought.

MC Lazy did not have any fans or pull in the industry either. No one bought any of his merch, because it was some Christian religious rap symbol of the cross and all the people that were left at the show were his family who probably already had his corny shirt. None of his so-called fans bought any of my merch, either. What a terrible slum fan base. The Ape DJ and MC Lazy, whom I thought had a lot of fans, only had their families come.

Never have gangsters ruin your show, unless they are truly established and can bring the loot. Otherwise, you just may get stabbed.

MC Lazy's set went for forty-eight minutes of terrible in-your-face, exhausting trap rap. By the time my band got on stage, I was literally playing for my few friends, and all the musicians, bands and their families. I didn't even get to play for the crowd I had at the beginning of the night. Not that it was a crowd I wanted anyway.

As I walked off the stage to the back room, a girl I knew stepped out of the shadows. It was the same lady who gave me a blowjob while I was in the studio, when the Waco bass player caught us. She came up to me when I had literally four minutes before stage time.

"Hey, Digger," the slut greeted me."I came to see you. You look good."

"What are you doing back here?" I asked her.

"Why didn't you come back here an hour ago? We could have fucked already and I would be in a good mood by now. Do you expect me to run downstairs with you in the next few minutes and run back onto the stage? I hate when people try to make everything rushed for time."

Hang on, everyone made me wait, now why can't they can wait for me, I thought.

I grabbed the girl by the hand and started kissing her. I knew she could just be trying to get me in trouble for harassment too. Nothing at this point I didn't care.

When the system turns on you, billions of dollars is at its disposal to create a nightmare against you. Just stay calm and survive.

Just then, of course, cock-blocking JCulture barged through the doors.

"What are you doing, Digger?" asked JCulture. "We're on!"

"I'm coming!" I told him.

"Yeah," the slut added with a smile. "Not in me!"

Everyone laughed, except me.

I walked on stage to start my set and saw an almost empty club. I guess this entire night was a practice night! What a waste of time, money and energy.

Close Encounter

During the show I had some great banter with the remaining audience. I told jokes about paying rent, adding a little comedy history lesson for *Burning Dido*, and made fun of my friend who was locked up in jail for accidently burning his own garage. The crowd really enjoyed my comedy skits and overall stage presence. I even made a music video slide show with pictures of the band in studio recording the album, with nice band logos, posters and welcoming slides.

My set list consisted of a rock/rap set of four songs, a rock set of four songs, back to a rock/rap set of four songs and finished with four straight trap hip hop songs. My band, on the other hand, sounded terrible. When our set started, I could only hear the boomy drums that were way too loud. Remember, they had spent way too much time on the drums in sound check. I knew that the Soundgoof would be of no help, so I took it upon myself to guide the musicians through.

During our set, I made very few mistakes, even though I heard the band make almost every transitional mistake you can imagine. The breakdown sections for the bass that really created some dynamics in the songs were always missed and drums rolls came one bar too late. When certain sections were supposed to be featured like horns or lead guitar, the volumes were too low. The whole thing was a drum and bass booming nightmare. It became a recurring theme that either my lead guitar player would be playing a wicked solo while the Soundgoof had his volume so low nobody could hear him, or my lead guitar players amp would be way too hot, and he would start screwing up. It was the worst venue my guitarist ever played as well.

Most annoyingly, when I had to turn to direct the Soundgoof, my amp chord would get tangled with my guitar. When I moved out of position, I accidently stepped on my own patch chord and twice ripped it right out of my guitar. The first time, the Soundgoof laughed and I wanted to kill him. The second time was in the middle of the song *Treemen*. I literally grabbed the mic, knelt down with it, plugged the patch chord back in and was able to hit the change in chord progression right at the perfect time the rhythm guitar comes back in. It was so professional and hard to do, even the haters in the crowd started clapping.

DJ Digger Jones

For my hip hop song at the end, I sang every song flawlessly, even though I was tired and had a dry mouth. Blaze forgot all his lyrics on the stage and was the worst side man in history. He was worse than Robin for Batman, worse than Mega Sonic Teenage Warhead, worse than the guitar player for the band Tool. Thinking back, they must have been all paid to stall me or they had been high out of their fucking minds.

By the time the disaster at the show had come and gone, and I knew I hated working with over-emotional, childish wannabe musicians, I was ready to start my new life. I had already protected myself legally from them. I knew if anything went awry, they would try to sue me, so I got each rapper and session musician to sign a contract stating that I owned all lyrics and riffs. Now, when I get famous, no one can say they co-wrote anything, because all of the lyrics and riffs are mine. Plus, the camera crew and dancers, opening band and club owner all know they can be sued for incompetence and negligence, so I never heard from them again, even though I only paid them half of what they expected. Trust me, half was still too much.

After the Disaster

As soon as I was rushed out of the night club on that last disastrous night in Toronto, I immediately hopped on a train to Vancouver. On the one-week trip I had time to think about everything that had happened. I was first angry at my own band for performing so poorly, but then I realized we just needed more time to practice. I knew that because I spent weeks correcting the printing error from Plane Crash Records, the band didn't get the last crucial time together that we needed. I had to rush them, and they sucked, because things suck when you rush them. My girlfriend saw us play that night and said we looked like a pathetic ensemble. My band however, are very talent musicians and with proper rehearsal time are just as good as The Dave Matthews Band.

After the show, the piece of shit band, Behind The Cage, that tried to sabotage my show, even had the audacity to bombard me with texts and emails for months, trying to get a rise from me, saying: "Fuck bud, wow, you didn't even pay your own band."

Why would I pay any of the assholes who bombed, stalled and sabotaged, even if you all think you're better musicians then you are. I had to spend the first two months in Vancouver literally avoiding Toronto online. Don't try to make me look like the guy from the documentary *Fire Fest,* I am not being ripped off my incompetent people anymore.

Chapter 32: Plane Crash Records

If you have already come to a point where you have recorded your album, mastered it and want to produce a physical product, you must chose this next step carefully. You have already read about my terrible experience with Plane Crash Records. Well, the second attempt was even worse.

Here are both experiences from the beginning.

When I was first interested in finding a manufacturer for the first album, *Burning Jerusalem,* I phoned a Toronto-based CD duplication manufacturer named Plane Crash Records. There was no answer, so I was about to look to another company. Against my expectations, some goof phoned me back. You will learn why I call him Goof by the end of this chapter. Goof was very good at making me feel that everything would be taken care of.

I agreed to do the first album with his company.

I should have known it would all be a mistake when I first asked about the six panel DigiFold, for a nice press kit. Goof responded that they didn't have those capabilities anymore and that the website had not been updated.

To give a little background about this company, it was supposedly started by a musician wanting to press his own CDs and who had found a broken CD press in a garage sale. Well, judging the way the company handled my order, they must still be using the same garage sale CD press.

I sent the original artwork and mastered music to Plane Crash. Then, I noticed that my original album artist had accidently put two song titles next to each other, thinking it was one song. The hidden song that should not have been on the text at all, was now the final song on the track list. I immediately called my artist in a panic, got my album artist to fix it immediately and sent it back to him. I phoned Plane Crash in a panic, and Goof picked up the phone. I explained everything to him. He assured me nothing had been printed and that they had gotten the revised Photoshop images. He also assured me that the album would have the twelve song track list and the hidden song would not be seen.

The first thousand units of the album were sent to me in five boxes with the error on them. The song track list on the back was in the wrong order. They had used the first mistake images. I was so furious I wanted to sue the company. The sales rep didn't know what had happened. I had to go over all the previous emails, and I found that the sales rep had sent the sales team the wrong files, after I had done everything to make sure that wouldn't happen.

So here I was, at my studio, when a thousand units were couriered to me. I opened the boxes so excited, but what I saw horrified me. The track list was all wrong. I thought that maybe the songs were just rearranged in a different order, and if they aligned with the songs on the album, I would accept it. To my dismay the track list did not match what song was playing at the time. What a disaster, a real plane crash.

To make matters worse, Goof blamed me when I phoned him. No discount was offered, and he had the audacity to tell me to manually take all the CDs apart and switch the back tray panel myself. This took me a whole week, when I could have been doing so much more to promote the album.

After I had finished replacing all the back trays with the revised track list, I had roughly a hundred cracked or damaged units. That is roughly a thousand dollars profit down the drain. I thought about never doing business with Goof again, but the owner felt so humiliated that he assured me I would get a huge discount if I ever ordered from there again. I later realized Plane Crash was one of the biggest reasons nothing worked, because of the time it stole from me to do more important things.

Watch out for the one variable company that purposely throws a wrench in your plans.

For the *New Legacy* album about two months later, Plane Crash Records' owner was happy to hear my voice again and assured me a discounted price, even though I needed a rush order. I also wanted to check Number 10 Studios, in the east side of Toronto. I had wanted to record and print there for so long, but the owner was so rude on the phone that I just hung up. It was kind of disappointing, since I always wanted to record and duplicate my product there. It was also right up the street from where the *New Legacy* album was mastered, but first impressions are crucial. Plane Crash owner phoned me right back, and was eager to set things straight and do a good job on the second album. I should have spent another couple months planning to get a publicist, promoting the *New Legacy* album and finding a new duplication company. Instead, I thought that this company would help me faster, since they already knew what I expected from them. What happened next showed me to always take your time. Never rush. If things are not working out, then stop, recalibrate and find another avenue. Never push on through with the same idiots that ruined the first attempt. Of course, Plane Crash ruined the second album release, too.

I got the mastered version of *New Legacy* on Friday at 2:00 p.m. I sent it to Plane Crash Records five minutes later. I didn't receive an email that night, or the next day or even Sunday. Then, randomly at 9:30p.m. on Sunday night, I got a call from Goof screaming: "I don't think we can make your deadline for Thursday!"

"What! What Happened?"

"I have been waiting all weekend for your response. Now I can't have the team set the machines till Monday and that will cost you another thousand dollars if you want them for Thursday, bud."

"What the fuck! Am I being hustled?"

"Hustled?" screamed Goof while using the Rogerian restatement in order to elicit a response from me.

He resumed screaming at me on the phone. Then, when I hung up on him, he phoned me back with a completely split personality, apologizing, like a bipolar patient.

"Listen," I said."I don't know what happened. I sent the files as soon as I got them from the mastering. I also already sent a thousand dollars. Then I waited for a response all day Friday and Saturday from you. When nothing came, I thought you had just gone ahead and started printing on Saturday, like you said you would. I even sent another thousand after that. Now you phone me up last minute on Sunday, saying I have to pay you another thousand dollars, because you have to rush the order, when it is you who procrastinated. Remember, I'm also getting a discount, because you ruined the last album."

"We were ready to print on Saturday," he retorted. "But I didn't get an approval from you. I looked really bad to my team!"

"It is not my fault that you stalled because you were worried about screwing up another one of my orders. Everyone was ready to go, and things were already approved. It is you who caused us all to wait. Tell your team that."

This guy even had the nerves to say how mature he was, because he had two kids. Well, buddy, if you're reading this, I feel sorry for your kids. He had already overcharged me a thousand dollars for duplication, and he never gave the discount he promised. The *Burning Jerusalem* album cost fourteen hundred dollars for a thousand copies (roughly $1.40/per unit) a very reasonable price, although it took three weeks for me to fix the error after. The *New Legacy* album cost me thirty-one hundred dollars ($3.10/unit), a complete rip off. The worst thing about it was that price started out as nineteen hundred for a rush delivery and then skyrocketed to three thousand because of the fuck up again.

What an arrogant prick!

Chapter 33: Industry Discrimination

Not only does the industry discriminate against overweight artists, it also discriminates against people of lower financial status. This is because it is a liability to invest in pulling an average Joe from the streets or the countryside, up to fame. It is risky promoting a white trash rapper, if there is already Eminem, just ask Machine Gun Kelly. Even certain cultures such as First Nations, Somali and Vietnamese, to name a few, are very rarely invited into feature films, Hollywood, or the red carpet of the music industry.

What the industry tries to do is actually test you in your quotidian life with something or someone that is so insurmountable that when you don't do it, they feel they can use that failure against you for life. Like it was a test to get into the industry that you failed. It is all a cheap mind game. Ironically, those people are actually usually in the background of life, the peanut gallery, constantly spying on others or criticizing. The real stars, who end up making it, know how hard it was, and they secretly are rooting for others to make it as well. People who are not that good at life seem to have the biggest egos. Besides, they only enjoy distracting people like a pop up ad and they like to create competition for a newcomer. They do this to make things so hard, so they don't feel so bad for not making it themselves.

Criminal Musician

I have had many experiences with musicians, who basically steal money. They will lie to about practicing your music at home, then when they show up to rehearsal practice, they are oblivious to the changes but want the money nonetheless. Many musicians are actually dangerous. If you try to fire them or slightly insult their fragile egos, they will want to fight you and may even phone their gangster buddies to wait for you outside the studio. I also know musicians, who fight each other for prime busking spots, or territory battles for dive.

The music industry is a dog fight at the bottom and a bunch of crabs in a bucket when you start to rise up, but I heard it is cloud nine at the top.

Up to now, you have heard of my financial misfortunes dealing with mixers and audio engineers. However, I have heard of how people working in studios get ripped off as well. Musicians will see someone playing a cool chord progression and will go home, change the sequence of it and then pawn it off as their own, I have heard of singer songwriters coming into a smaller studio, sitting down with the mixer for a couple days, then actually spying on all the plug-ins, techniques and templates that the mixer uses. Obviously, no one can replicate an auditory knack for music and mixing. However, once you know the EQ settings a mixer likes to use, it isn't hard to deviate slightly to make your own. I have heard of musicians coming in, stealing plug-ins, along with mixing techniques, and then starting their own studios and stealing customers. I do not doubt that at all! People are always afraid to create from scratch and would rather rest, be lazy and steal something at the last minute, when all the hard work has been done.

I Wanna Be Famous

The first question on the first day of school at Seneca College was: Who wants to be famous?

It is like the music industry keeps promoting this pipe dream of fame for people to keep following and pumping money into it. Sorry to tell you, but becoming famous has nothing to do with hard work. I know people who can fill buckets with sweat more than five famous people combined. It is all about working smart, surpassing oneself when everyone is watching, and then sowing the seeds of longstanding relationships with people who will create a great team. The latter will save you the trouble of breaking your back. There is no fame apart from those whom have already been chosen. Even school systems start to shift from simple theory, choirs and big bands to more industry-related pressure. I know from experience that Seneca's Independent Music Production (IMP) program is funded every year by kids who think it will make them famous. I was one of the best students — both academically and musically — the school had ever seen. Oddly, I had nothing but walls to pound in lieu of help, while cute blondes could fill a stadium barely playing three chords.

In school, I met a bunch of cool talented individuals seeking to be famous. Being famous means no more struggling to pay for the simple necessities of life. In my school, however, a lot of these kids either had huge egos or limited talent. Instead, they would network their asses off to compensate for the lack of talent. I felt like it was just literally one big dog fight to get all the attention, literally making the whole scene a mess. It saddened me that on the flip side, others would be more talented than they even realized and would always be second-guessing themselves because of the fear of the dogs ripping their hearts apart with criticisms. Those types of musicians were my favourite to work with, because in the studio, when I unlocked their potential, I would literally just sit there and watch them make magic in front of me. Two examples of this are in the songs *Light up This Track* and *Lonely West*.

To this day, I don't know why Seneca College's staff would try to block me. I guess the teachers were embarrassed that I was a better musician than them and a University grad. One day in one of my more ridiculously impractical song writing classes, I had a teacher admit that she didn't know the relative minor of a major note. Right then I knew I was in the wrong place.

Being a poor student for a decade got so hard. When you are a poor student, other students that love to party will never let you rest. I would be bothered all night and day with garbage trap music, screaming girls that barely got laid and people coming in and out of my residence's bathroom. Worst of all, as soon as I would flip out, start practicing my vocals loud, drumming or even plugging in my guitar in the amp, they would get self-righteous. In addition, a female student would usually try to tell me to turn it down. I would have to become the bad guy and tell them all to fuck off. I felt like the hero of the comic book *Scott Pilgrim vs The World*.

Of course, in Seneca, there was even some tool who constantly bragged about being accepted into Berkeley. I found this so suspicious and comical. Supposedly, he didn't want to travel across the continent to study there. So this guy gave up his chance at a great career from Berkeley in order to downgrade to the worst music college in the country. Indeed, he wanted to stay around mommy and daddy. I said, yeah right bud, something smells fishy here. We all know, where there's fish, there're flies.

Black Flies Matter

In my personal opinion, working with some black people in anything music-related is tantamount to working with Emotional Retards when you have something important to do. Now, I must clarify the difference between a black person and an ignorant asshole. Like Chris Rock said: "There are niggers and there are black people....Even the black people hate niggers." In my experience working with some coloured individuals in the music industry, I found that they will suck all the energy for themselves and are just waiting to be offended. In fact, it always felt like they were trying to play the race card. I am sick of being labelled a racist in my own country. I am half-Native and have witnessed my people struggle in poverty as well as obscurity. Racism is a way for some non-white people to gain advantage over others by using guilt tactics and social shaming. I personally felt in working with some black people that they were one word away from starting a fight. If you choose anything that does not go with their agenda, you are labelled a racist. If you try to negotiate their price point, you are a racist. I literally had all my Asian investors plead with me to not do any business with black people. I was in a catch-22. I enjoyed my black musician friends for their vibe and groove. But when it came to business, it was like they were Trojan horses. Instead of being on my team during rough times, I was being sabotaged by my own teammates from within. Whenever an outsider came along to do business with me, if that person was black, my own band mates seemed to allow this person to "fuck me".

Meanwhile, they seemed to never get "fucked" themselves. Everything became a racial thing at one point or another, and I felt like they were just using me to get where their black faces were not allowed. For instance, when it came to dealing with bank loans, certain festivals and promoters, I felt like the middleman. I never thought about racism, until I seemed to be around a bunch of black guys, who were racist but tried to hide it and then blamed others for being racist. I got sick of their intimidating jail tactic manipulations, so I ended the band.

Black lives matter, but so do Native American lives. Besides, I would argue they probably matter more, because at least we are not killing each other in such high statistical numbers and then blaming racism for our plight. Don't believe me about black-on-black crime? Check the FBI's yearly statistics on homicides. Native Americans believe that they have been screwed systematically. But they are at least willing to work with the government to address problems for their youth generations. They do not blame Trump, they do not blame the government solely. All lives matter, and to single one out as more important seems to be the most racist thing of all. Oh, and what about black flies...Black Flies Matter as well!

While I was in Seneca College, I found a picture of a black fly, and I put the words "Black Flies Matter" under it. I was almost expelled for it. Fucking liberal colleges! Some things are just *Better Left Unsaid*.

By this point in the book, you may hate everything I have said, think I am a racist and are about to put this book down. I do not blame you. However, I say what everyone thinks, but is terrified to say in this politically correct society of bullshit. I pray every day for the starving children in Africa. Apparently the "bling bling" rappers, making millions, forgot to pray and donate to those kids themselves, yet they promote their blackness every day. I am not racist; I am realistic. In fact, I probably have more black friends than you. I have played basketball my whole life, do rap music, and have a nickname, Digger. That sounds pretty urban to me. I have loved and hated individuals from every race, culture and denomination. In fact, if you say you love everyone, you are probably going to hell. Jesus didn't love everyone; he hated the serpent and his people. I am proud to be a Native Canadian with European ancestry who has friends from around the world. I can only comment on what I have observed, and if what I have observed up to now looks racist, maybe some groups of people should change. After all, heaven knows I have changed enough to accommodate and tolerate them. So please don't put this book down. There is more knowledge in here than in most books you will read in your entire life. It is a music industry bible not written from the point of view of the Romans or the Pharisees, but from a poor disciple, or *The Last Saint*.

Chapter 34: Digger's How To's

This chapter is probably the most important chapter in this book. Up to now, you have read some hilarious stories, some angry rants and some questionable ideology. This chapter, however, is all about the facts. This is a step-by-step formula to become successful in the music industry. Here is a list of the quickest, most cost-effective and bullshit-preventing way to do it. Here is a whole bunch of tips that Drake will never give you:

HOW TO:

Make a Band

1. First, write a song. If it sucks, you need a band to write the song for you. If it is good, you need a band to perform it with you. Know your priorities.
2. Meet musicians, try to start a band for free, find like-minded people and jam together. Start simple. Then, progress. Elect a leader or be prepared to be very sensitive to decisions by committee.
3. Audition a band by going to music schools, churches and bars, finding musicians, putting up posters, and posting online ads.
4. Hire a band of professional musicians or session musicians.
5. Try to get musicians, who live close to you and have either their own equipment or their own rehearsal/jam space.
6. Keep your band happy and hydrated; not hungry or horny.
7. Rehearsal space costs are high. They are necessary if you need to perform at paying gigs, but not when you are first starting out, unless you are all willing to pitch in on the costs.

Make a Music Video

- Find the song you want the video for. Make sure it is mixed and mastered!
- Set your budget for the video.
- Create a story, a theme or at least a reason why you want to do a video (even if it is just cool shots of you).
- Create a simple shot breakdown of each shot, location, movement, camera angle, costume and mise-en-scène.
- Create a simple storyboard to visualize how the video will look.
- Scout locations and receive a filming approval.
- Get people to act and/or sing in the video.
- Get a dance crew/models if needed.
- Get a director if needed.
- Get a camera.
- Get a camera guy and/or crew with lighting capabilities.
- Make sure to rap/sing your words verbatim.
- Make sure that your lips sync up on exact timing.

- Have snacks, catering, refreshments and/or payment for people involved.
- Have cool cutaway shots of people, places and things. Those could be cool cuts from drones flying above the city, colourful lights and beautiful locations.
- Depending on where you live, secure a permit to operate drones.
- Edit the best shots only.
- How to Edit a Music Video
- Create a folder for junk material.
- Move unused shots into junk folder.
- Create a folder for your best material.
- Put your unedited and raw best shots in the best folder.
- Now, sift through shots and arrange them according to your story/video either chronologically, aesthetically or categorically.
- Start to place shots in the order that you want the rough storyline to follow.
- Allow for an overlap between same time/space shots from different takes/cameras.
- Start to edit down shots to selected timeframe and size, disregarding leftovers and dumping them into the junk folder.
- Allow for best cutaway shots, even if not logical yet, to be left at the end of the video. You can add them into the video later.
- Once you have selected the best shots, location shots, lip sync shots and cutaway shots, start to assemble them into the exact order for the video, even if they are raw and unedited in timeframe.
- Always edit in relation to the actual song being played in image/audio sync-up (link).
- Once the shots are in order, start to perfectly edit shots down to timeframe (average: 1 shot/second - 1 shot for every 3 seconds).
- Use 24 frames per second as the frame rate of your video.
- Be careful of filters, lighting and colour palettes.
- Be sure to keep the flow and momentum of the beat matching with your shot transitions.
- Once your shots are edited to appropriate lengths, start looking into unique, artistic and non-distracting transitions. Those are edits that move from one shot to another (i.e. dissolve).
- Once your transitions are almost done, start looking into any SFX, filters, moving texts, animations and so on. This may take a while. If you have a minimal budget, the simpler, the better.
- The video is almost done. Now, it's time for titles and credits. Take your time with those. You do not want to forget someone, misspell something or miss an artist's name or label.
- Go over the video multiple times, correcting, adjusting, adding, omitting, refining and editing, and finally get another professional to look at it and give advice.

I followed those steps for each one of my first music videos that were filmed and edited by me:

"Treemen"

"Bright Lights"

"Better Left Unsaid"

Album Artwork Check List:

1. Front Cover: Image, theme, legible band/artist name and album name, all within a colour scheme.
2. Inside jacket: Info page, special thanks, lyrics, images, a poster, pictures of band, or whatever fits and is relevant.
3. Tray Card: A unique picture/logo or band symbol that will be seen behind the CD.
4. CD: Have the band's logo, a unique picture and the band/artist name, as well as album name. Maybe some record company info, as well.
5. Back Cover: Track list, a picture to tie the front cover to the back. I like to use a poster spreadsheet that can be folded out and connects the two images of the front cover, inside jacket, as well as back cover.

PROMOTIONS

1. Decide if you want and are competent enough to do your own design (Photoshop, Adobe InDesign, etc.). If not, hire a professional publicist, graphic designer and/or friend.
2. Design your unique image as an artist or a band, consisting of wardrobe, colours, symbols, a logo, sounds and one defining picture.
3. Design a band logo with the intention of not infringing on other bands' and companies' trademarked logos.
4. Match your album covers to your image and logo or vice versa.
5. Create an official website; not another social media account.
6. Create an event page for your concert.
7. Create an artist/band page on YouTube, Facebook, Twitter, Instagram, CD Baby and other sites.
8. Try to get the authentic, official and verified stamp on your social media.
9. Make two posters for your upcoming album release and concert. One of the posters will be more generic with your name, links, pictures and album image/logo. It is for just promoting you as an artist or band in general. The second will be specific for the upcoming concert. This should have your name, logo, dates and locations in large fonts. Remember, you are trying to attract random passersby or clubbing fans, not the fans you already have.
10. You may want to go a step further and get a print company to print a few more promotional ads for you, such as a concert signage stand, a canvas banner to hang behind the band, stickers to sticker bomb relevant locations, and even flyers that are similar to your posters to be delivered in residential areas by yourself, your band or hired flyer distributers.

11. Send your press releases and EPK to radio stations, bloggers, publicists and record company A&R reps.
12. After you have done all the above, you may want to speak to your band about getting a manager, booking agent and most importantly, a publicist, or the backing from a production company.
13. Register your album release party on Ticketfly, so people can purchase tickets online before the show.
14. When your band's name and logo are officially chosen, trademark and register them as a business.
15. Get an entertainment lawyer or at least consult with one.

Make a Website

1. Draw a rough idea of how you want your website to look like and create a site map.
2. Use existing templates or create your own.
3. Buy a domain on a web hosting company, such as GoDaddy, or HostGator.
4. Set up a folder of the most usable material, such as pictures, logos, one-sheets, posters, banners, album covers, music videos, media write-ups, quotes, links to musical samples and "buy" buttons (linked to PayPal, Ticketfly, Amazon and iTunes). Lastly, make sure you have all the contact information for booking agents or for record companies to contact you.
5. Start designing your website slowly, with areas, borders and players for each desired part.
6. Add sections like Home, About, Band, Merch, Videos, Tours and Blog.
7. Create an EPK page with a one-sheet as your website or as one of the subpages.
8. Link your finished website to your social media accounts and CD sales pages.

One-sheets

1. A one-sheet is like the resume of an artist or a band. But it is augmented with pictures. There are many different formats, but you will want to create a one-sheet that shows your face well, has a consistent colour theme and is easy to read. My first one-sheet consisted of all of the following items:
2. Title
3. Website/social media links
4. Contact info/record label
5. Pictures of the artist and band, playing a live concert, etc.
6. The recent album cover and track list (perhaps discography).

7. A background image, location and landscape that is not distracting but adds to the other material.
8. A short biography of the artist/band
9. A few pertinent quotes from industry people or media journalist
10. Anything else you think promotes you effectively.

Electronic press kits (EPKs)

1. Create a music CV. If you do not have one, make one. It is like a resume with gig experience, music education experience, any accolades and whatever else makes you look good in the entertainment industry.
2. Incorporate your one-sheets.
3. Add a press release. It must encompass a description of the album and artist (you).Add concert information for your album or concert, as well. If you are doing a special show for a cause, a festival or some other newsworthy event, prepare a press release. Remember to write "-30-" at the end of the press release.
4. Add any news story written about you or your band. It could either be an article, a review, an interview or even just a quote.
5. Add your most famous poster/flyer.
6. Have the mixed and mastered album at hand for easy listening (physical CD or USB).
7. Biographies of the band members.
8. Discography and music links.
9. Album artwork.
10. Social media links.
11. Free downloads.
12. Gather all of these digital files, and either put pieces of them into a press kit or section the website off, so that viewers can look at them in their entirety.
13. Send the press release and EPK to radio stations, bloggers, publicists and record company A&R reps.

Merch

1. Before doing any merch, decide who will pay for it, because this will eventually be an expensive endeavour.
2. Next, choose a printing company for your merch. The company responsible for your CDs may be different from the one producing your t-shirts. Just remember that if you go cheap, the quality may suffer. And if you are not already famous, quality equals sales.

3. Decide what what's at hand: CDs, t-shirts, hoodies, hats, stickers, mugs, posters, press kits, business cards, etc.
4. Design your album covers in relation to all your merch items, (i.e. sticker, band logo should also be on t-shirts and CDs).
5. Have two options for the print teams to look at. Then, allow them to help you design what fits best for marketability and sales. They do this for companies, bands and people, every day.
6. Create stickers with a logo and name design possibly to go on items on stage as well (i.e. my own DJ headphone brand with logo stickers).
7. When creating t-shirts, do not allow the print company to squeeze an album cover too small or too long. Create a rounded edge so things don't look "cut and paste". Also allow room for a logo on the back or shoulder. Remember that large logos and texts work better than condensed images.

Magazine & Newspaper Ads

1. Do not overpay for ads, because sometimes an ad will not attract random fans for you. You can put the best ad in the best magazine, but unless there are other media attracting buzz, it will be a waste of money since those media outlets and their classified sections are expensive.
2. Ads are most effective either in grassroots bombardment on the street level or with very expensive positioning. The latter could be on the first page of a newspaper or the entertainment section. Ads are not very effective in the classifieds, alongside the ads of hundreds of other bands, unless your band already has a decent following. If your band has some magnetism, then the ad is more of a reminder.
3. Try to become friends with an editor or journalist of a media outlet. Befriending either one of them is your chance to find out who is the best person to network with to get a cheaper, larger advertisement.
4. Decide which magazines and newspapers are best for your niche. If you are a string quartet, choosing a magazine like *The WholeNote*, some other magazine from the classical music industry and a local paper may be the best route. On the other hand, if you are an emerging pop singer, you may opt for a larger distribution as a full size page in *Now Magazine* or *The Toronto Star*, even at any price.
5. Research the pricing for local newspapers and free commuter papers.
6. Research concert listing newspapers like *Now*, *Eye Weekly* and *Fringe*.
7. When dealing with concert listing papers, do not let them pick which images work best. After all, their main concern is not how many people show up to your show,

but rather how your ad works within the aesthetics of their paper. Pick and create your own.
8. Make sure the picture of the artist/band is effective in representing the style of music at the venue.
9. Make sure all contact info is present on the ad for the artist and show's date/location.
10. They all overcharge, so you can either opt for a long-term campaign with cheap newsprint classifieds, or a one day bombardment of the entire city with the largest newsprint companies you can find and afford.
11. Send your press releases and EPKs to radio stations, bloggers, publicists and record company A&R reps.

Radio Ads

1. Do not allow some disc jockey to rush the creation of your advertisement. Make sure you get ad demo versions long in advance of your final payment date and show date.
2. If you do get a response from a radio station wanting an interview, suggest giving them a free "bumper" as well (an audio ad that says the band's name and the radio stations name): "This is [band's name] and you're listening to..."
3. If the ad sounds terrible, has bad audio, or is too busy, do not hesitate to tell the sales rep. If they flip out, hang up and don't pay. Move along to another station. It is not a burnt bridge if you are polite and then do not agree to pay the final payment.
4. Write your audio ad out yourself, with a headliner, and a theme or funny saying to catch people's attention. Then add all the dates, times and locations of the venue, the artists involved and any freebies or discounts available. The public loves this.
5. Decide the songs you want to be behind your ad voice and where exactly the music will come in and fade out. Do not leave it to the radio station. They will screw up somewhere, because they do not know your band or your mind.
6. Send the promo ad with your press release and EPK to radio stations, bloggers, publicists and record company A&R reps.

Stage Presence

1. Come up with a list of all the things you would like to say to your audience.
2. Make a list of ten ways to tell your audience this information without speaking (singing, jokes, acting skits, hand gestures, someone else speaking, etc.)
3. Practice your banter between songs, in front of a mirror.
4. Practice a few ways to introduce a song in front of a mirror.
5. Create an iconic walk from the backstage to the stage.

6. Have a slideshow or video playing behind or beside the band. That video can have pictures or videos of random stuff that highlights the songs, the recording process with the band in the studio, or other material for boring parts.

ONLINE DISTRIBUTION:

After finally getting two albums fully mixed and mastered, it was time to put the stuff online. I thought this would be easy and fun. But boy was I wrong! It is such a hassle to put music online. Everything is expensive and fragile. Maybe uploading files on SoundCloud is fun, but to get serious in the industry and to do what record labels and agents would be doing for your music, is an entirely different ball game.

Spotify only accepts music filtered from a distribution site like CD Baby. The latter has a person go through rigorous screening and documentation just to get an album on their site. You have to make biographies, album art, perfectly formatted 44.1 kHz, 16-bit uploads, then ICRCS, contract agreements and barcodes. Then they take almost half of the profit off every unit sold, on top of the registration fee to join and upload one album. At roughly one hundred dollars, the fee is way too high. Then finally, after sending them documentation and getting the shrink-wrapped physical copies from the manufacturer, CD Baby demanded me to send them five units to start with. That cost me twenty dollars to ship from Shoppers Drug Mart. So in total, I will make about two dollars a CD. Thanks, CD Baby and an untrustworthy scam of a system for musicians!

For online sales, plays, clicks and other interactions, make sure your publicist, manager and label are familiar with royalty tracking. Register with SOACN and BMI to make sure you are getting the passive income you deserve.

After all this, sometimes I felt that it was better to do this all in a yard sale, instead of the burden of all these online sales. If you have a family member, friend or manager who is fine with sitting at the computer all day and promoting the album, then great, because it is way too much to be a musician, who writes, edits and performs everything and then goes online for hours. It will catch up with the artist and band and actually take away from the music itself.

There are many ways to sell an album. Merch tables are an obvious choice. The Internet (i.e. online sales, iTunes, etc.) is the busiest market now, but another overlooked market is the consignment segment. Consignment is actually better for you if you are of mid-level popularity. Another great market I found during my smaller tours was the untapped markets in small towns and northern parts of Canadian provinces. Native reserves, powwows and colleges always have huge untapped markets full of fans waiting to discover you.

ITUNES - Requires membership, Gracenote data details and more payments to put it on their site, too. For a system that is supposed to be user-friendly and has worldwide availability, it is very glitchy, time-consuming and not cost-effective.

SPAM - Try not to join too many list serves and music publications, or you will get thousands of unwanted junk emails from everyone and their grandma, telling you about some shitty band coming to town or some effect pedal (which you will never use) that just came out. Avoid ANNOYING EMAIL HITS FROM RANDOM MUSIC GARBAGE and avoid online bombardments.

SPOTIFY - This service is vital for promoting your music, but it is a pain in the ass. It is expensive to go through CD Baby, then you have to send them documents, register everything, have proper formatted songs, then when all is said and done, you have to literally send them hard copy CDs to a random address in Ohio. The postage cost is almost the same amount as the profit you will make off the CDs themselves. So annoying. But at least, it gives you an inventory to sell CDs out of. This will all take you about a week.

TICKETFLY - This service is one of the most annoying online music services I know. I thought it would be easy to get a local concert on their website for people to buy tickets in advance. The truth is, the venue themselves must register, and an independent band has a very hard time to do this for the venue themselves. Ticketmaster is for big acts, but where is the middle man for the emerging smaller acts?

VINYL - A great medium for already established artist with a fan base that loves the nostalgic records. Not a good medium for emerging artist, because a production on vinyl costs three times as much as one on CD. And who is going to buy a vinyl, which can cost between forty and fifty dollars, of a nascent band? Maybe one fan out of a hundred will.USB sticks are a safer, cheaper, technological and savvy alternative. You're welcome!

RADIO AIR & ARTIST PR- Provides credits for new artists to get radio air time on satellite radio stations. But after using them for a year, I found out that it is a scam run by an online company, which barely promotes any new artists. They spend more time and money hooking new artists to sign up than they do promoting artists, who have already signed up.

FEEDSPOT–This is a good place to find bloggers and get press releases out to the public and media companies. However, be careful. They will try to downgrade you to a mere customer, as well by constantly bombarding you with other artists' info, instead of helping you become famous. In short, get a publicist to spend weeks and months handling those responsibilities for you or your band. This will take some weight off your shoulders.

HOW TO PRACTICE...

Guitar

1. The most efficient way to hold the guitar is to economize on space and movement.
2. Learn why your basic chords are shaped like they are first and what notes are in them.
3. Do string skipping exercises.
4. Learn scales - choose only what you need (There are hundreds of scales).
5. Practice sequences for every scale. You will find that sixths and fourths are the hardest, because of string skipping or rolling of the fingers.
6. Do spider stretch exercises on the guitar, or on a flat surface, when you do not have a guitar handy.
7. Stretch your fingers every day.
8. Learn new chords.
9. Learn new chord voicings (open chords, inversions).
10. Learn arpeggios to chords (minor, major, diminished triad, the dominant seventh chord, etc.).
11. If you prefer bass guitar, practice how to do octaves and slapping.
12. Learn how to practically apply theory to chords such as add 9's and add 7's.
13. Once you feel comfortable repeating patterns using the alternate picking methods, start to learn riffs from your personal ear, guitar books or online.
14. Practice finger picking and sweep picking according to your style of play.
15. Learn soloing techniques that add colour to your playing, such as hammer-ons, pull-offs, trills, bends, slides and more.
16. Solo to backing tracks to practice soloing.

Singing

1. Find a vocal coach either in real life to be paid or online in free videos.
2. Lip rolls.
3. Lips trills (if you can do them).
4. Do circular scale vocal exercises, such as "Goog", "La Ga", "Yah Yah", and "Uh Uh".
5. Don't eat spicy or overly creamy foods.
6. Vocal fry.
7. Drink tea.
8. Stay healthy and exercise.

9. Learn the difference between chest, head and falsetto voice. Don't scream notes at the top of your register to avoid vocal damage.
10. Sing to a simple vocal melody using sheet music to learn the basics of sight reading.
11. Sing your favourite songs on a low volume.

Drums

1. Stretch your whole body.
2. Get familiar with the drum kit and your position sitting around it.
3. Practice on the snare first, until it feels comfortable to move on to new things.
4. Buy a beat pad you can practice on anytime or a pillow to practice harder timings.
5. Learn what are paradiddles and paradiddle diddles. Learn to alternate between left and right hands doing them gradually at faster tempos.
6. Practice ghost notes on different beats of the bar (on the 1,2,3,4 etc.).
7. Practice to different BPMs on a metronome from 60-160 is a good start.
8. Get comfortable with different grooves.
9. Practice creative rolls. It doesn't have to go from snares to toms to cymbals. Switch it up.
10. Learn and practice to keep the kick pedal independent of the groove.
11. Learn different styles with different sticks, like brushes, pallets, etc.
12. Build hand speed using strength and economy of movement as a technique.
13. Explore quintuplets.
14. Manoeuvre around the kit with fills and combos, increasing your chops within the groove.
15. Only until you get good with one pedal should you explore double kick pedal.

Piano

1. Learn scales - choose only what you need (There are hundreds of scales).
2. Stretch fingers every day.
3. Learn new chords.
4. Learn new chord voicings (open chords, inversions).
5. Learn to make the left and right hands independent in timing.
6. Learn arpeggios to chords (minor, major, diminished triad, dominant seventh chord, etc.).
7. Play to backing tracks to practice soloing.
8. Learn to read music, start with basics, then take exams Grade 1,2,3 Harmony & Counterpoint.

True Teachers on YouTube

- Eric Arceneaux of AApproach.
- Justin Stoney of New York Vocal Coaching.
- Brett Manning of Singing Success.
- Marty Schwartz.
- Steve Stine.
- And my favourite, Guitar God, Andrew Wasson of Creative Guitar Studio.

Show Preparation Checklist:

1. Strings changed and tuned. Have spare strings and a capo, just in case.
2. Make sure the patch cable is not dangling and does not keep pulling out. Failing to do so can cause no sound if you accidently step on it. Moreover, the sound system can't provide a direct line.
3. Tap or place patch chords around your guitar strap to be secure and out of the way.
4. Check all guitar pedals for batteries and power.
5. Check all amp settings.
6. Have multiple guitar pictures in your pocket for safe keeping spares.
7. Stretch your fingers to avoid injury.
8. Have a piano song, or a back-up song, in case a string breaks on stage.
9. Have a friend or roadie prepared to restring a guitar on short notice.
10. Have a funny story or banter to buy time, if a string breaks, an amp pops or a drum skin breaks.
11. Do some vocal warm-ups (lip rolls and vocal fry) thirty minutes before going on stage.
12. Go for a run, walk or jump around to get your heartbeat elevated one hour before the stage time.
13. Make sure clothing is not too tight, unless it is part of a gimmick.
14. Make sure you have all merchandizes, float and a merchandize table area ready.
15. Make sure you have a door man, host/greeter, MC, security guard, merchandize table rep, musicians, sound guy and hype fans, who will jump around and hype others during the show.
16. Make sure to book with a venue that will promote your show on their website, have similar acts play there and are easy to communicate with.
17. Tune drum kit skins.
18. Put a pillow or blanket in the kick drum to muffle the vibration.
19. Double check all instruments.

20. Go to the back of the venue, while your band plays, and hear how it sounds for yourself. If something feels or sounds off, tell the sound guy or venue owner ASAP.

Great Performances Have:

1. A great set with the dynamics of loud and soft sections.
2. Great guest musicians (horns, classical, a different genre).
3. Great connection with the audience.
4. Combinations of new material and familiar favourites.
5. A strong light show that compliments the songs.
6. A mystery, not letting the coming audience know what exactly they're getting into.
7. A funny or interesting entrance (e.g. Kurt Cobain wheel chaired onto the stage).
8. A good show, no matter how many people come, is pivotal to launching a career.
9. A good vibe.
10. A good dress code.
11. A good sex appeal.
12. A good sound guy.
13. A good backdrop.
14. Good energy.
15. A buzz before the show.
16. Some media present.
17. The venue (meaningful like Folsom Prison).
18. A stadium of fans singing every word and screaming "I Love You".
19. Showmanship.
20. A funny gimmick (*The Tingler* - Vincent Price).

Chapter 35: Stay Healthy

Don't blow your money on blow

There is a rampant epidemic in the music industry to do cocaine. The reason is that the industry gatekeepers make everything so fast-paced to weed out the amateurs that no human being can keep up with them for a sustained period of time. Many people turn to cocaine to keep that high energy, to continue to feel confident and to schmooze with their idols. Even producers and audio engineers, who have a deadline for a song or album and have listened to a song a hundred times to the point of insanity, have to push on, so they do a line of the white. Do you blame them?

Don't blow your money on blowjobs

If you are a real star, the ladies will line up at your hotel room's door. If you do not get this, be careful about your sex life. You do not want people to find out you spend all your money on whores, because you can't get your own for free. I am not saying don't splurge a little. But if it gets in the way of waking up in the mornings, performing or looking at your wife in the eyes, then stop, recalibrate and find a new way to refresh. Hookers are fun. But if you need them to have fun, you are no fun. People love to associate celebrities, especially fresh emerging ones, with child molestation, rape, human trafficking and adultery. Have fun, pay the ladies you choose very well, have contracts, have respect and keep it hush-hush. Enough said, you horny dog. There is a reason Shaq never had adultery charges and Kobe Bryant did.

Don't blow your money on friends and family

Yes, it is nice to show off to the friends and family, who said that you would never achieve what you have now, but be careful. As Cypress Hill once said, "that first single don't last very long".

Invest to blow up

Invest in something not related to music, such as real estate, stocks and companies; not in pipe dreams or drug dealing. You are all so welcome for this priceless advice from someone, who did all the hard work before you had to. I have jammed a lifetime of knowledge into a quick chapter.

Haters Blow Me

Everyone is a pro at dealing with haters these days. Any criticism is a hater. Any advice is a hater. Anything negative is a hater. What kind of delusion is the next generation on? It is funny. Someone will adamantly hate a hater rather than go and make fun of someone else where that other person sees them as a hater. I hate it. During my whole life, I have been dealing with the most hate-filled haters around. I always got people with either a little hatred in their eyes or extreme aloofness to the point of being condescending. Those people always had a little snide remark, saying:

"Hey bud, if you didn't make it, you know, you probably weren't good enough, or didn't have enough chops, or sorry bud, guess you didn't have the right connections."

Like somehow everything I did wasn't right, when I was a lot more talented than most the people on the radio, who honestly don't have to work as hard as most to getmuch more than they deserve. Ironically, the people telling me that I wasn't good enough or didn't have the right chops are the same people, who didn't make it and kiss the asses of the people, who did. Worst off, they are usually the old gatekeepers that had a tiny bit of success in the 1970s, when it was easy. Now, they just hang on this, holding it over people's heads. To make things worse, I experienced teachers in school, who not only tried to discourage me and take my confidence, but also tried to steal my scripts and chord progressions.

To be honest, someone who has truly made it, looks back, doesn't say anything negative and says: "Wow man, it's a dog fight, I barely made it through, and I really hope you do, too."

The industry didn't want me to get famous, maybe because I was a little chubby, or because I had a criminal record, or because I was from a poor family, or because maybe one day I was having a rough singing day and couldn't hit the high note. Whatever it was, there was no support from my family or friends and especially not the music industry.

Stay Healthy

Many stars in both acting and music burn out and then have mental problems. The worst part about this is that the industry will not let them fully deal with those problems. A slightly struggling artist is easier to exploit and manipulate. Remember, the people giving you orders cannot do what you do. If you are feeling burnt out or dealing with issues from the past that keep rearing their ugly heads, take some time off. Trust me, the industry will make you feel like if you take time off, your chance will pass you by. That is a lie. The world will always wait for you, especially if you will be more effective when you return. Plead with them to "give you one more chance" if you have to. When you take some time off, truly heal. Heal your voice from drugs, go to therapy, get a personal trainer and start to get back in shape.

Chapter 36: Mixing Genres

Mixing Genres Are Good

In our day and age, people will listen to various types of music and genres. Mixing music style can be very fun, refreshing and awesome, if done well. Look at bands like Rage Against the Machine and Linkin Park. They were the pioneers and forefathers of Nu metal or as I like to refer to it, Rap Rock. Rage specialized in heavy chord progressions and politically charged anti-government lyrics. Linkin Park, on the other hand, perfected melodic piano riffs with metal guitars and Asian-style hip hop beats. If one of those bands were to add horns or acoustic guitars, it may have all gone south. Many artists, myself included, find the joy in music and instruments so much that we try to incorporate too much into one song instead of leaving certain instruments for only one song at time.

If you can choose a genre and stick to it, the industry and fans will allow you to deviate tastefully from your chosen genre for the music's sake. For example, the band Dream Theatre may be fully seen as a metal band. However, if you randomly skip to the middle of one of their songs, they sound like a folk band, or a piano singer songwriter. There are many dynamics in their songs and many genre crossings.

Fans will, however, come to expect a certain sound from you, from which you can deviate slightly. Nevertheless, do it too much, and they'll just drop you and find a band in the same genre. Some of the greatest sounding bands look like a generic copy of themselves, pieced together by some image consultant for a record label. Take the instrumental band, Polyphia. They are musical geniuses. But they all literally have the same haircuts, the same comb-overs and the same dark-sweaters-under-jean-jacket look. They look like brothers or generic replicas. It is like every church youth group I have ever seen, which got some money from their parents and decided to form a band. They had it so easy. Fucking "emo" musicians baffle me.

*Furthermore, what is with this enslavement of genre categorization anyway? I remember when you went to a record store and you only had a choice between:

Country	R&B
Rock	Classical
Hard Rock	Dance
Metal	World
Hip Hop	and Pop

Those were the days...

Now there is...

- Art Punk
- Alternative Rock
- Thrash
- Experimental Rock
- Folk Punk
- Goth / Gothic Rock
- Grunge
- Hardcore Punk
- Hard Rock
- Indie Rock
- New Wave
- Progressive Rock
- Punk
- Shoegaze
- Steampunk
- Acoustic Blues
- Chicago Blues
- Classic Blues
- Contemporary Blues
- Country Blues
- Delta Blues
- Electric Blues
- Avant-Garde
- Baroque
- Chamber Music
- Chant
- Choral
- Contemporary Classical
- Classical
- Opera
- Orchestral
- Alternative Country
- Bluegrass
- Contemporary Country
- Country Gospel
- Country Pop
- Traditional Country
- Dance
- Club / Club Dance
- Breakcore
- Breakbeat / Breakstep
- Brostep
- Chillstep
- Deep House
- Dubstep
- Electro House
- Glitch Hop
- Glitch Pop
- Hardcore
- Eurodance
- House
- Jungle / Drum'n'bass
- Liquid Dub
- Regstep
- Techno
- Trance
- Trap

- Bop
- Lounge
- Swing
- 2-Step
- Ambient
- Crunk
- Electro
- Electronica
- Electronic Rock
- Industrial
- Trip Hop
- Alternative Rap
- Dirty South
- Gangsta Rap
- Hip-Hop
- Latin Rap
- Old School Rap
- Rap
- Underground Rap
- West Coast Rap
- Indie Pop
- Christian Metal
- Christian Pop
- Christian Rap
- Christian Rock
- Contemporary Gospel
- Gospel
- Praise & Worship
- Instrumental
- J-Pop
- J-Rock
- Acid Jazz
- Avant-Garde Jazz
- Bebop
- Big Band
- Contemporary Jazz
- Dixieland
- Fusion
- Latin Jazz
- Mainstream Jazz
- Ragtime
- Smooth Jazz
- K-Pop
- Latin
- Alternativo & Rock Latino
- Bossa Nova
- Contemporary Latin
- Flamenco / Spanish Flamenco
- Pop Latino
- Reggaeton y Hip-Hop
- Salsa y Soca
- New Age
- Meditation
- NatureRelaxation
- Adult Contemporary
- Britpop
- Bubblegum Pop

- Dance Pop
- Dream Pop
- Electro Pop
- Pop/Rock
- Contemporary R&B
- Disco
- Doo Wop
- Funk
- Modern Soul
- Motown
- Neo-Soul
- Soul
- Reggae
- Dancehall
- Ska
- Acid Rock
- Adult Alternative
- Alternative Rock
- Arena Rock
- Blues-Rock
- British Invasion
- Death Metal / Black Metal
- Glam Rock
- Gothic Metal
- Hair Metal
- Hard Rock
- Math Metal
- Metal
- Metal Core
- Jam Bands
- Post Punk
- Prog-Rock/Art Rock
- Progressive Metal
- Psychedelic
- Rock & Roll
- Surf Rock
- Singer/Songwriter
- Contemporary Folk
- Indie Folk
- Musicals
- Soundtrack
- Spoken Word
- Chicano
- A cappella
- Barbershop
- Gregorian Chant
- World
- Africa
- Afro-Beat
- Asia
- Calypso
- Celtic
- France
- Hindustani
- Indian Pop
- Japanese Pop
- Polka

*I don't even know what genre I am anymore.

Mixing Genres Is Bad

With diversity comes confusion. People enjoy knowing and anticipating what they are going to hear. Yes, people in hip hop will stomach a bit of rock and vice versa. But if you try to stretch their preferences too far, you will not be picked up by a label. That's because the honchos of a given label will see your style as a liability for sales. Besides, you will lose your fans to confusion and whimsical scepticism.

This happened to me at my show at The Mock Club. Too many genres, not enough fans.

Maybe you think all those genres are better, since it more accurately places musicians with like-minded sounds and fans. I understand you can't label the Dave Matthews Band, Moist and Disturbed as merely rock, because they are so different. Nevertheless, if you keep referencing bands to the point of marginalizing them, it gives them only a very small niche. Like when someone asks me if I like pop, I would say I like Bieber and Beyonce. But if someone refines his or her question by asking me if I like bubblegum pop, I would probably say no. There are too many categories that people now actually have what is called a "paradox of choice". This is defined as the possibility for people to stay in their comfort zone more easily, rather than learning new bands and styles. In life that is fine, I guess, but not in music. Embrace something new. Isn't that how you found your favourite band? It is just similar to going to the drug store to buy a tube of toothpaste. Twenty years ago, you used to go and see three or four brand names. Then, you picked what you liked. Now, you go and there are five hundred different choices with different features. You almost feel sick about being wrong, so it makes choosing one actually harder. The same thing is happening with the music industry. People are actually not even buying one tube of toothpaste at all.

Chapter 37: Unique Gigs

VIA Train Musician

I once had a gig, for a summer, playing guitar as a singer/songwriter on the national trains between Winnipeg and Vancouver. I loved that job. Every afternoon, I had to play two sets that lasted forty-five minutes each. I played for both first class and coach passengers. I met so many great people who were either trying to start a new life in a new city, just visiting different parts of Canada as tourists or living adventures as retirees.

Each one of my shows was completely planned by me. This became one of the best practice/rehearsal times I have ever had. I was able to practice new material, and gauge how spectators, from different walks of life, reacted to each one of my songs. It was like getting paid to practice in an intimate setting for larger shows in the future. I also got used to the train's cars consistently rocking along with people coming and going in-between sets. Usually, a show would have about twenty people present at any given time, but by the end of the three-day trip, everyone would have heard and appreciated at least one of my songs.

My designed sets would go like this:

I usually dimmed the lights and had a candle on the table. As for instruments, I kept an acoustic guitar, a keyboard and a bongo. For my last couple of trips, I would even use a backing track of my own chord progressions when I got really good. I loved playing acoustic versions of my songs. The most loved songs of mine would make up my set. I had a keyboard for specific songs that reached people of any age, such as *Light One Candle, Change, Secret Cities* and *Strength in Identity.* I would also do special songs for special occasions, such as birthdays and famous covers. I would mix covers with my original tunes to create a pleasant unpredictability. Covers included anything from *Another Brick in The Wall, Wish You Were Here,* parts of *Bohemian Rhapsody,* Eric Clapton's *Layla,* Oasis' *Wonderwall* and *Don't Look Back In Anger,* to Our Lady Peace, Tracy Chapman, The Police, Johnny Cash, Elvis, Buffy Sainte-Marie, John Denver, The Beatles, Nickelback, Silverchair, Nirvana, R.E.M, Radiohead, and even Robert Johnson.

An average set would look like this:

Set # 1:

Intro with a stand-up comedy routine, while lighting the candle.

Launchpads

Dive

Find it for Yourself

Wonderwall & Don't Look back In Anger (Oasis)

Roxanne& Message in a Bottle (The Police)

Hold Your Hand & Yesterday (The Beatles)

SmokeStop

Sixteen

Treemen

Best Ones

Folkume Prison Blues & Ring Of Fire (Cash)

Talkin' About a Revolution (Chapman)

Heartbreak Hotel &All Shook Up (Elvis)

Light One Candle (Piano Song)

Meet Again

For the last two or three songs, I would usually ask someone to come accompany me on the bongos. This usually got the crowd excited for the ending. For the closing moment, I would thank the audience, collect tips, and ask for special requests for people having dinner. I would tell a couple of jokes and then give an invitation to the next show in a couple of hours.

Set #2

A Gift

Comedy Sketch about the Electric Car

CarBones

Wish You Were Here (Pink Floyd)

Layla (Clapton)

Squirrels and Sparrows

Into My World

Losing My Religion (R.E.M)

With or Without You (U2)

Spies (Coldplay)

Starwalker (Buffy Sainte-Marie)

Burning Dido

Waiting On A Train

I Wonder (Sixto Rodriguez)

Take Me Home, Country Roads (John Denver)

Dust in the Wind (Kansas)

Simon & Garfunkel (Mrs. Robinson)

Sorry (Bieber)

Strength In Identity (Piano Song)

My Country

Good Knight

Sometimes, if it was later in the evening, and the crowd was a younger crowd of student travelers, I would perform acoustic versions of some of my hip hop songs such as *Indoctrination, Fly with Me, Note H, White Rabbit Ninja,* and even *Lonely West*. I would throw in covers that were more risky for the younger crowds, because most of the time, they were drunk. Those sets would be free, but I usually made the best fans, connections, networks and tips. Years later, I still talk to some of those younger travellers. Moreover, they often come to my shows or keep in touch on social media. One free show would usually be something like:

Free Set:

Intro: Jokes about the train

Indoctrination

Fly With Me

Note H

Bulls On Parade (Rage)

White Rabbit Ninja

Creep (Radiohead)

4am (OLP)

Emotional Retards

Drain You & On A Plain(Nirvana)

Savin' Me (Nickelback)

Here Without You (3 Doors Down)

With Arms Wide Open& What's This Life For (Creed)

Lonely West

My Country

Good Knight

Meet Again

Wonderwall (Oasis)

A night of drinking, jokes and occasionally sex.

Powwow Gigs

When I was still in poverty, I went to an amazing powwow in Brandon, Manitoba. It had great Aboriginal dancers, drummers, musicians, food, vendors, and was very well organized. Many people from around the province joined, and the traditional dancers wearing bustles were just amazing. I wanted to just buy a hand-carved drum, go on stage and beat the drum with the country singer during the half time show. They needed a drummer. Everyone was eating and busy. I was so poor that I couldn't afford the fifty dollars for the hand drum and twenty dollars for the handle. I just sat there watching and planning. I saw how I could better any powwow. I could have a band play for free or at minimal cost to the venue, bringing more people to the actual powwow, via my music. Then to assure that I was not the focal point, I could design my set to be very traditional and Native-like, with Native big drummers and singers backing me up on a few of the starting songs. Then later in the set, I could have the traditional dancers come out onto the floor and dance to a few of my tunes. Finally, as we were playing, I would get my assistant to buy a bunch of clothing, artwork and accessories (dream-catchers, drums, etc.) from the vendors at the back, and I would throw all the gifts to the crowd on my final song to complete my portion of the show. Then, I would quickly have the MC move into another section of the powwow, and I would nonchalantly slip out the back to stand by my own merchandize table, selling albums and swag bags and giving a few away for free. I would also sign free autographs with every purchase. Then, after a couple hours, I would quietly leave out the back, showing my final respects to the participants and organizers.

My Set List would be:

<table>
<tr><td>Set # 1:</td><td>Set # 2:</td></tr>
<tr><td>My Country</td><td>A Gift</td></tr>
<tr><td>Treemen</td><td>One Day In June</td></tr>
<tr><td>Indoctrination</td><td>Burning Dido</td></tr>
<tr><td>Launchpads</td><td>Best One's</td></tr>
<tr><td>Find It For Yourself</td><td>Birthdays</td></tr>
<tr><td>Close Encounter</td><td>Lonely West</td></tr>
<tr><td>CarBones</td><td>Change</td></tr>
<tr><td>Light One Candle</td><td>Bright Lights</td></tr>
<tr><td>Strength In Identity</td><td>New Legacy</td></tr>
<tr><td>Missing Angels</td><td>Better Left Unsaid</td></tr>
<tr><td>Meet Again</td><td>Good Knight</td></tr>
<tr><td>Break Time</td><td></td></tr>
</table>

Chapter 38: Flake

I never really got into Drake, but I never disliked him, until I started doing research on him. Drake is not all loving and caring to new Toronto rappers. Instead, he stifles the city. Drake had a decade long campaign to convince young Torontonians that he is the official poster boy for Toronto's music scene. The truth is he was nothing but a well-managed gimmick, created, maintained and promoted to bombard the airwaves until every single secondary student knew every single song, and listen to something else was seen as blasphemies. It is like he and his well-educated industry devils have successfully brainwashed the youth with auto tune and redundant lyrics. Maybe people like to have sex to his music, but when was the last time he did anything really meaningful for Toronto? I mean something that was uncomfortable or hard for him to truly show his love for the city. When was the last time he donated to missing Native women or a food bank in Toronto? No! Instead, Drake claims he put Toronto on the map by going to every Toronto Raptors' game. What a selfish rapper! Drake stifles the city. He doesn't heal it. I'll never forget when Kevin Durant said he doesn't "give a fuck about no Drake night"! Then, he went off and won the NBA title.

Drake has got to be the luckiest SOB around. Drake will murder you if you don't do the music route his way. Drake is not trying to inspire new young rappers. He is pointing down from the mountain top ready to snuff out any competition. We could hear him shout: "It's my hill!" To be honest, I heard a whack story once that I would not doubt has some truth to it.

Supposedly, there was this rapper from Jane & Finch, once a low-income neighbourhood of Toronto that is gradually becoming dominated by Vietnamese immigrants. He was a phenomenal rapper with no capital, and not a big crew. Supposedly, Drake heard about this guy and offered to take him aboard. Obviously, the thing was a setup. Drake only felt threatened by this guy's talent and thought he might bump him out of the Toronto's Best Rapper spot. Drake's crew sent this guy down to a show in Detroit, a place they knew was shady. But they paid all inclusive, so the guy didn't know. Next thing you know, there is a beef between Drake's crew, the promoters and some mafia dudes. Well, the rapper from Jane & Finch got taken into the back alley, supposedly mistaken identity and had the shit kicked out of him so bad by Drake's entourage that he was left paralyzed. Drake, the kid in the wheelchair in *Degrassi: The Next Generation* is now putting kids in wheelchairs. Isn't it ironic? Come to Manitoba, Drake. I'll knock you out at the corner of Portage and Main. Evil people hide behind the world's mistakes! Drake is a Flake!

Here are a few articles that may change your opinion about the most popular rapper of this decade.

1) https://nationalpost.com/news/toronto/drakes-company-loses-trademark-dispute-over-exclusive-use-of-torontos-6ix-

nickname?fbclid=IwAR0uZPC36e6Jmk7KI3k1choQmsimlc34bZkaydzSBaVdXEfqfLm8zvZD5
Xo

2) https://www.thestar.com/entertainment/2016/04/06/city-employee-claims-drake-bullied-him-
after-he-snapped-pictures-of-famous-rapper-getting-off-
helicopter.html?fbclid=IwAR0JhW3cR33GR96xIwmDQHxIAmyKyjDSIRldRNMg7JwIKBkc_
KXQ58Tf5sI

3) https://www.thestar.com/news/crime/2017/09/25/questions-raised-about-the-company-drake-
keeps.html?fbclid=IwAR0X0FmnPtUs1M4uDS842P5ciC58ajYlCabgTbguReXGAsgvz_RPdl4a
_O4

Chapter 39: Song Synapses

I am glad you have made it this far. By now, you know who I am and what I like to write about. As a little reward for tolerating my endless rants, I will give you a chapter that will explain the reasoning behind all my albums' titles, song names and the lyrics to many of my popular songs. No one in the world knows this information except you and I, and I hope that it makes listening to your favourite one of my songs even more memorable now.

Burning Jerusalem: The Metal /Progressive Rock Album

Why Burning Jerusalem?

Many people might question the motives and meaning of this album title. To some, it may be controversial and it may be offensive, especially in our current political atmosphere. The point is that the music creates a story. To be honest, the name has nothing to do with a specific race or religion. Instead, it has everything to do with what is sacred in general. Years ago, while I was composing those songs, I came across a news article on terrorism and violence murdering innocent people in churches, synagogues and mosques around the world. In a fit of rage, I screamed out: "Why don't they just bomb Jerusalem, Mecca and the Pyramids, while they're at it? Blow up Niagara Falls, too, assholes. Just destroy the most sacred places on Earth until there's nothing left. Maybe then these needless bombings will stop. No one cares about the sacred anymore!" My band was all lounging around our studio and stopped what they were doing in shock, when I blasted this out. They immediately said I should name the album *Burning Jerusalem*, and maybe even have "I heart BJ's" on a t-shirt. Well, the Toronto Blue Jays already stole that idea. Hence, *Burning Jerusalem* was born! This album is a journey through the past, present and future, and I hope that to you it will become sacred as well!

 1) Burning Assholes: Started as a love ballad actually, and then turned into a slightly jazzy song with metal undertones. While I was living in a youth shelter, going a bit crazy in my mind, I met an insane Korean kid, who kind of inspired me to write this song. This song is directed at all the asshole gatekeepers in the entertainment industry that don't know how to share. They are usually only tough to the point of a dog's impulsiveness, until you slam your fist on the table and say:"I'm fucking you up outside." Then, they all turn into pussies, because, let's face it, sound guys, directors, camera guys and producers are not running the track or pumping the iron every day. Ironically, *Burning Assholes* is the first song on my first released album. As you will later find out, all the recordings and albums were done in the reverse order. The album *Shadows and Machines* should have been released first, as I wrote all this material in the early 2000s.

2) Dreams: Came up with this metal riff, while trying to write a jazz song. Once I made the motif lead guitar part for the chorus, I was hooked. It is definitely one of the harder rock songs I have made.

3) Dog Walkers: Tired of the noisy neighbours always lurking around your house and the public parks? Tired of people spying on everything you are doing, hiding behind the fact that their dog has to take a piss? One day I was jogging, and some Rottweiler came running up beside me, biting at my legs. I turned around in order to kick the dog in the face, and the owner ran over to fight me. "I've had enough," I screamed at the guy. "I am sick of loser people taking their dogs around with no leash, and no respect!" Seriously, those owners treat those dirty dogs better than their own kids! Then, they get defensive, when people flip out at how their dog shits everywhere and animals keep intimidating our children. Dog Walkers always come around like they own the streets and parks. I have a neighbour, who has the loudest dog I have ever heard. The mutt barks when I am just trying to do some exercise in my backyard. When I scream "shut the fuck up", the neighbour pouts and takes the dog inside.

4) Into My World: A beautiful Jazz song with one of the nicest chord progressions I have ever come up with. I wrote this song, while dating a wonderful Japanese girl, and we used to always laugh hysterically at how cheesy the lyrics as well as the melody were. She said that it would be my most famous song, LOL.

5) Burning Dido: I won't tell too much about this epic story, because I actually want you, dear readers, to go research who the real Dido was and why she lit herself on fire. Hint: the only country to ever defeat Rome!

6) Lies: This song was one of the most intense experiences I have ever felt, while writing a song. It was like a counselling session with many troubling truths finally being stated. It was actually a song of pain, as the lyrics kind of yell truths at my parents. In general, my parents lied to me about music...period! Lyrics include: "Worst mother, cock block, worst father, crack head."

7) Noah's Song: It's like watching a movie, with Russell Crowe.

8) Emotional Retards: Enough said, LMAO!

9) Burning Jobs: Almost like a dance song on a metal album...it was the only filler on the album... don't judge. However, I love this song. It has a catchy chorus that purposely doesn't rhyme. It is about the greatest time in my life, when I played sports all day made love all night.

10) Waiting on A Train: Came up with this awesome white trash rock riff, while watching Woody Harrelson in *Zombieland*. The song eventually progressed into multiple parts, including the call and answer section that I thought up while watching a Spanish busker on the TTC in Toronto. This busker seemed to play rhythm and lead guitar at the same time.

11) Strength in Identity: The best piano song I have. It took me a while to write and perfect it. I really am proud of this one. I got a cool hillbilly guitar player from Seneca College to play an iconic riff on it, which sounds like Carlos Santana. It is a real pretty song.

12) My Country: The only country song I have ever written. I had to for a class at Seneca College. Even after being forced to re-write it, I made this masterpiece. It has really profound lyrics about Western films. I broke some hearts writing this one.

Hidden Song: The Citadel: This is a cultural appropriation historical song, about the Mayan temples. It is a bit of a joke song, which features the automaton.

New Legacy - Hip Hop Album

1) Bright Lights: I wrote this song after speaking to a Nigerian friend about hardships in Africa. Then the same friend made the beat for me- and I added guitars along with vocals. The song turned out to be one of my best, and can be applied to other poverty stricken communities as well (e.g. Native Reserves).

2) Light up This Track: This song was made in a day. Sometimes the best things happen quickly. I wish all of life were like that.

3) Kush: Needed a song for the potheads. Kush is a banger with a real cool trap beat.

4) Hollywood Harmony: I love the rain SFX and the melancholy beat at the beginning. This song has a special place in my heart, and has one of the nicest vocal choruses I have ever written. Move over, Chester Bennington (I wrote that last sentence before he committed suicide and I decided to keep it).

5) The Truth: My Eminem diss, that I hope doesn't get me killed. The rap game is terrible. Egos, idiots, pimps and PhDs, I honestly was so fed up with all the whining and lyrics that are just pointless. So I let Wab Kinew and Eminem have a piece of my mind. The song is pretty raw! IN THE END, BEEFING WITH EMINEM MADE ME FAMOUS ANYWAYS! That's just like Machine Gun Kelly.

6) Lonely West: Also a song made in a day. It was an assignment for school, which consisted in writing a country song, and my friend was a rapper. He begged me to help him, because writing a country song was not his forte. So we made a country rap song. It's a mellow banger.

7) New Legacy: A wicked beat I made with midi horns, and NBA sound FXs. I then came up with a really unique rapping style. I am glad I named the album after this song.

8) Note H:I wrote this song for my friend George, who went to jail for two years for lighting a school bus on fire. I know that makes him sound nuts, but honestly, he is a great guy, a great rapper, a clean soul, and an unlucky chap, who just allowed bad people to influence him. On top of that, he came from a broken home. One day, I was tutoring George in music theory and I asked: "What note comes after G sharp?"George responded H. Needless to say we died laughing.

9) Fly With Me: My favourite song on the album. The chord progression is amazing. Imagine Jamiroquai meets Nas, and it is definitely one of the singles for the album.

10) City Of Bones: I always have a bass heavy dance beat song as one filler. This is the one for this album. It is about Russia's history. My first two albums surprisingly have a lot of historical references.

11) White Rabbit Ninja: By far, the funniest song to play live. Many men like the power and uniqueness of this sound. It is also a hard song to replicate.

12) Better Left Unsaid: This song was also written in a day. The beat was one of my only songs created on Logic Pro. The latter is one application acting as your digital workstation and MIDI sequencer for the macOS operating system. I added live drums, live basslines and some wicked groovy lead guitar. If you have ever had problems talking with the opposite sex, listen to this song. Hidden Song: About the Great Wall of China!

Shadows and Machines - Rock Album

1) Launchpads: Actually, this song is the first song on the first album. I wanted a catchy chorus that was inspirational, but with a wicked metal sounding bridge. This song is like Linkin Park.

2) Dive: A song about paying rent in Toronto. I was so fed up with bait and switch ads, promising a "beautiful three-bedroom" only to hurt your eyes with a rundown halfway house. I got so angry once that I screamed at a landlord: "It's a DIVE!" Hence the hip hop rock song *Dive* came about. The chord progression for the verses is actually the first chord progression I have ever written, when I was fourteen years old.

3) Indoctrination: My Linkin Park metal hip hop version of a manifesto. The song is about questioning university and the learning processes in general. I love the lead guitar that sounds like Coldplay on a bassline that sounds like a 90's hip hop song.

4) Find it For Yourself: This song is actually the first song I have written, when I was fifteen. I was really into finger picking at the time, and the song was written to inspire society to not give into the temptation, peer pressure and hype of forced trends and to seek out the world.

5) SmokeStop: This is a really cool song that took me years to piece together from three different songs. The lyrics are profound, kind of like a rap in a metal song. The chorus melody is pretty catchy, but everyone just loves the melodic bridge in the middle. It has a double meaning: either stop smoking or go stop to have a smoke.

6) Sixteen: Kind of my angst song for teenagers, who are sick of their parents' bullshit advice. I sing pretty high in this song, and the chorus has a Dave Matthews feel. The bassline is what makes the song.

7) Treemen: The easiest song I have. It is the easiest to play live. Besides, *Treemen* is always a throwback to Tracy Chapman, Oasis and other acoustic folk hits. The song was my first music video, done entirely by myself, and talks about political issues such as deforestation, corruption and First Nations' proverbs. One of those proverbs is: "Only after the last tree has been cut down, will mankind find that money cannot be eaten."

8) Best Ones: I wrote this song for my friend Brad Barnes, who committed suicide. In fact, I was stuck on a lyric line once in my twenties, and I asked him to help. He leaned over and nonchalantly gave me the most incredibly obvious line to close the verse perfectly: "A team of heavily wheels circle around, put it back on, maybe it's time to let the king be crowned." The song is about why the world always tries to block and destroy the best ones, so it doesn't look bad.

9) Close Encounter: The band was named after this song. It is a political song about Native poverty and building an international community to share resources instead of war. I love the trance type dance beat in the chorus.

10) Band-Aids Over Bullet Holes: Now, normally I am not one for progressive emo type music, as it usually is like a wave that leads people into depression. Yet, the melodic melody and chord progression to this song are legendary. The lyrics were written on a beach, with an amazing bass player. This song will go down as one of the nicest sounding songs I have that is accompanied with some powerful lyrics.

11) Light One Candle: Every album has a bass heavy dance song. This is the best one I have. It was the first song I composed, produced, mixed and performed all by myself at Seneca College.

12) Meet Again: This song is a ballad. It was written to be performed in intimate settings and as a closing song for concerts. It is a beautiful song about losing a loved one. I always play it at funerals.

Hidden: Quest (To an intense destination) This song made me sweat while making it. It was hard to perform in the studio, and I hardly ever play it live. It reminds me of a few songs of the band Rush that were so hard to create that the band never played them again. What a Quest, there is only spoken word, trust me, worth listening to.

FunHole - Soft Rock

1) A Gift: This is the second simplest song I have written. I was playing in a church band at the time. You can tell by the chord progression and lyrics that it has a somewhat Christian feel. I spent countless hours making the basslines and lead guitar parts special to compensate for the simplistic rhythm guitar.

2) One Day in June: I wrote this kind of like a ballad, when I was listening to a lot of The Dave Matthews Band. However, when we started adding the basslines, the song turned into a fun dance rock song. I love playing this live, as it is challenging but fun to dance to.

3) CarBones: By far the most popular song on this album. I love the guitar intro, the catchy chorus, the swing bass lines and most of all, getting a chance to tell the story about the first Electric Car fiasco. The song is about the story of the E1. Research it yourself, you will hate the government and oil companies as much as I do.

4) Change: Every album has a piano song, and this is the catchiest. It is like a 90s R&B song done to a rock piano chord progression.

5) Fed Up (Just Hold Her):I wrote this song for a girl I allowed to get away. I was not mature enough or ready for commitment at the time, but when I look back I get so fed up with my insecurities that I wrote this song. I played this song for one of my loves and it made her cry, especially the line "just hold her".

6) Stick: When I wrote it, I intended to give birth to a ballad. But when I heard my boy rap on it, and put a sick beat to it, the song instantly became one of our best hip hop songs. You may ask why I kept it on this album and didn't put it on the *New Legacy* album. The truth is that I wanted to surprise people. I felt that this album already had enough rock and jazz, so I wanted to throwa curve ball song. If it is considered a filler song, then what a filler it is!

7) Good Knight: I really like the *Wonderwall* feel of this song. I wrote this song for a girl I met at the camp that I worked at, when I was going through one of the most peaceful times in my life. The lead motif riff in this song is so fun and catchy. It is no wonder that it became a single. It is also a great song to play at the end of a concert.

8) Squirrels and Sparrows: This song took awhile to write. Then, it almost got scratched. I eventually came up with a chord progression that sounded like *Layla* by Eric Clapton, and a drum beat that really pushed the song forward.

9) Birthdays: So I hope this song becomes a song that people play for each other on their birthdays. I wanted a humorous type song that was a bit tongue and cheek, like Jim Morrison and The Doors. I played this on the day of Merle Haggard's death in college. Of course, the teacher nearly had a fit, claiming that Mr. Haggard would be rolling in his grave if he knew I considered that a country song. I had to redo the assignment, and I used *My Country*. Fuck teachers.

10) Plastic Warehouse: Here, I had written a really funky, progressive bassline that I was going to establish a song around. I had really witty lyrics, but when I heard my rap friends rapping on it, I knew I had a hit. It is so funky rock/rap. It was supposed to be a rock song, but we made it a quick rap/rock song. The boys had a hell of a time trying to rap to this fast of a tempo.

11) PSalt/Solar Eclipse: This is the only time I have ever played one song into another while performing live. The song *PSalt* comes from the Bible, and *Solar Eclipse* was written around the same time as *PSalt.* I recorded *PSalt* in a friend's attic, when I was in my early twenties, and I almost added it to the *Shadows and Machines* album. Other songs beat it out. I like how those songs are kind of esoteric. One is about Jesus, and the other is about fame and handling fake people. Coincidence?

12) The Last Saint: I always wanted to write this song. It had many versions, but the chord progression always stayed the same. It is almost a funky ballad about the burdens of being a saint. I always believed that I was like a saint. I am not implying that I am better than others. I meant I have always had a strong moral compass and a sense of holding the world up on my shoulders like Atlas, the Titan from Greek mythology. Besides, I like the New Orleans Saints.

Hidden: Echoes in Eternity: This was written when I was into Spanish finger picking guitar. I wrote this challenging song and I wanted the lyrics, if there were any, to be very simple. It ended up being a perfect calming hidden song, based off of the line Russell Crowe uttered in *Gladiator*: "What we do in this life echoes in eternity."

Digging Deeper / Feeble Hands / Hydro

I am currently working on three albums of the best material I have ever written. *Digging Deeper* is a rock rap album like *New Legacy*. The next albums are on the drawing board. We have a few songs finished for them already. Songs like *Black Human Oil, Rain City Brats, Ghost Valley, Turbulence, Born Orphan, Sex@Sunrise, Secret Cities* and my favourite, *ColorBlind.*

Chapter 40: Thoughts On The Music Industry

The most successful and respected people are like mob bosses with no remorse. It is like this:

Intimidate the most people, fuck the most insecure women and you are king.

What does music have to do with this? That is why music now, especially rap and dance is so repetitive, intrusive and low-level energy. It has literally become the anthems for orgies between human animals and their disgusting sexual partners. Remember, the devil was a musician. That is why all the evil lurks in the music industry. A bunch of egos thinking that they're better than God. Unfortunately, it is also transforming our youth into horny retards. Be careful, music can be a great motivator and/or a great brain-washing technique.

The more I was involved in the Canadian music industry, the more I felt that it was a dusty, disorganized attempt to be like the American industry. Anyone who is a truly phenomenal musician is scooped up by American production companies and management. Canada lacks truly adequate venues, promotions, funding programs and financial infrastructure. Now, I know some Canadians will argue with me on this. And although there are grants, the amount of money for the many talented Canadians is finite. In fact, many Canadians are left to get rusty and discouraged, when they should be advancing in the industry. Yes, there are decent venues in big cities, like Massey Hall, Roy Thompson Hall and the Scotiabank Arena (formerly the Air Canada Centre).However, for average venues across the country, they just don't pay well. Compared to average places in the United States, if you are good, they pay you very well. That is why many artists are forced to head below the forty-ninth parallel. When those Canadian artists are there, they finally achieve fame or at least some level of financial comfort, while Canadian musicians back home are some of the hardest working, underappreciated workforce I have ever met. What can I say? It is dusty, cold and old in Canada. So is the music industry. Our American neighbours may have a higher crime rate. But at least Americans get more excited for their domestic entertainment industry. I like the West Coast as well!

Nickelback is Radio Fodder

How many bands do you know that are literally put together by tool parents promoting tool children to become tool bands? I don't mean the actual cool band Tool! I have seen so many bands that play generic music day in and day out, but have no direction or true connection to music on a spiritual level, let alone want to share that connection with their audience. It is more like a bunch of assholes showing off. Tool musicians trick tool fans into buying their tool products for tool bands. Fools with big egos! Speaking of tool musicians in tool bands with big egos...Nickelback!

Chad Kroeger is like a child, who was given too much! He is homoerotic and is one of the biggest rock stars in the world. With all the women he could ever want, I heard he spend his time frolicking around with his band and other men, playing the teenage frat boy until he dies. This reminds me of the loser arrogant homoerotic chump from high school actually getting to be student president. To be honest, I actually liked a few of their songs like *Savin' Me, Hero* and *How You Remind Me*. But once you get passed their few catchy singles, shit goes downhill quick. Watch the footage of him throwing a tantrum on stage in Portugal. That country gave it to them. Nickelback does not donate money like I think they should. Thank God the Internet ruined Nickelback and gave humanity a platform to meme the shit out of their souls. I love when people distort their lyrics.

"Look at this photograph, every time I think I'm gonna yack" or *"Look at this Instagram, in Canada you can have 28 grams."*

I have even heard stories of Kroeger being abusive towards women, like a child who hates his mother and then is given every girl in the county to abuse as his healing process. Of course, like a hillbilly with a million bucks and an excited pecker, only Kroeger prefers crying, pissing and hitting women, to cuddling and caressing.

Theory of a Dead Band

This is an example of the cannon fodder in an industry turning out the same sound to leverage a spin off. It is so white trash that it makes anyone from a Midwestern state look bad. It is like co-writing for bands that sound like Nickelback. They should have named the band Theory of an Oil Crisis!

Other tool bands include...a lot. Who names their band Death Cab for Cutie? That name sounds morbid and ripped from the Illuminati's playbook, but I like a few of their songs, lol.

In general, the music industry is a very finicky thing. One moment they are all about the music, the next minute they are all about the image and sometimes they are all about destroying what they have built up, so they can rebuild in front of the eyes of the world. I will always respect Enigma, the musical project founded in 1990 by German-Romanian musician Michael Cretu. The same goes for his desire to create his music the way he sees fit. Yes, he changed with the times, and some albums were better than others. However, for the most part, he kept true to *The Eyes of Truth* and *Returned music to its Innocence,* even though the music industry wanted to only promote the *Principles of Lust* and *Sadness.*

The industry tried to make me deaf:

I learned after years of observing people, places and things around me that the operating system of life tried to make me deaf. It did this with constant overstimulation, loud unexpected noises, bad audio headphones and anything else that would be detrimental to my ears. I started to get pain in my left ear and a ringing sound. Therefore, I took extremely good care of my ears and often wore noise cancelling headphones with nothing playing in them when I went outside. I also had to be conscious of staying away from loud speakers and overly loud clubs. After about a year of caution, I noticed a serious improvement.

My advice to starting musicians: wear ear plugs more than you want to, because you will never regret it later.

Another thing, the system will always try to get singers to use their voices in conversations more than they want to. This is a coercing attempt to damage your vocal chords permanently and get you to lose high notes of your top register. Be careful of this. If you don't want to talk or have a sore throat, tell people that you are not talking. End of discussion.

Fuck 50 Cent! Here's my two cents:

"Hey, mommy, I got what you need. I'm into having sex, I ain't into making love."

Wow! Can you believe that is the message from supposedly cool guys? Well, I bet you a million bucks that is not what a mommy needs. A mommy needs a million dollars from a good caring man. To have more sex, get pregnant from a guy with no love to spare and have another bastard child are not what a mommy needs. I'll tell you what she needs: someone to help pay the daycare costs, to drive the kids to soccer practice, and to take a whole night off, babysitting the poo poo pants, so that her and her girls can go out and have fun, like she hasn't done in a decade.

Rodriguez - Cold Facts

I always felt that Canada took care of rich and poor immigrants better than its own people. I always felt bombarded by multiculturalism to the point of having to compete for the smallest things with people from around the world. In my own country, I felt that many immigrants had more money, work, living arrangements, schooling, sports, opinions, debating, support from the government and even in the entertainment industry than I did. People talk about white privilege. Well, I can assure you that only a small portion of rich white society gets that. The rest of us have to slave for a government that cares more about adaptation and saving face with other cultures than it does about the Canadian culture. In fact, what is the Canadian culture? Is it poutine, beer and hockey? Come on! Immigrants are given more than the First Nations people.

When I was struggling to pay rent and put food on the table, I thought my music career was like Sixto Rodriguez. He was a talented songwriter with catchy songs who got fucked by the music industry. You have to research this guy's story yourself. But I can tell you that people in suits, who worked for record labels made millions off this guy's music for years, before he even saw a penny of it. Worse yet, when he did finally get notoriety, he was like sixty years old and the money didn't really hold as much value to him. What a waste of time and success. I prayed to God every night that I would become rich and famous in the entertainment industry before I get old. Watch the movie *Searching for Sugar Man* for more details. What a lesson about the music industry!

Chapter 41: Best Advice Ever!

The next chapter will be all the most important quotes I think every reader should remember. Get you notebook or laptop ready and take notes. If you do not read any of this book, at least read this chapter and pass it on. It is the best of the best.

I had a friend giving me great advice once, he said...

You cannot do more than one illegal thing at a time.

In the music industry...

If you give them an inch, they take a mile; if you give them a mile, they take the world. At this point, I felt like I was against the whole world, with a sword on my neck.

Do theory, but don't kill it, unless you enjoy it.

After a certain point, nobody but esoteric jazz lovers (small market) will care about an E diminished 7th, flat five over C. as the old proverb goes:"You play a million chords for four people, or you play four chords for a million people."

Here's a whole bunch of tips Drake will never give you:

I actually had a dream once that LeBron James told me the following principles to success:

Four Principles to achieving success

1) External Stimulus

- Weather, location, timing, chemistry, networks, support.

2) Competition

- No respect, glitches too close, avoiding cheaters, not letting people come around and affect your internal clock, taking people's energy if needed.

3) Internal Motivation

- Winning at all costs, hatred of losing, fatigue recovery, knowing when to rest and when to work. Avoiding overworking, avoiding stagnation, staying progressive, learning to harness anger, pain, fear and happiness.

4)Practice

- Repetitive motions, muscle memory, stopping on errors and examining them and then fixing them, when work becomes play, the more something is done, the easier it becomes.

Chapter 42: Extra Thoughts

This chapter is nearing the end of this book. Thank you for coming this far on this journey using *the Rock Star's Survival Guide*. I hope one day something in this book will help you navigate the mine field of the industry. Here is a list of important thoughts I thought of, while writing this book. Something's may be straight divine inspiration, while others may be garbage, but take everything with a grain of *Psalt*.

- Our parents' generation ruined this world. Anyone born after World War II (1939-1945) had a bright future; technology was just starting; and the environment was not depleted. Then the baby-boomers came into existence, and anyone born between the 1950s and 1970s completely ruined this world.
- It was wars, not of people, but of ideologies, famine, Africa's plights, gossip, the wrong use of technology, corporations getting their first glimpses of the billion, environmental destruction, all by somewhat simple-minded assholes.
- Then, our generation gets blamed. Yes, we may be lazy and emotional, but it is your fault. We have a burden to save the world, and honestly, with our sacrifices for veganism and the proper use of technology to create antibodies, drones and GMO's, we are doing much better than you, in regards of keeping up with an obscene population growth, while still sharing the Earth with animals.
- I never wanted to associate violence with music. I chose my weapon of choice (Guru) and that will always be my pen and my guitar. Speaking of criminal musicians, I have read that a lot of so-called "famous musicians" are actually just dangerous criminals that the industry was intrigued with their willingness to kill. I bet half the rappers in the industry in the last twenty years have killed more people with bullets and crack than any other industry besides the military or the mob.
- If you work too much, time to play; if you play too much, time to work!
- I loved the dynamics of most songs by the band Nirvana! They are like a clinic in writing happy songs about hating the world. They didn't want to be part of the perfect creepy world that didn't exist anymore.

There are four types of people:

1) Bad people who suck

2) Bad people who are efficient

3) Good people who suck

4) Good people who are efficient

Chapter 45: Show Me the Money

Conclusion

I guess it's time to burst some fragile egos. All those people that got in your way, said discouraging things, and had no good avenues for you to reach your goals, let them have it. Become successful, and tell them you didn't appreciate their arrogance, inconsiderate pressure, insults and attitude. Then walk away into the sunset.

I finally made it online. I am all over Spotify, iTunes, Apple Music and even Amazon. *Thanks, CD Baby!* I took a train across the country to come back to Vancouver, where my journey began. I stayed there for a bit and then made my way down to where I belonged all along, Hollywood!

LA

I live in Los Angeles now and frequently travel between Jasper, Alberta, Vancouver, BC, Big Sur, California and Hollywood. Sounds like a good life to me! It only took me two decades. My ultimate question to you is: can you do it in a shorter time?

Last Thoughts:

Now that I am a Rock Star in a famous band and an actor, I get laid all the time. I don't have to slave for it like a dog anymore. Go figure! Now that I am not homeless, wearing the same pants every day, I often see girls from my past that are so impressed with how far I have come. I do not take anything for granted and I will always remember the friends and enemies along the way and what they taught me. Now that I ride off into the sunset, I hope you take this book as your bible to the music industry. Remember you do not have to be me or anyone for that matter to have success with music.

I am Canadian, I am a Musician, I am a Lover, and I am an Actor. Oh I also am an author, athlete, criminal, DJ, and screenwriter. I am an asshole. I am a compassionate individual. I love my family, and I hate corruption and lies.

Who are you?

References:

by Joe Tangari

https://pitchfork.com/reviews/albums/12189-cold-fact/

by Patrick Sisson

https://pitchfork.com/reviews/albums/12994-coming-from-reality/

https://nationalpost.com/news/toronto/drakes-company-loses-trademark-dispute-over-exclusive-use-of-torontos-6ix-nickname?fbclid=IwAR0uZPC36e6Jmk7KI3k1choQmsimlc34bZkaydzSBaVdXEfqfLm8zvZD5Xo

https://www.thestar.com/entertainment/2016/04/06/city-employee-claims-drake-bullied-him-after-he-snapped-pictures-of-famous-rapper-getting-off-helicopter.html?fbclid=IwAR0JhW3cR33GR96xIwmDQHxIAmyKyjDSIRldRNMg7JwIKBkc_KXQ58Tf5sI

https://www.thestar.com/news/crime/2017/09/25/questions-raised-about-the-company-drake-keeps.html?fbclid=IwAR0X0FmnPtUs1M4uDS842P5ciC58ajYlCabgTbguReXGAsgvz_RPdl4a_O4

Goleman, Daniel. Social Intelligence: The New Science of Human Relationships. Bantam; September 2006

Waitzkin, Josh. *The Art of Learning: An Inner Journey to Optimal Performance.* Free Press; May 27 2008

Movie References:

- *8 Mile*
- *Three Axe Circle*
- *Ghostbusters*
- *Highlander*
- *Harry and the Hendersons*
- *The Matrix*
- *Who Killed the Electric Car?*
- *X-Men*
- *The Pursuit of Happyness*
- *The Greatest Showman*
- *Scott Pilgrim vs. the World*
- *Zombieland*
- *Gladiator*
- *Misery*
- *Searching for Sugar Man*